french

language
life
& culture

CELIA DIXIE

TEACH YOURSELF BOOKS

To my mother and father who have given me a lasting love of language, both English and French

For UK orders: please contact Bookpoint Ltd, 39 Milton Park, Abingdon, Oxon OX14 4TD. Telephone: (44) 01235 400414, Fax: (44) 01235 400454. Lines are open from 9.00–6.00, Monday to Saturday, with a 24 hour message answering service. Email address: orders@bookpoint.co.uk

For USA. & Canada orders: please contact NTC/Contemporary Publishing, 4255 West Touhy Avenue, Lincolnwood, Illinois 60646–1975, USA. Telephone: (847) 679 5500, Fax: (847) 679 2494.

Long renowned as the authoritative source for self-guided learning – with more than 30 million copies sold worldwide – the *Teach Yourself* series includes over 200 titles in the fields of languages, crafts, hobbies, business and education.

A catalogue entry for this title is available from The British Library.

Library of Congress Catalog Card Number: On file

First published in UK 2000 by Hodder Headline Plc, 338 Euston Road, London, NW1 3BH.

First published in US 2000 by NTC/Contemporary Publishing, 4255 West Touhy Avenue, Lincolnwood (Chicago), Illinois 60646–1975 USA.

The 'Teach Yourself' name and logo are registered trade marks of Hodder & Stoughton Ltd.

Typeset by Transet Limited, Coventry, England.
Printed in Great Britain for Hodder & Stoughton Educational, a division of Hodder Headline Plc, 338 Euston Road, London NW1 3BH by Cox & Wyman Ltd, Reading, Berkshire.

Impression number   10 9 8 7 6 5 4 3 2
Year   2005 2004 2003 2002 2001 2000

CONTENTS

Acknowledgements

I should like to thank

the editorial team at Hodder & Stoughton, and in particular, Sue Hart and Rebecca Green for their skilful guidance and very hard work

Jean-Claude Arragon, Gabrielle Bélance, Viviane Dunn, Aline Gueury, Stuart Hood, Kathleen Llanwarne, Nadia Llanwarne, Emmanuel Mermet and Phil Turk for all their suggestions and invaluable advice on the manuscript

Dave, Anna and Rose Dixie, my very patient husband and children for their love and support throughout this project.

Celia Dixie

INTRODUCTION

This book is designed to give you as full a basic overview as possible of the main aspects of France: the country, its languages, its people, their way of life and culture and what makes them tick.

You will find it a useful foundation if you are studying for examinations which require a knowledge of the background of France and its civilization, or if you are learning the language in, for example, an evening class and want to know more about the country and how it works. If your job involves travel and business relations it will provide valuable and practical information about the ways and customs of the people you are working with. Or if you simply have an interest in France for whatever reason, it will broaden your knowledge about the country and its inhabitants.

The book is divided into three sections:

■ **The making of France**
Chapters One and Two deal with the forces – historical, geographical, geological, demographical and linguistic – that have brought about the formation of the country we know as France and the language we known as French.

■ **Creative France**
Chapters Three to Eight deal with the wealth of creative aspects of French culture from the beginnings to the present day. These chapters take a look at the main areas or works of literature, art and architecture, music, traditions and festivals, science and technology, fashion and food and drink, together with the people who have created and are still creating them.

■ **Living in France now**
Chapters Nine to Twelve deal with aspects of contemporary French society and the practicalities of living in present-day

France: the way the political structure of the country is organized, education, the environment, the workplace and how people spend their leisure time.

Taking it further

Each chapter ends with a section entitled 'Taking it further', where you will find useful addresses, websites, suggested places to visit and things to see and do in order to develop your interest further and increase your knowledge.

The language

Within each chapter you will encounter a number of terms in French, whose meaning is given in English when they are first introduced. If you wish to put your knowledge into practice, we have provided in each chapter a list of useful words and phrases to enable you to talk or write about the subject in question.

We have been careful in researching and checking facts, but please be aware that sources sometimes offer differing information. Of course a book of this length cannot contain everything you may need to know on every aspect of France. That is why we have provided so many pointers to where you can find further information about any aspect that you may wish to pursue in more depth. We trust that you will enjoy this introductory book, and that it will provide leads to further profitable reading, listening and visiting. *Bon voyage!*

Phil Turk
Series Editor

1 | THE MAKING OF FRANCE

France today

For centuries France has had a political, economic and cultural impact on the rest of the world. Today it plays a key role in the European Union and in international politics; it is the world's fourth largest economy; and it remains a pre-eminent cultural centre. However, these bald facts do not explain the continuing fascination that other countries feel for France.

Although the national symbol, Marianne, gazes impassively from French postage stamps, one can't help thinking that if she were a real person she would be a complex and sometimes contradictory personality – a mathematician and an artist, both cerebral and sensual, conformist and individualist, authoritarian and libertarian.

From Roman times France has been a nation that values engineering and mathematics; for centuries, and still today, most of the country's governing élite have been trained in these skills. It is no coincidence that France is known to the world by a feat of nineteenth-century engineeering, the Eiffel Tower, or that the French refer to their country as a mathematical figure, *l'Hexagone*. Logic, and the way of thinking which establishes general principles before proceeding to the particular, runs through much of French culture and is exemplified in the French passion for ideas and public debate, in the centralized and hierarchical systems of government and education, and, at its worst, in the inflexible 'rules is rules' attitude of some French bureaucrats.

However, this love of system and order is constantly challenged by an equally powerful and subversive individualism, epitomized by the jaunty Gallic cockerel which still features on the seal of the Republic, which has given its name to thousands of *Coq Hardi* cafés, and which patriotic fans still smuggle in to international sports events and release to wreak havoc on the pitch!

It was French individualism, together with the multitude of regional differences that fifty years ago caused de Gaulle to testify, with exasperation but also with some pride, to the difficult task of uniting *'un pays qui compte 265 spécialités de fromage'* ('a country with 265 varieties of cheese'). Today there are over 350 types of cheese which reflects the fact that, although France has recently made room for the hamburger culture, she is far from submitting to it.

Despite the creeping uniformity of modern life, France is a nation of multiple identities, not only regional but ethnic, as testified by the backgrounds of the footballers in the French team which so brilliantly captured the 1998 football world cup. But such diversity is not new. France owes her rich cultural heritage to the different peoples that have settled on this land, their passions, skills and languages and the determining events of their history. Because of this, France is often described as a 'melting-pot', which in French is also the name of her world-famous make of cooking pot – *le Creuset*.

Le Creuset

Before examining the contents of the pot, let us turn to the land and its climate – the pot itself!

How France began

500 million years ago, 496 million years before there was any human life in the world, France's oldest high land was formed – the

Massif Central, the Vosges, the Ardennes and Brittany, and in the far south Maures, Esterel and Corsica. Then 200 million years ago, sea covered most of the land, leaving sediment in what were to become the fertile Paris and Aquitaine basins. Alpine folding 50 million years ago caused the formation of younger mountains – the Pyrenees, the Alps and the Jura – and the appearance of volcanoes in the Massif Central. It was not until 100,000 years ago during successive periods of extreme cold, that glacial erosion gave these mountains their present appearance. After many changes in sea level, the coastline too became the one that we know today.

Un embarras de richesses! (An embarrassment of riches!)

Because of France's varied landscape, her climate and a wealth of natural resources, she has often been the envy of her neighbours. Shakespeare's Henry IV declares 'This best garden of the world, our fertile France ...', while a German saying common in the nineteenth century was, 'Happy as God in France'.

Landscape and climate

Ma France de toujours　　My eternal France
que la géographie　　　　that geography
Ouvre comme une paume　opens up like a palm
aux souffles de la mer　　to the breath of the sea

Louis Aragon (1897–1982)

With low-lying land in the north, west, and centre, and the high land of the Massif Central, the Pyrenees and the Alps to the south and south-east, France does look like an open palm. This combination of mountains and plain, the presence of the Atlantic Ocean to the west and the land mass of Europe to the east, together with her temperate latitude, give the country four types of climate which help to give each region its distinctive character.

The northern and western coastal regions are frequently swept by rain driving in from the Atlantic, while the central and eastern areas have a drier, continental climate of hot summers and cold, often snowy winters. The mountainous Vosges, Jura and Alps in the east, as well as the Pyrenees in the south-west have long, harsh winters

French mountains and rivers

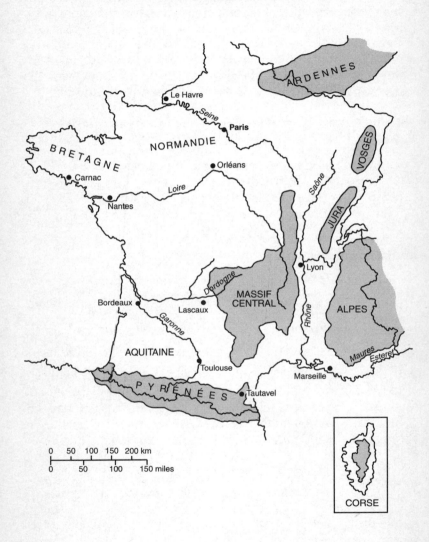

and short rainy summers, although the Alps and the Pyrenees also have their share of hot sun, given their southern position. Because of its southern latitude, the Midi has baking hot summers and mild winters, but it also has the Mistral, a searingly cold wind that whips down the Rhône valley at the end of the summer.

The soil

It is to France's varied and fertile terrain that we owe the abundance of fine wines and regional produce in which the French take such pride. Farming was central to many people's lives until the mid-twentieth-century, and although now it only creates a small part of the country's wealth, it remains close to the French person's heart. France still has a quarter of all the farmed land in the European Community and is its primary producer of wheat, wine, sugar, barley and beef.

Diverse traditions and techniques of cultivation have shaped the landscape to give the vast, often treeless open fields of the north and north-east; the smaller, irregular fields enclosed by banks and hedges in the west and centre; and the terraced vineyards and olive groves on the dry, rocky slopes of the Mediterranean area.

Rivers

Throughout France's history her dense network of rivers has played a major role in the country's trade and communications. After the Second World War, the government's huge investments in hydro-electric power stations on the Garonne, the Rhône and the Rhine on France's eastern border, helped the country's dramatic economic recovery.

Minerals

Minerals, too, have helped shape France's landscape and her history. Coal in the north, and coal, iron ore and salt in Lorraine, caused the rapid industrial development of these areas in the nineteenth century. But now the coal fields are depleted and the empty pits are silent reminders of a way of life that Zola portrayed at its most brutal in his novel *Germinal*. However, government incentives have attracted other industries, such as the car industry, to the north which is still a major industrial conurbation.

Today it is on uranium, not coal or water, that France depends for her energy supplies. Since the 1970s, the government has determinedly pursued its nuclear power programme, using uranium from le Limousin, le Forez and la Vendée. Nuclear electricity production currently represents over three-quarters of France's electricity consumption, which is the highest proportion of any country in the world. After the United States, France is the world's biggest producer of nuclear power.

Coastline

In the past, France's 3,000 kilometres of coastline have naturally given rise to fishing, salt production and ship-building. But in the twentieth century, tourism has been the coast's growth industry. Eight stretches of coast entice the holiday-maker with their poetic names: in the north – *la Côte d'Opale* (opal); in Normandy – *la Côte d'Albâtre* (alabaster), *la Côte Fleurie* (flowery), *la Côte de Nacre* (mother-of-pearl); in Brittany – *la Côte d'Émeraude* (emerald), *la Côte de Granit Rose* (pink granite); in the south-west – *la Côte d'Argent* (silver); in the south – *la Côte Vermeille* (vermilion) and the world-famous *Côte d'Azur* which speaks for itself!

The contents of the pot – the people and their history

Early ancestors

From the earliest times of human history, France has been marked by successive invasions, conquests and immigration from the north, east and south. Her first known inhabitants, whose remains were found at Tautavel in the Pyrenees, are thought to have lived around 450,000 years before Christ. However, most is known about Cro-magnon man, who lived around 15,000 BC, because of the wealth of evidence of this culture, discovered in the Dordogne in particular. The culture of these early cave dwellers must have come to an end with the gradual melting of glacial ice, between 10,000 and 8,000 BC, making settlement possible throughout the land.

France's first village societies appear to have been formed by invaders from the east, a people known as the Ligurians. However, they were not responsible for the mysterious standing stones, stone tables and alignments found in Britanny and the Dordogne. The earliest of these, and possibly the earliest stone construction in Europe, is the tumulus of Kercado at Carnac in Brittany which was built around 5,700 BC, predating the Egyptian pyramids. Very little is known of the megalith builders except that their constructions span 5,000 years and that they probably had more in common with the builders of Stonehenge in England, and Newgrange in Ireland than with the rest of what is now France. Their civilization appears to have been untouched by the first Celtic invasions which took place between 1000 and 800 BC.

Gauls and Romans

The warlike Celts, who were said to scorn shields and to go into battle bare-chested, swept across western Europe and into the Jura, Burgundy and the Auvergne. These Celts were the Gauls who gave their name to the land that is now roughly France and Belgium. The contents of the melting-pot were mixed further as Celts mingled with Ligurians in the south-east, Iberians in the south-west and with Greeks who settled in Marseille in around 600 BC.

Some French people claim to owe their individualism, indiscipline, a certain daring spirit and a love of argument to the Celts of Gaul who lived in about 500 tribal units which all had their own leaders, customs and gods, and who were constantly fighting each other! The fact that throughout the world 'Gallic' means something quintessentially French shows the importance that this part of their heritage has for the French today. All French children know that higgledy-piggledy Gallic resistance to the invading Romans under Julius Ceasar, was led by the valiant Gallic leader Vercingétorix who was finally defeated in the siege of Alésia in 52 BC. But they and many other children in the world want to believe that one outpost of resistance to Roman centralism survived in Brittany, home of the cunning little warrior, Astérix and his bumbling side-kick Obélix.

The success of the Astérix books, translated and sold in 77 other countries, lies in the appeal of the universal myth of the resourceful underdog, the oppressed minority, winning through against dehumanizing, hostile forces. This myth has remained particularly powerful with the French, threatened by invasion over the centuries and for whom the Nazi occupation is within living memory. Astérix and Obélix are standing up for regional identity, but at another level they are defying the uniformity of modern life. In protecting the French film industry and through the efforts of the Académie Française to protect the language from a flood of Americanisms, many French people are resisting what they see as American cultural imperialism, just as their Gallic forebears resisted the culture of imperial Rome. But perhaps too, the French recognize in themselves the contradictory characteristics epitomized by both Gauls and Romans.

Roman Gaul

The Roman legacy to France includes hierarchical government, engineering skills, Latin, logic and wine, all of which are at the heart of French culture today. The Romans' influence is particularly visible in the architecture of the south where the Provincia Romana was established three-quarters of a century before Julius Caesar set about conquering the whole of the country in just seven years (58–51 BC). The Romans developed a sophisticated urban culture, with Lyon, modern France's second city, as the capital of Roman Gaul.

The Franks

Five centuries of peaceful Roman rule were brought to a violent end by a series of invasions from the east and north by Vandals, Visigoths, Alamans, Franks and Huns. The Huns were renowned not only for their ferocity but also for their legacy to French cuisine. According to legend, hasty Huns ate on the move without dismounting, and softened raw meat by riding with it under their saddle, so producing a particularly flavoursome *steak tartare*!

In the late fifth century, the Franks succeeded in establishing control over what had been Gaul. They later gave their name, meaning 'free', to the country – *la Francie*. However, many Roman influences remained, including Christianity which had replaced Gallic and Roman gods and was too well-established to be supressed. The King of the Franks, Clovis, who converted to Christianity and was baptized by the Bishop of Soissons, is known to most French people from the incident of the vase de Soissons. The newly devout Clovis was so incensed when one of his soldiers stole the Bishop's vase that, on encountering the culprit a year later, he promptly split the soldier's head in two with his sword and uttered the immortal words '*Souviens-toi du vase de Soissons*' • ('Remember the vase of Soissons'), thus giving the French their favourite catch-phrase for getting even with an enemy.

More significant however, is the fact that Clovis was crowned King of Francia in Reims Cathedral. This meant that henceforth the king had the material and moral support of the Church which proved to be vital to later medieval kings in their efforts to consolidate their lands and gain the allegiance of the people.

The Carolingians and Charlemagne

In 732, Charles Martel (said to strike his enemies like a hammer! – no relation to Clovis) protected France from a further invasion, this time from the south. He fought back Moors who, after conquering Spain, had ridden as far north as Poitiers. This meant that Charles gained for the Crown the lands of Aquitaine and Provence that had eluded royal control. Charles' son, the diminutive Pépin le Bref, who was crowned King of France by the Pope, became the first of a line of hereditary monarchs, the Carolingians, which included the redoubtable Charlemagne. True to his name, Charlemagne thought big in more ways than one. He is reputed to have been very tall, although with a thin, piping voice, and to have had 20 children from nine marriages. Under him, France became part of a vast empire that extended eastwards to include the lands that are now Germany, Austria, Switzerland and Italy. When Charlemagne died, so did his empire which was split between three of his sons. The western section, controlled by Charles le Chauve (Charles the Bald), covered much of what is modern France.

The Normans

The last violent invaders to add their characteristics to the French racial mix came from Denmark and Norway. These Vikings arrived in their long-boats in northern France in the middle of the ninth century, about 200 years before they invaded England under William the Conqueror. Although they reached as far south as Toulouse and

Bordeaux, they were pushed back to the north and made their home in what is now Normandy where some of today's tall, blond inhabitants have inherited the nordic looks of their ancestors.

Although in later centuries France absorbed the cultural influences and racial characteristics of foreign visitors and immigrants, the nature of the country was never again radically transformed by sudden invasion.

The English

In the eleventh and twelfth centuries the king's power diminished and the country was controlled by feudal lords who wielded power in their own areas and often fought amongst themselves. Consequently, opportunistic English kings saw French land as ripe for the taking, particularly Guyenne in the south-west which they coveted for its fine wines. The Plantaganet kings were so confidently settled in France, in the south-west, Brittany and the north, that many only spoke French. Old conflicts between France and England flared up again in the fourteenth century when Charles IV of France died with no direct successor. His nephew, Edward III of England, was so enraged when the throne went instead to Charles' maternal grandson, Philippe de Valois, that he led his army on a rampage along the whole northern French coast. So began the Hundred Years War. The hostilities were long and bloody, with other French factions (Brittany, Burgundy, Orléans) coming to the support of either side as it suited them. Finally, the English forced the *Dauphin* Charles (the heir to the throne) to leave Paris, and when Henry V of England married the French King's daughter in 1420, it looked as though France was in the English bag. Enter Jeanne d'Arc (Joan of Arc).

Jeanne d'Arc – la Pucelle d'Orléans (the Maid of Orleans)

Jeanne was a seventeen-year-old peasant girl from Lorraine who, guided by her 'voices', believed she had a divine mission to free France from the English. Her unswerving conviction inspired the French troops and emboldened the vacillating *Dauphin*. She played a crucial role in halting the English advance at Orléans and in defeating the English at Patay in 1429, allowing the *Dauphin* to be crowned as Charles VII in Reims cathedral. Finally, the English were driven out of France, but not before Jeanne was captured by the Burgundians and handed over to the English to be burnt at the stake for heresy and witchcraft.

Jeanne contributed to a new French national consciousness, and as this grew in the centuries that followed, so did her importance as a national heroine. She figured as a symbol of France during the First World War and has been used as an icon by France's nationalist extreme right-wing party, the Front National.

However, Jeanne's appeal has been much wider than French nationalism. Throughout the world she has been the subject of plays, films, children's books and countless history books. Her story has the vital ingredients of legend – adventure, a heroic cause, religious mysticism and a young, vulnerable and courageous protagonist fighting against the odds. In common with other female saints (Jeanne was canonized in 1920), and also like non-religious modern female icons (Marilyn Monroe, Princess Diana ...), Joan has appealed to people on many different levels, and is important for what people have chosen to see in her, as much as for who she really was.

A new France

Towards the end of Charles VII's reign, at the beginning of the fifteenth century, the rigid hierarchies of the feudal system were giving way to the growing power of the bourgeoisie. Charles' son, the wheeler-dealer Louis XI, who was known as *l'universelle araignée* (the universal spider), made further, lasting changes for France as a nation. He surrounded himself with civil servants instead of power-hungry lords, introduced the first national postal service and consolidated French territory. He rid France of the English by offering them their favourite tipple – 300 cartloads of best Guyenne wine! Through further bribery and an alliance with the Swiss he gained Burgundy by winning over his old enemy, Charles le Téméraire (Charles the Rash). Brittany, which had remained independent, finally became part of France when Louis' son Charles VIII made a judicious marriage to Anne of Brittany.

France, mère des arts, des armes et des lois
France, mother of arts, of warfare and of laws

> Joachim du Bellay (1522–1560)

With universities established in Paris, Toulouse, Montpellier and Orléans, France in the fifteenth and sixteenth centuries was at the heart of humanism, a movement that was concerned with man's fulfilment on earth and that defied religious restrictions on knowledge. A new openness and vigour was evident, in particular, in the work of writers such as Rabelais, Montaigne, Ronsard and du Bellay, forefathers of modern French literature. However, the questioning of received truths in religion ultimately led to a hardening of attitudes and the opposition of Protestantism to Catholicism, for which the country paid a high price.

The wars of religion

In the sixteenth century, Catholic nobles saw the Huguenots (Protestants), many of whom were successful artisans, intellectuals and army officers, as a threat not merely to their beliefs but to their power. The result was the bloody wars of religion of which the most famous incident was *la Saint-Barthélémy* – on St Bartholomew's Eve 1572 the Catholics massacred 3,000 Huguenots in Paris and a total of 30,000 throughout France. Thirty years of civil war and Protestant persecution came to an end when the Protestant Henri IV inherited the throne and in a famous example of realpolitik converted to Catholicism, proclaiming '*Paris vaut bien une messe*' ('Paris is well worth a Mass'). When he issued the Edict of Nantes four years later, he was the first European king to formally grant freedom of conscience to all his subjects. Henri permitted Protestants to hold public office and allowed them public worship in certain castles and towns in the south-west, including La Rochelle which still has strong Huguenot affiliations.

Today 800,000 French people are Protestants. Protestantism has long been associated with dissent and hence with left-wing politics – the Prime Minister Lionel Jospin and a Socialist predecessor, Michel Rocard, are both Protestants. Some French historians go so far as to claim that without the Protestant challenge to Catholic complacency and tradition, France would not have become the advanced industrial power and secular republic that she is today!

L'Ancien Régime

The *Ancien Régime* was the system of government under the Bourbon kings Louis, XIII, XIV, XV and XVI. It was a period of flamboyant art and architecture and of rigid royal control that came to a violent end with the Revolution of 1789. Royal power reached its apotheosis in the absolute monarchy of Louis XIV, but not without the ruthless suppression of opposition. Louis XIII had executed dangerous nobles, destroyed castles likely to be used as centres of resistance and subjected the Protestants of La Rochelle to a year-long siege. His son, Louis XIV, revoked the Edict of Nantes, so causing 200,000 Protestants to take their skills and their money to other countries. Freedom of worship did not return until after the Revolution.

Le Roi-Soleil (The Sun King)

In and outside France, Louis XIV is probably the best-known French king. His love of extravagant celebrations is legendary, but it was also a way of keeping his nobles in check. In exchange for tax exemptions he gave them ceremonial duties at court and then encouraged them to spend ruinous sums on lavish entertainments.

Louis' legacy as a patron of the arts is evident in his palace of Versailles which remains a monument of French architecture, painting, sculpture, interior decoration, landscape gardening and building technology. Here, life for the 5,000 inhabitants was conducted according to a series of elaborate rituals designed to reinforce Louis' god-like status. A chosen few were permitted to attend the rising of the Sun King in the morning, and the day ended for everyone when he went to bed at night. However, in some ways the King was more accessible than modern leaders as the palace was a place for all and sundry to come and see him, eating his dinner or sitting on the toilet!

France before the Revolution

Louis XIV's inglorious legacy was an economy severely weakened by costly wars. This meant crippling taxes, which, combined with the effects of poor harvests, spelt poverty and famine for the peasants. The result was widespread popular unrest which intensified in the reigns of the ineffectual Louis XV and XVI.

Despite France's impressive commercial growth in the eighteenth century – she became one of Europe's richest trading nations – discontent spread amongst the bourgeoisie who, like the peasantry, bore a hefty tax burden and bitterly resented the tax exemptions enjoyed by the clergy and the nobility.

However, this was not the only reason for the growing opposition to the *Ancien Régime*. Just as the ideas of the Renaissance had gradually undermined the rigid systems of feudal society, so a new spirit of rationalism and scientific enquiry was shaking the foundations of political and religious absolutism. The libertarian ideas of French writers such as Montesquieu, Voltaire and Rousseau inflamed political and social debate across Europe and America. Within France the old structures could not contain the thirst for knowledge, the thirst for freedom, and in some, the thirst for blood.

The 1789 Revolution

Within just a few months in 1789, the structures of the *Ancien Régime* were overturned and modern France was born.

In May 1789, Louis XVI was forced to call a meeting of the *Etats Généraux* (Estates General), a body representing the nobility, the clergy and the bourgeoisie, to vote on the burning issue of taxation. The members of the Third Estate, who were drawn from the bourgeoisie, declared that they constituted a national assembly and vowed not to disband until they had given France a constitution.

When the King's troops forced the defiant Third Estate members to disperse, the people of Paris took up arms and seized the Bastille prison, a symbol of the king's arbitrary power to lock away political subversives without trial or sentence. The fact that there were only seven prisoners to be released did not diminish the significance of the event which marked the end of absolute monarchy and which is celebrated with fireworks throughout France every 14th July.

In a single all-night session in August, the new Assembly abolished all feudal dues and privileges, hereditary nobility and titles. A few weeks later *La Déclaration des Droits de l'Homme et du Citoyen* (The Declaration of the Rights of Man) affirmed the right to *liberté, égalité, fraternité* (freedom, equality, fraternity), and the principle of citizenship upon which French law and all French constitutions have been based. In December, the old provinces were replaced by *départements* and the administrative division of France became roughly what it is today. However, the revolutionary calendar which made 1792, the year of the First Republic, 'year one', and which renamed the months more poetically e.g. *Thermidor* (hot) July; *Ventose* (windy) March; *Brumaire* (misty) November, did not survive.

Napoléon Bonaparte

Modern France suffered a violent childhood as the euphoria of revolution gave way to fear during the period of *la Terreur* (Terror) when Robespierre and Danton gained power. Throughout the country, tens of thousands of people suspected of opposition were shot, drowned or guillotined, including King Louis XVI and his Austrian wife Marie-Antoinette. The time was ripe for Napoléon Bonaparte to offer a return to order and absolute rule.

Although considerably smaller than his role model, the towering Charlemagne, Napoléon was not short on ambition. For fifteen years he brought military glory to France by dominating much of Europe, and like Charlemagne he was crowned Holy Roman Emperor. However, not wishing to be upstaged by the Pope, Napoléon placed the crown on his own head. His military gains were lost when he was beaten by the Anglo-Austrian alliance and finally by the English at Waterloo in 1815.

France today is a highly centralized state because of measures introduced by Napoléon to control the whole country from Paris, and to spread uniform justice and educational opportunity throughout the land. A less significant but enduring innovation was Napoléon's decree enjoining Europeans to *rouler à droite* (drive on the right), for no known reason unless it was to spite the English who for many years had been driving on the left!

After Napoléon's defeat, monarchists took their chance to restore the unsuccessful kings Louis XVIII, Charles X and finally Louis-Philippe who was unable to address the needs of a newly industrialized society and was forced to abdicate following further revolution in 1848. It was not until the Third Republic of 1870 and following France's defeat in the Franco-Prussian War that the country settled into a period of economic growth, free of civil or external wars, but not free of political conflict.

L'Affaire Dreyfus

Dreyfus was a Jewish army captain wrongly accused of having given military secrets to the Germans. In 1897 his case caused a political storm in France and united in his defence the left-wing artists, intellectuals and politicians of Europe, one of whom, Emile Zola, wrote an open letter to the government beginning '*J'accuse ...*'

The affair brought to a head the continuing conflict between republicans on the Left, who believed Dreyfus was the victim of a miscarriage of justice and blatant anti-semitism, and monarchists and clericalists on the Right, who were more concerned that the army was being discredited. The outcome of the affair in France was a further attack on the Church which resulted in the closure of 3,000 Catholic schools. In 1905 Church and State were separated, making France the secular state that she is today.

La Belle Epoque

French confidence at a time of commercial expansion and industrial change is epitomized by the 300-metre high *Tour Eiffel*. It was completed in 1889 for the centenary of the Revolution and for the Paris Universal Exhibition which exhibited goods from all over the world. This was the time of French colonial expansion in Africa and Asia which, despite subsequent decolonisation, forged lasting economic amd cultural links. It was also a time when literature and the arts flourished, although they criticized and shocked bourgeois society. First the Impressionist painters, and later Matisse, Picasso and Braque, made Paris the art capital of the world.

As in England, industrialization in France gave rise to Socialism and the growing confidence of the workers to form Unions. In 1906 alone there were 1,300 strikes demanding better conditions of employment. The Socialist politician and workers' leader, Jean Jaurès, who is commemorated in street names all over France, was a pacifist who tried in vain to avert world war.

The world wars

Both world wars left France terribly scarred. Although France was a victor in the First World War, her industrial north-east was devastated and she lost nearly 1,400,000 men, a quarter of all Frenchmen between the ages of 18 and 30. In the inter-war years she had little chance to recover her former industrial strength and was understandably slow to rearm following Hitler's occupation of the Rhineland in 1936. She was subsequently unable to prevent the German invasion of northern France in 1940.

For the four years of the Second World War in which France was occupied by the Nazis she was governed by the collaborationist Vichy regime of Maréchal Pétain who represented the right-wing forces that had in the past opposed the Revolution and the Republic. During this period, the revolutionary emblem of '*liberté, égalité, fraternité*' was replaced by the sober slogan '*travail, famille, patrie*' ('work, family, country').

Resistance to the occupation was led from London by an unknown general, Charles de Gaulle. However, today it is the bravery of de Gaulle's second in command, Jean Moulin, that symbolizes heroic resistance to the Nazis. De Gaulle was a powerful but remote figure fired by the belief that '*la France ne peut être la France sans la grandeur*' ('France cannot be France without greatness'). Jean Moulin, on the other hand, won a place in people's hearts for his sacrifice in the name of freedom – he died in 1943 following capture and torture by the Germans.

The Free French forces who joined de Gaulle, together with the British, Americans and Canadians, helped turn the tide of the war against Germany when they landed on the Normandy beaches on 6 June 1944. Paris was liberated on 25th August 1944 and the last German stronghold, Bordeaux, was freed in May 1945.

The Vichy regime still casts its shadow over France. In the post-war years there was an understandable desire to focus on the heroism of the Resistance rather than on the extent of French collaboration with the Nazi deportation and murder of 75,000 Jews. Official collusion, including that of President Mitterrand, with war-time collaborators, protected many of them from being brought to justice before they died. But in recent years, the trials of the Lyon SS chief, Klaus Barbie, the Vichy militia official Paul Touvier, and the Bordeaux head of the Jewish Affairs service, Maurice Papon, have contributed to public soul-searching and greater openness about this painful period of recent history.

The economic devastation of the Second World War caused France to throw herself into far-reaching economic and social reforms including the nationalization of many industries, the modernization of agriculture and the introduction of social security and a guaranteed minimum wage. By 1949–1950, industrial production was higher than it had been pre-war. It was because of her fervent desire for political peace as well as economic stability that France, alongside Germany, became a committed founding member of the embryonic European Economic Community in 1957.

Général de Gaulle

Outside France, Charles de Gaulle was the best-known Frenchman of his time because of his role in the Second World War and in France's recovery, and also because of his impressive physical presence and the authority of his oratorical style. Being able to understand de Gaulle's measured tones on the radio reassured many students of French previously dispirited by their failure to communicate in a *boulangerie!*

De Gaulle was the architect of the current Fifth Republic, introducing a new constitution to greatly strengthen the president's role. He successfully negotiated an end to the bloodshed of the Algerian war and independence for the former colony; and he led France into a period of material prosperity. But during the late

1960s he lost touch with the mood of the country and failed to address underlying social tensions. As so often before in French history, a period of authoritarian control was followed by violent revolt – *les événements de mai '68* – when striking students and workers brought the country to a standstill.

Up to the present

Educational reforms and improved working conditions were introduced while France was still in a period of expansion. However, in common with other European countries, from the mid-1970s to the 1990s France experienced varying degrees of recession, and despite an economic upturn, French unemployment is still worryingly high. Even in such times, French presidents have embarked on ambitious cultural projects. The style and confidence with which the French embrace the future, while at the same time respecting the past, is exemplified by the the gleaming glass *Pyramide du Louvre* which is a stunning complement to its gracious sixteenth-century neighbour.

Far from forming a homogenized mixture, the contents of the French cooking pot resemble an exciting ragoût of ingredients that have been added through the centuries. The pot is as old as history, but the distinctive flavour of the dish continues to surprise.

VOCABULARY

la formation de la terre *formation of the Earth*
le relief *relief*
le climat *climate*
la préhistoire *prehistory*
paléolithique *paleolithic*
réaliser *to execute, achieve*
les gravures (f.) *engravings*
les peintures (f.) *paintings*
les parois (m.) des grottes (f.) *cave walls*
évoluer *to evolve*
néolithique *neolithic*
les mégalithes (m.) *megaliths*
les alignements (m.) *alignments*

les menhirs (m.) *standing stones*
les dolmens (m.) *stone burial chambers*
les archéologues (m.) *archeologists*
la fouille *dig, excavation*
découvrir *to discover*
les Celtes *Celts*
se défendre *to defend oneself*
la conquête romaine *the Roman conquest*
les peuples barbares (m.) *barbarians*
envahir *to invade*
s'installer *to settle*
le Moyen Age *Middle Ages*
la féodalité *feudalism*
les seigneurs (m.) *lords*
les paysans (m.) *peasants*
construire *to build*

les **châteaux forts (m.)** *castles*
la **Renaissance** *Renaissance*
la **cour** *court*
les **découvertes (f.)** *discoveries*
inventer *to invent*
l'**imprimerie** *printing*
les **guerres de religion (f.)** *wars of religion*
l'**assassinat (m.)** *murder*
la **monarchie absolue** *absolute monarchy*
convoquer *to call*
la **prise de la Bastille** *taking of the Bastille*
les **sans-culottes (m.)** *townspeople who fought for the Revolution*
les **Jacobins** *hard-line republicans*
prendre le pouvoir *to come to power*
se proclamer empereur *to declare himself emperor*

la **restauration de la monarchie** *restoration of the monarchy*
la **classe ouvière** *working class*
s'organiser *to become organized*
réclamer *to demand*
la **Première Guerre mondiale** *First World War*
la **crise économique** *economic crisis*
le **Front Populaire** *Popular Front*
la **Seconde Guerre mondiale** *Second World War*
le **débarquement** *Normandy landings*
rétablir l'ordre *to restore order*
les **trente glorieuses** *post-war years of relative economic stability*
occuper (les usines, les facultés) *to occupy (factories, universities)*
manifester *to demonstrate*
la **fracture sociale** *social breakdown*

Taking it further

Places

Le Parc de Saint-Vrain, 91770 Saint Vrain, tel. 01 64 56 10 80 (dinosaur park)

Les Eyzies, Dordogne (prehistoric finds and cave paintings):
■ le Musée National de Préhistoire, Place de la Mairie, tel. 05 53 06 97 03
■ la Grotte de Font de Gaume and la Grotte des Combarelles, tel. 05 53 06 90 80
■ la Grotte de Rouffignac, tel. 05 53 05 41 71

Lascaux, Montignac, Dordogne:
■ Lascaux II, tel. 05 53 51 95 03 (fine replica of original cave paintings)

Carnac, Brittany:
■ le Musée de la Préhistoire, 10 Place de la Chapelle, tel. 02 97 52 22 04

■ Alignments of 3,000 menhirs north of Carnac town centre (Tourist info, 74 avenue des Druides, tel. 02 97 52 13 52)

Books

Besson, Jean-Louis, **Le livre de l'histoire de France**, Collection Découverte Cadet (Paris: Gallimard, 1985) – delightfully illustrated summary of French history for children

Jones, Colin, **The Cambridge Illustrated History of France** (Cambridge: CUP, 1994)

Braudel, Fernand, **The Identity of France Vol I – History and Environment** (London: Fontana/HarperCollins, 1988)

Michaud, Guy and Kimmel, Alain, **Le nouveau guide France** (Paris: Hachette, 1996)

Tocqueville, Aude Grouard de, **Guide Tocqueville des musées de France** (Paris: Minerva, 1997) – beautifully illustrated, town-by-town guide to museums

Le Roy Ladurie, Emmanuel, **Montaillou: Life in a medieval village** (London: Penguin, 1978)

Warner, Marina, **Joan of Arc, the image of female heroism** (London: Weidenfeld and Nicholson, 1981)

Roberts, J M, **The French Revolution** (Oxford: OUP, 1997)

Zeldin, Theodore, **France 1848–1945** – 2 vols (Oxford: OUP, 1977)

Burrin, Philippe, **Living with defeat, France under the German occupation, 1940–1944** (London: Arnold, 1996)

Gildea, Robert, **France since 1945** (Oxford: OUP, 1996)

Ardagh, John, **France in the new century** (London: Viking, 1999) – comprehensive and very readable overview of France today

Levieux, Eleanor and Michel, **Insider's French** (London: University of Chicago Press, 1998) – very useful explanation of terms used in current affairs

Aplin, Richard, **A dictionary of contemporary France** (London: Hodder & Stoughton, 1993)

Films

Astérix et Obélix contre César, dir. Claude Berri, 1999
Jeanne d'Arc, dir. Luc Besson, 1999

La Reine Margot, dir. Claude Berri, 1995 – the wars of religion

Le Ridicule, dir. Patrice Leconte, 1996 – satire of court life under Louis XVI

Le Colonel Chabert, dir. Yves Angelo, 1994 – Napoleonic wars

Germinal, dir. Patrick Border, 1996 – grim tale of nineteenth-century mining families

Le Chagrin et la pitié, dir. Marcel Ophuls, 1971 – wartime collaboration

Au revoir les enfants, dir. Louis Malle, 1987 – persecution of Jewish pupils in occupied France

Lucie Aubrac, dir. Claude Berri, 1997 – Catherine Deneuve and Daniel Auteuil as Resistance fighters

Websites

Ministère de la Culture – **www.culture.fr** (in Fr and Eng)

UREC, *Made in France* – **www.urec.fr/France** (directory of French websites, in Fr and Eng)

2 | THE LANGUAGE

French is spoken as a first language by an estimated <u>100 million</u> people throughout the world. Leaving aside the variations of French spoken by France's European neighbours and former colonies, the language of metropolitan France is as rich as the country's geography and culture. It is the result, on the one hand, of the diverse inventions, mistakes, abbreviations and borrowings of individual speakers, and on the other hand, of a process of rigid standardization. These conflicting elements are an important part of a French person's linguistic heritage. Consequently, whether they are farmers in remote Corrèze, Parisian business people or rap singers in run-down suburbs, the French are very conscious of their language. They may not all speak it with attitude, but they certainly have attitudes towards it.

The French and their language

In 1784, the writer Antoine de Rivarol proudly declared '*Ce qui n'est pas clair n'est pas français*' ('That which is unclear is not French'), suggesting that precision and logic are intrinsic qualities of the French language. This belief was echoed two centuries later by François Mitterrand who, when opening an exhibition about the French language, heaped praise on his native tongue for '*sa clarté, son élégance, ses nuances, la richesse de ses temps et de ses modes, la délicatesse de ses sonorités, la logique de son agencement*' ('its clarity, its elegance, its nuances, its rich tenses and moods, its delicate tones, its logical structure').

Such pride in the French language goes back to the seventeenth century when the Académie Française was founded to determine and preserve a pure form of the language. However, the language approved of by the Académie was not exactly in everyday usage. It was the fine language used in the works of the philosopher Descartes and the poetic playwrights Molière, Racine and Corneille. Of course, a writer possessing similar intellectual and poetic skills might express himself in any language with the clarity and elegance traditionally associated with French. Nonetheless, the prestige of the language enshrined in the Académie's first dictionary was established. It is difficult to say if its seventeenth-century members would be appalled or delighted if they could witness the 1694 edition of the dictionary in use today on CD-Rom!

Today, the Académie Française still acts as a kind of word police, nosing out impurities (it is particularly sniffy about anglicisms) and attempting to maintain rigid standards of grammar in public life. In 1998, it even reprimanded the Minister for Education for making minor spelling errors in a formal letter!

Given the restraints imposed by the Académie Française on the natural evolution of the written language, it is not surprising that written French is often very different from spoken French which has been freer to develop and diversify.

However, the idea of a correct norm to be emulated has carried over from the written to the spoken language. As a consequence, many French people today still feel that the way they speak is inferior to, rather than simply different from, the 'correct French' taught in French schools. It is quite common to hear older French people apologizing for what they have said – *'ce n'est pas français'* – or even admitting to 'mangling the language', *'estropier le français'*. Even those French people who take pride in speaking in the manner of their region, or of their social or ethnic group, retain a sense that they are deviating from 'standard' French.

French respect for the complexities of their written language is evident in the importance French schools place on *la dictée* (dictation test) which requires a thorough grasp of grammar as well as vocabulary. Despite the *dictée*'s association with irksome school tests, an annual televised dictation competition, *Les Dicos d'or*, is immensely popular and undeniable proof that French people not only respect but delight in their language. The competition finals are always held in august surroundings (l'Assemblée Nationale, la

Bibliothèque Nationale de France, l'Opéra-Garnier...) and are broadcast live to enable three million viewers to tackle the *dictée* at home along with the finalists. In vain they make their past-participles agree, and distinguish between same-sounding third person singulars and plurals – there is always something to trip them up. Ten mistakes in a text of 35 lines is a result to be proud of. The majority of candidates can console themselves with the performance of Napoléon III in a dictation compiled by the writer Prosper Mérimée – he made 75 mistakes!

Bernard Pivot, the presenter of TV culture programes who hosts the finals of the *dictée* competition, explains its widespread appeal: *'Les français aiment bien l'Arc de Triomphe, le Louvre, la Tour Eiffel ... et la langue française, c'est aussi un monument historique.'* ('The French love the Arc de Triomphe, the Louvre, the Eiffel Tower ... and the French language too is a historic monument.')

History of French

The first languages known to have been spoken in the land that is now France were those of the early settlers – the Iberians, the Ligurians and the Aquitainians. Today, the language of the Aquitainians survives as Basque, spoken in the extreme south-west of the country as well as over the border in Spain. The oldest language still spoken in France, Basque bears no relationship to the Indo-European languages of later invaders and appears to have had no part in shaping modern French.

Le gaulois

Little written evidence remains of the Celtic languages spoken by the Gallic tribes who arrived between 700 and 500 BC. Their culture was mainly oral. However, about 70 Gallic words – among them, *bec* (beak), *boue* (mud), *chemin* (road), *mouton* (sheep) – still testify to the Gauls' agricultural preoccupations. Place names too reveal their Gallic past, as towns were often given the name of the local people: the Celtic Parisii tribe gave its name to Paris, the Pictavi named Poitiers, the Remi Reims, the Turones Tours.

Latin

The first true ancestor of modern French was the Latin spoken by invading Roman legionaries in the first century. This oral form, *le latin vulgaire* (Latin of the populus) which differed in many ways from the classical Latin used in the Roman Senate and by writers such as Cicero and Virgil, became the official language of Roman Gaul. Although, by the end of the sixth century, the various different Gallic languages had ceased to exist, they left their mark on Latin as its pronunciation varied from region to region.

The Franks

The period that followed was decisive in the development of the language. After the fall of the Roman Empire in 476 and before the appearance in 842 of what is believed to be the first official French text, *les Serments de Strasbourg*, diverse languages and dialects developed from Latin.

It was the fifth century Germanic invasions of the Burgundians, the Visigoths and most importantly, the Francs, that precipitated dramatic changes. Frankish influence was strongest in the northern part of the country (with the exception of Brittany) as far south as the Loire. The way in which the Franks pronounced the Latin of this area led to the development of *la langue d'oïl* (*oïl* meant 'yes' in this area). However, in the southern part of the country where Roman control had been strongest, the language remained closer to Latin and was hardly affected by the relatively brief incursion of the Visigoths. It developed into *la langue d'oc* (*oc* also meant 'yes'). *Franco-provençal*, which shared features of both languages, came to be spoken in the area dominated by the Burgundians, what is now Bourgogne, Franche-Comté and part of Rhône-Alpes.

Pronunciation

The Franks made a lasting impact on pronunciation. The adoption of Germanic stress patterns meant that in many words the final syllable was no longer pronounced even if it was written e.g. *table*, formerly *tavola*. Beyond Frankish influence, in the south of France, the last syllable of a word continued to be pronounced. In the same way, many southerners today still tend to pronounce a final 'e', whereas their northern compatriots do not.

'H' aspiré

This bug-bear of French language students is another legacy of the Franks. They introduced words in which an initial 'h' was pronounced. Even when the 'h' eventually became silent, it was still treated like a consonant and became known as *'h' aspiré* ('h' aspirate) as in *le hêtre* (beech), *la haine* (hatred) and *la haie* (hedge). But in spoken Latin introduced by the Romans, an initial 'h' was treated like a vowel and therefore was not pronounced. This explains why in French words derived from Latin, initial 'h' is treated like a vowel and gives rise to elision or liaison. Elision means that the preceding vowel of the article is dropped, as in *l'homme* (man), *l'honneur* (honour), *l'heure* (hour or time); liaison means that a preceding consonant which is not normally pronounced, will be heard, as in *les hommes* (pronounced *les-z-hommes*) or in *un homme* (pronounced *un-n-homme*).

However, knowing the origin of 'h' aspirate does not necessarily help the language student to recognize one! Unfortunately, the only answer is to learn the pronunciation of 'h' words together with a preceding article. The dictionary indicates 'h' aspirate words with * or ', before the word itself or before the phonetic symbols in square brackets.

Le francien

In the centuries following the Frankish invasion, the development of feudal fiefdoms throughout the land meant that the main languages of the country *(breton, langue d'oïl, langue d'oc, basque* and *franco-provençal)* became further divided into a multitude of local dialects. *Le francien*, the dialect of the tiny area around Paris known as *la France*, was simply one dialect among many until Hugues Capet who was *duc de France* was elected king in 987. By the end of the twelfth century, the royal domain had grown and *le francien*, known today as *l'ancien français* (old French) had become not only the language of the court in Paris, associated with political power as well as with fine manners, but it was also the language of literature.

By the sixteenth century, what we now call *le moyen français* (middle French) had acquired the status of a national language. The

Ordonnance de Villers-Cotterêts of 1539 established that all legal and administrative documents should be written in French. Since, in many regions, Latin had already been supplanted by local dialects in official documents, the new ruling meant diminished status for these dialects and for those who spoke them. At this time too, French began to replace Latin as the medium of education. But with few children having access to schooling, French remained unequivocally the language of power and privilege, and as foreign to most people as Latin had been.

French and the Renaissance

For those who spoke and wrote French, the sixteenth century was an exciting time of innovation and discovery, in science as well as literature. Ambroise Paré, the founder of modern surgery, scandalized the world of medicine by producing all his works in French; Jacques Cartier's accounts of his Canadian expedition were published in French, as were the *Prophéties* of Nostradamus.

One of the first attempts to classify the language was William Palsgrave's French grammar written in English in 1530. Ironically, the first French grammar to be published in France was written in Latin and appeared a year later.

Many writers of the time delighted in discovering and creating new French words formed from Greek, Latin, Hebrew and local dialects. The poet Ronsard declared *'Plus nous aurons de mots dans notre langue, plus elle sera parfaite'* ('The more words our language has, the more perfect it will be'). Du Bellay's *'Défense et illustration de la langue française'*, which praised the beauty and richness of French, was the manifesto of young writers of his generation.

L'Académie Française and *le bon usage* (correct usage)

Although the seventeenth century became known as the great age of French literature which emulated the writers of classical times, it was also the period of a new orthodoxy. As the official language of the state, and a political tool in the geographical extension of the king's power, French became subject to the constant surveillance of the Académie Française. Louis XIII's powerful minister, Richelieu, founded the Académie in 1635 to analyse and regulate the language and to produce a definitive grammar and dictionary. The author of the first dictionary, Vaugelas, coined the term *le bon usage* which has cast its shadow over French speakers for nearly four centuries. As the 40 members of the Académie, known as *les immortels*, met to determine a correct spelling for every word, the first dictionary took 60 years to complete and only contained 24,000 words as any word deemed too vulgar or too outmoded was excluded. French spelling continues to confound foreigners and natives alike, thanks to the seventeenth-century *académiciens'* decision to retain many twelfth-century forms in order to distinguish '*les gens de Lettres d'avec les ignorans*' ('the cultivated from the uneducated')!

In the seventeenth and eighteenth centuries, French became the language of international diplomacy until it was supplanted by English in the Treaty of Versailles in 1918. It was also the chosen language for many foreign writers such as the German philosopher, Leibniz, and Casanova whose prodigiously long philosophical *mémoires* have been the subject of serious literary debate in France.

French and the Revolution

The French language was just as much a tool of the Revolutionaries as it had been of the *Ancien Régime*. The new Republic aimed to replace *les patois* (local dialects), still spoken by the vast majority, with '*l'usage unique et invariable de la langue de la liberté*' ('the universal and uniform use of the language of freedom'). However, although teachers, known as '*les hussards noirs de la République*' ('the black hussars of the Republic'), were responsible for introducing elegant Parisian French to the wooded valleys of the Auvergne and to remote Alpine villages, they did not succeed in eradicating the dialects in which most people still spoke in all but formal circumstances. In the nineteenth century, about half of the population were bilingual, having a command of both French and their local dialect. While a further quarter could understand French imperfectly, the remaining quarter could not speak French at all.

It was not until the twentieth century that French spread to the whole population as the standard means of communication.

Improvements in transport, and the birth of radio and television meant that communities no longer remained isolated from the outside world and often their livelihood depended on a common language. Nonetheless, the French language spoken throughout the country today, unlike the revolutionary ideal, is far from uniform.

Regional languages and dialects today

Regional languages and dialects are quite distinct from standard French. Some are now only spoken by old people in rural areas. However, the old dialects have left their mark in the pronunciation, vocabulary and syntax of *les français régionaux* (regional forms of French) which are widely used in everyday speech throughout the country.

In some areas, local languages are still a vital part of local culture. In Brittany and parts of the Midi, regional movements dedicated to preserving the old local languages have to some extent halted the decline in their use and have encouraged young people to take an interest not only in the language but in local history and folklore. In Corsica and the Basque region many people are bilingual in French and the local language. In these areas, where autonomy movements have frequently used violent tactics, speaking *le corse* or *le basque* is not just a means of affirming local identity; it is a political statement. In Alsace-Lorraine *l'alsacien* and *le lorrain* are flourishing, partly because these Germanic languages resemble the type of German spoken nearby in the Black Forest, and partly because of the region's history of German ownership.

Despite this enthusiasm for regional languages, France's official attitude to them has been ambivalent. In 1999, after years of equivocation, France signed the European Charter on Regional and Minority Languages. But the following month, the Conseil Constitutionnel, France's highest court, ruled that the charter posed a threat to French unity and violated the French constitution whose Article 2 declares the Republic's language to be French. To the dismay of France's regional language speakers, a mere 2 per cent of the population who hardly constitute a threat to republican values, President Jacques Chirac refused the Prime Minister's request to

France's languages and dialects

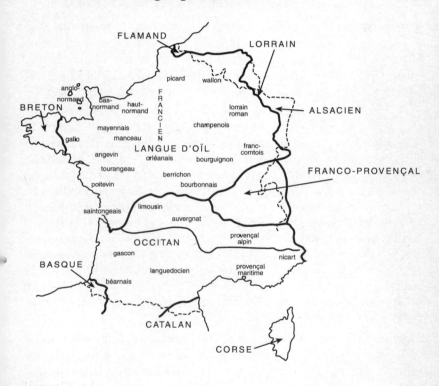

alter the constitution. Such a change would have given regional languages official recognition and would have enabled Breton-speaking schools, which are currently funded mainly by parents, to enter the state education system.

France's regional languages

Non-romance languages (not derived from Latin)

language	area	no. of speakers	features
le basque	800 square miles around Bayonne	80,000	
le breton	Finistère and west of Côtes-du-Nord and Morbihan	500,000	similar to Welsh
le flamand	northern tip of le Nord dept. and Belgium	50,000 (est.)	place names end in *-ghem* or *-ghen*
l'alsacien	Alsace	n/a	similar to German (from lang. of Aleman tribe)
le lorrain	Lorraine	n/a	similar to German (from lang. of the Franks)

Romance languages (derived from Latin)

language	area	no. of speakers	features
la langue d'oïl	from Britanny and Bordeaux to north-eastern border	n/a	dialects include: *le picard, le wallon, le francien* and *l'anglo-normand* (the Channel Isles)
l'occitan	from dept. of la Gironde in west to Hautes-Alpes in east	2 million speakers but 8 million understand one of the *occitan* dialects	dialects: *le limousin, l'auvergnat, le provençal, le niçart, le languedocien, le gascon, le béarnais*

le catalan	Roussillon area and over the Spanish border	260,000	similar to *l'occitan* and to *valenciano* in Spain
le corse	Corsica	125,500	northern dialect similar to Tuscan; southern similar to Sardinian
le franco-provençal	from west of Lyon to the Jura, Switzerland and Italy and south to Valence	n/a	'yes' is *wa*

French in the world

Because of France's colonial past, French is used all over the world, in some cases as the offical language only, in others as the language of everyday use. The French of each of these ex-colonies and of Belgium, Switzerland and Luxembourg differs from the language of metropolitan France in pronunciation and in certain structures and items of vocabulary.

Main countries with French-speaking population	
Belgium	Southern half of the country and Brussels region
Switzerland	West of Basle and Sion
Canada	Quebec (*le québécois*) Acadians in Nouvelle-Ecosse (*l'acadien* or *le cajun*)
America	Louisiana (*le vieux français créole, le cajun, le black créole*)
West Indies and Guyana	Martinique, Guadeloupe, and dependencies (*le français* and *le créole*)
North Africa	Algeria, Morocco, Tunisia
Black Africa	Mauritania, Mali, Senegal, Nigeria, Guinea, Ivory Coast, Burkina Faso, Togo, Benin, Chad, Cameroon, Central Africa, Gabon, Congo, Zaire, Rwanda, Burundi

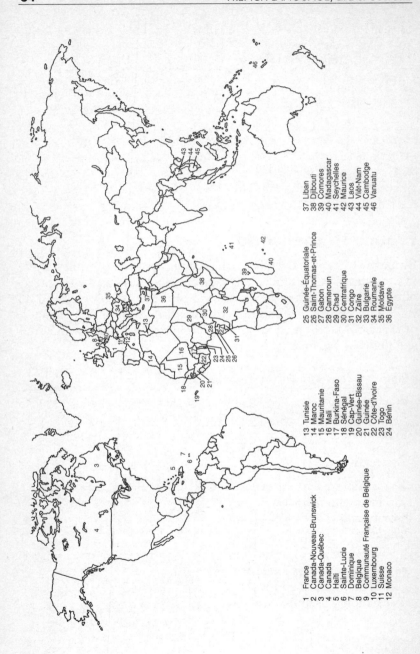

1 France
2 Canada-Nouveau-Brunswick
3 Canada-Québec
4 Canada
5 Haïti
6 Sainte-Lucie
7 Dominique
8 Belgique
9 Communauté Française de Belgique
10 Luxembourg
11 Suisse
12 Monaco

13 Tunisie
14 Maroc
15 Mauritanie
16 Mali
17 Burkina-Faso
18 Sénégal
19 Cap-Vert
20 Guinée-Bissau
21 Guinée
22 Côte-d'Ivoire
23 Togo
24 Bénin

25 Guinée-Équatoriale
26 Saint-Thomas-et-Prince
27 Gabon
28 Cameroun
29 Chad
30 Centrafrique
31 Congo
32 Zaïre
33 Bulgarie
34 Roumanie
35 Moldavie
36 Égypte

37 Liban
38 Djibouti
39 Comores
40 Madagascar
41 Seychelles
42 Maurice
43 Laos
44 Viêt-Nam
45 Cambodge
46 Vanuatu

Aspects of French

Pronunciation

The myth that the purest French is spoken in Touraine seems to have originated not in France but in texts written by foreigners, such as the French grammar written by Palsgrave in the seventeenth century. Possibly prestige was accorded to the French of this area because the French court was based there in the fifteenth century and later continued to make frequent visits to the king's châteaux. Be that as it may, it is the pronunciation of the Paris area which has been taught as the norm. Today, standard pronunciation emerges not as the eradication of regional variations but as a blurring of the many differences in speech of the educated middle classes who may have come from the provinces to live in Paris. Thus the range of pronunciation accepted as 'standard' French is now much greater than it was a couple of generations ago.

One change in pronunciation has occurred in words such as *un*, *brun*, *commun*. There is a growing tendency for *-un* to be pronounced as *-ain*, although this is by no means universal. In addition, the use of liaison (pronouncing a normally silent consonant when it occurs before a vowel) is now less common in cases where it was previously optional. While it is essential to pronounce the 's' of *vous avez*, the 's' of *pas un jour* is often omitted in informal speech. On the other hand, there is a growing tendency for the final consonant of words such as *but* (goal), *nombril* (navel) to be pronounced, whereas once these letters were silent.

Structures

The structures of informal spoken French are increasingly at variance with formal written language, generally in the interests of brevity and simplicity, which is welcome news for students of the language.

It is very common for speakers in an informal situation to drop the *ne* of a negative: *je sais pas* (I don't know), *on va pas* (we're not going) etc. As in the previous example, the third person singular *on* is commonly used for 'we' instead of *nous*. Interrogatives have also been streamlined, so that questions are frequently spoken as statements with rising intonation: *tu aimes ça?* (you like that?), which is easier than inversion: *aimes-tu ça?* and considerably quicker than the cumbersome *est-ce que tu aimes ça? Ça* is now used almost universally in speech instead of *cela*.

Nowadays, the imperfect subjunctive sounds impossibly precious in speech and has been dropped in favour of the present subjunctive, except in the most formal or literary style. Consequently, with blatant disregard for the rules of *la concordance des temps* (sequence of tenses), 'I wanted you to know' will be rendered as *je voulais que vous sachiez* and *not je voulais que vous sussiez*.

Similarly, while a grasp of the *passé simple* (past historic) is still essential for studying French literature, this tense only rarely appears in contemporary written narrative and has hardly been used in speech since the end of the eighteenth century.

Tu or *vous*?

The question of which form of address to use is particularly tricky, not only for Anglo-Saxons who do not have this problem in English, but also for Spaniards and Flemings (from Flemish-speaking Belgium) who, when speaking their own language, are accustomed to use the familiar form in a far wider range of situations. In France *vouvoiement* is still the rule when speaking to people you do not know well, although young people and students commonly address each other as *tu* straightaway.

The circumflex

This 'little hat', as language teachers love to call it, occurs in words where an 's' has been dropped. Many related English words have kept the 's'.

modern French	old French	English
fête	*feste*	festival
château	*chastel*	castle
hôpital	*hospital*	hospital

Vocabulary

Vocabulary, perhaps more than any other aspect of language, reflects values, attitudes and social change. While the Académie Française continues to carefully select each word for the ninth edition of its dictionary, French people speak as it suits them, changing their vocabulary consciously or unconsciously, in accordance with the fashion of the day.

Abbreviations and *les sigles* (acronyms)

The everyday speech of the young in particular is peppered with abbreviations which seem to denote familiarity with, and a certain affection for, commonly used words e.g. *le bac* (*baccalauréat*, equivalent of 'A' levels), *accro* (*accroché*, hooked), *un ado* (*adolescent*), *un appart* (*appartement*, flat), *une caric* (*caricature*), *une cata* (*catastrophe*), *déb* (*débile*, stupid), *un dico* (*dictionnaire*), *la doc* (*documentation*), *McDo* (McDonald's), *le p'tit déj* (*petit déjeuner*), *pro* (*professionnel*), *la pub* (*publicité,* advertising), *un quadra* (*un quadragénaire*, a forty-something), *un quinqua* (*un quinquagénaire*, a fifty-something), *la sécu* (*sécurité sociale*, social security), *spéc* (*spécial*, cool/unusual). Whether or not an abbreviated word attains normal status in written French seems to depend on its frequency of use and place in society. For example, while *auto* and *métro* have become more acceptable than *automobile* and *métropolitain*, *ciné* reverted to *cinéma* when cinema-going lost popularity to television (*télé*) and video.

A love of *les sigles* (initials and acronyms) is another characteristic of both spoken and written French: *les BD* (*bandes dessinées*, strip cartoons), *le CAPES* (*Certificat d'aptitude pédagogique à l'enseignement secondaire*, secondary teacher training certificate), *EDF* (*Electricité de France*, French Electricity Board), *une HLM* (*Habitation à loyer modéré*, council accommodation), *un SDF* (*Sans domicile fixe*, a homeless person), *le Smic* (*le Salaire minimum interprofessionnel de croissance,* minimum wage), *le Sida* (*le Syndrome immuno-déficitaire acquis*, Aids), *le TGV* (*Train à grande vitesse*, high-speed train).

French concepts

Certain French words which have only clumsy equivalents in English denote concepts less familiar to Anglo-Saxons e.g. *estivant(e)*, summer holiday-maker (with the sense of 'summer/sun lover' – not so easy in England); *aoûtien* (*-ienne*), August holiday-maker (reflecting the traditional mass exodus from towns to coast and country, see p. 220).

Dates associated with events can give their name to people in a more general way. English has no equivalent for *les soixante-huitards*, individuals who were active in, or who still espouse the ideals of, *les événements de mai* (the nation-wide student and worker protests of 1968).

France's pre-eminence in the field of cooking and catering is reflected in the abundance of French cooking terms adopted in English (roux, bouquet garni, croutons, to blanch, etc.) and in the terms denoting the hierarchy of cooks and kitchen staff (sous-chef, commis-chef ...) elaborated by Georges Auguste Escoffier at the beginning of the last century.

Another area of vocabulary which is far less-developed in English than French is that relating to inhabitants of regions, and towns in particular. In English, the inhabitants of only a few towns are graced with their own name: Londoners, Brummies, Mancunians, Liverpudlians, New Yorkers, Bostonians, Sydney-siders; the suffixe '-er' or '-ian' is added only rarely to other place-names. In France, on the other hand, thousands of names denoting the inhabitants of every town and most villages are in everyday use, as the sports reports of local papers testify. Such names are commonly formed by adding the suffix *-ais*, *-ien*, *-ois* or *-on*: *les Marseillais*, *les Parisiens*, *les Niçois*, *les Aiglons*. However, there are also many intriguing names derived from towns' Latin or Celtic names: *les Tourangeaux* (from Tours), *les Stéphanois* (from St Etienne), *les Biterrois* (from Béziers), *les Bordelais* (from Bordeaux and nothing to do with brothels!).

L'argot (slang)

At first used in medieval times to refer to a criminal brotherhood, the word *argot* subsequently came to mean the language devised by thieves and villains to make themselves unintelligible to outsiders. Today *l'argot* has lost its criminal associations and exists in many varieties which are constantly changing. *Le verlan*, a form of slang based on inversion (*verlan = l'envers*, reverse) and originally used by nineteenth-century convicts, has had a rebirth in recent years. It is very popular amongst certain groups of young people and in particular amongst second-generation immigrants from North Africa, known as *les beurs*, this word being *verlan* for *les arabes*. Speaking *verlan* is a way of marking adherance to this social and ethnic group and is pretty effective at confusing outsiders. While considerable mental agility is required to speak entirely in *verlan* and in turn to decipher it, the task is made easier through a mixture of *verlan* vocabulary, anglicisms and French words given new meaning e.g. *grave* (serious) to mean 'very' and *criminel* (criminal) to mean 'superb'. The most common *verlan* has found its way into the *Petit Robert: une meuf = une femme* (a woman), *un keum = un mec* (a guy), *un keuf = un flic* (policeman), *une reum = une mère* (mother), *une teuf = une fête* (celebration). Other dictionaries are dedicated to documenting the latest trends, but this is really a contradiction in terms as by publication date the language has always moved on.

franglais

The Académie Française has made most fuss about 'franglais' in the last twenty years, however the phenomenon is not recent. In the eighteenth century, a wave of anglo-mania led to the adoption of many English words. Some are now very well disguised e.g. *la redingote* (frock coat – from riding coat), *le boulingrin* (lawn – from bowling green). Present-day official hostility to the assimilation of English words stems from a fear that the integrity of the French language, and by extension, French culture itself, is under threat. However, in certain fields, such as technology and pop music, English words are used because there is, or was, no French equivalent. Despite the scholarly French alternatives (e.g. *oléoduc*, pipeline; *logiciel*, software), created by a succession of government commissions appointed for this purpose, the newly-constructed French words are rarely as popular as the English originals. In an attempt to stem the tide of anglicisms, in 1994 la loi Toubon restricted the use of foreign words in public life and in the media. As a result, disc jockeys found themselves scraping the barrel for mediocre French pop music, as songs with English lyrics were no longer allowed to hog air time. However, this measure did give a boost to the French pop music industry which is currently thriving (see p. 108).

The English words of the moment that are slipped into conversation as a kind of fashion statement may have only fleeting appeal. Others, which stand the test of a few years, rather than months, find their way into dictionaries, but rarely into the revered dictionary of the Académie. It did recently accept *un mel* for e-mail, but insisted that this was an abbreviation of *un message électronique* and not a 'frenchification' of English. However, there are many examples of such transformation, for example: *biper*, to bleep; *cliquer*, to click; *un outé*, a gay man who has 'come out'. Sometimes an English present participle is used as a French noun e.g. *un shampooing*, a shampoo; *un lifting*, a face lift. Building-site hoardings throughout the country describe future blocks of luxury flats as *immeubles de grand standing*.

English *Franglais*

Over the centuries, English has absorbed many French words, some of which are in such everyday use that their origins are forgotten: *bizarre, bureau, café, chic, cliché, ensemble, étiquette, fiancé, menu, milieu, régime* ... The list is endless. In England, as in France, borrowed words are often used in ways that mystify native speakers: *cul-de-sac* (literally 'bottom of a bag') suggests a very English, net-curtained suburbia, and *blancmange* (white food) can only be imagined quivering on an English tea table.

Les calembours (puns)

As it has so many *homophones* (same-sounding words) French lends itself to puns. Perhaps one of the most famous is based on Napoléon's alleged exclamation: *'Ma sacrée toux!'* ('My bloody cough!') which was interpreted by a minion as *'Massacrez-tout!'* ('Kill them all!').

Some derivations

le tennis	Although tennis was an English game, French was the language of the English court and players cried *tenez!* when they served
un charcutier	from *chair cuite* (cooked meat)
une cravate	the regiment of Louis XIII was *le Royal Croate*; their cavalry wore a thin scarf
un barbecue	a whole cow was turned on a spit and roasted *de la barbe à la queue* (from beard/head to tail) – *un barbe-à-queue*
la lavande	lavender was used for washing (*laver*)
une baïonnette	weapon made in Bayonne in the south-west of France
un chandail (sweater)	knitted garment worn in the Auvergne by *les marchands d'ail* (garlic sellers)
la sauce Béchamel	invented in the seventeenth century by Louis de Béchamel, financier and gourmet
la nicotine	tobacco was introduced to France by Jean Nicot
une silhouette	the first drawings of this type were caricatures of the very unpopular finance inspector, Etienne de Silhouette
une poubelle	almost as unfortunate as Sir Thomas Crapper, Eugène Poubelle who urged Parisians to bin their rubbish, is remembered by the name of the bin itself.

Gender and job titles

Until recently, most job titles in French were masculine irrespective
of the sex of the worker. But in 1998, the Jospin government
sanctioned the *féminisation* of male job titles when the worker is a
woman. The change was felt to be particularly urgent in the
education ministry where 63 per cent of staff were female. Despite
fierce opposition from the Académie Française, women ministers
are now addressed as *Madame la* (instead of *le*) *Ministre*, female
advisors as *conseillère* instead of *conseiller* and women head
teachers as *directrice* instead of *directeur*. The Académie's outrage
at the changes betrayed not only chauvinism but snobbery as the
feminine forms of more humble posts have long been in common
use: *une ouvrière* (female factory worker), une infirmière (female
nurse), *une institutrice* (female primary school teacher); and
nobody quibbled about *une chômeuse* (unemployed woman)!

Who said that?

Honni soit qui mal y pense.
Evil be to he who evil thinks.
>   Edward III of England
>   (whose first language was French)
>   Motto of the Order of the Garter (1348)

L'Etat c'est moi.
I am the State.
>   Louis XIV
>   (April 1655)

Je pense donc je suis.
I think therefore I am.
>   René Descartes
>   *Discours de la Méthode* (1637)

Après nous le déluge.
After us the deluge.
>   Madame de Pompadour to Louis XV (Nov 1757)

Qu'ils mangent de la brioche.
Let them eat brioche. (see p. 134)
Marie-Antoinette (c. 1789)

Du sublime au ridicule il n'y a qu'un pas.
There is only one step from the sublime to the ridiculous.
Napoléon I (1812)

Plus ça change plus c'est la même chose.
The more things change the more they are the same.
Alphonse Karr
Les Guêpes (Jan 1849)

L'enfer c'est les autres.
Hell is other people.
Jean-Paul Sartre
Huis Clos (sc. 5) (1944)

VOCABULARY

la langue *language*
la prononciation *pronunciation*
le vocabulaire *vocabulary*
l'orthographe (f.) *spelling*
le langage parlé *spoken language*
s'exprimer *to express oneself*
la langue étrangère *foreign language*
francophone *French-speaking*
l'étymologie (f.) *etymology*
les mots (m.) *words*
le sens *meaning*
signifier *to mean*
la grammaire *grammar*
la structure *structure*
le temps *tense*
le substantif *noun*
le verbe *verb*
le mode *mood*

conjuguer *to conjugate*
le français correct *standard French*
le français populaire *unsophisticated French of ordinary people*
la langue régionale *regional language*
le dialecte *dialect*
le patois *local, rural dialect*
argotique *slang (adj.)*
le barbarisme *made-up, incorrect word*
le néologisme *newly-created or borrowed word*
le gallicisme *structure particular to French*
le belgicisme *Belgian-French word*
le joual *Canadian-French*
le créole *language used by descendents of American slaves*
le bilinguisme *bilingualism*
le langage des signes *sign language*

Taking it further

Books

Walter, Henriette, **Le Français dans tous les sens** (Paris: Laffont, 1988) – excellent over-view of history, regional languages, current usage

Walter, Henriette, **Le Français d'ici, de là, de là-bas** (Paris: Lattès, 1998)

Grévisse, Maurice, **Le Bon Usage** (Paris: Duculot, 1980) – vast, worthy tome covering every nicety of 'correct' French

Battye, Adrian and Hintze, Marie-Anne, **The French language today** (London: Routledge, 1992)

Lodge, Armstrong, Ellis, Shelton, **Exploring the French Language** (London: Arnold, 1997)

Dictionaries in French

Le Petit Larousse Illustré 2000 (Paris: Larousse, 1999)

Le Petit Robert 1 and 2 (Paris: Dictionnaires Le Robert, 1996) – France's number one dictionary; volume 2: proper names

Le Dictionnaire étymologique du français (Paris: Robert, 1999)

Le Dictionnaire des expressions et locutions (Paris: Dictionnaires Le Robert, Collection les Usuels, 1993)

Merle, Pierre, **Le Dico du français qui se cause** (Paris: Milan, 1998) – current street French

Depecker, Loïc, **Les Mots de la francophonie** (Paris: Belin, 1988)

Dictionaries in English and French

Larousse Chambers, **Advanced English/French dictionary** (Paris: Larousse, 1999)

Burke, David, **Street French: The best of French idioms 1 & 2** (New York: John Wiley, 1996)

Levieux, Eleanor and Michel, **Insider's French** (London: University of Chicago Press, 1999) – current affairs terms

Regional languages

Diwan-Breizh, BP 147 ta sant ernel, 29411 Landerneau, tel. 02 98 21 33 69 – Association of Breton language schools

L'Institut d'Etudes Occitanes (IEO), 12 rue du faubourg Bonnefoy, 31500 Toulouse, tel. 05 61 11 24 87

3 | WRITERS AND PHILOSOPHERS

What is distinctive about French literature is the degree to which it embodies philosophical questions. This is not to say that all French writers of fiction are philosophers, though some are. But French writers belong to a culture which has a long rationalist, and an even longer humanist and moralist, tradition. In addition, the ideas of the eighteenth-century philosophers and the ideals of the Revolution are reflected in many aspects of daily life. For example, for the last two hundred years, children in the fiercely *laïque* (secular) state-school system have studied philosophy not religion. Philosophy is not necessarily academic or élitist, as testified by the recent trend for *cafés philosophiques* (philosophy cafés) where lovers of ideas from all walks of life can meet to tease out answers to life's big questions.

Ideas matter in France, and so do intellectuals. British or American philosophy dons might cut a dash on the campus, but unlike their French counterparts, they are rarely accorded prime-time television interviews. In France since the time of Voltaire, *les intellectuels* have been influential public figures. They may be philosophers, historians, sociologists, scientists, psychologists or novelists but they are ready to pronounce on current affairs and issues beyond the limits of their own discipline.

The French fondness for ideas is accompanied by an *esprit de système*, a desire for coherence, method and clarity which is apparent as far back as the seventeenth century, in the works of Descartes, in the strict rules of classical literature and in the rigid hierarchies of Louis XIV's government. In literature as in politics, when a system becomes a stifling orthodoxy it can be subverted only by the dangerous and the new, which in turn becomes fixed as another '-ism'. Thus it took Romanticism to challenge the spirit of classicism, individualism to break the hold of rationalism, spirituality to confront materialism. French literature swings between these polarities and it is not surprising, therefore, that particular literary forms have been dominant at certain periods and not at others. For example, lyrical poetry was not the favourite genre of the eighteenth-century *philosophes*, but it was eminently suitable for soul-baring Romantics.

The Legacy of the Middle Ages

French vernacular texts first appeared in the ninth century, but a flourishing oral tradition of legends and songs went far back to the Celts of Gaul. The medieval exponents of this tradition were minstrels, known in the north as *trouvères* and in the Midi as *troubadours*, who sang *chansons de geste* (epic poems describing heroic deeds) and songs of courtly love which had originated as *chansons de toile* (weaving songs). By the fourteenth century, the music and singing were dropped, and musicality or lyricism was incorporated in the text in the form of rhymes and repetitions, giving birth to lyrical poetry.

In the fifteenth century, François Villon developed the lyrical genre further, anticipating modern poetry by expressing his personal emotions and experience. In his violent and colourful life Villon had many brushes with death. When he was sentenced to be hanged he wrote *La Ballade des pendus* (The ballad of the hanging men). Here is an extract, no less powerful today for being more than five centuries old and written in *le moyen français* (middle French – see p. 27):

Illustration from *La Ballade des pendus*

La pluye nous a buez et lavez
Et le soleil dessechez et noircis;
Pies, corbeaulx nous ont les yeux cavez
Et arraché la barbe et les sourcilz ...

Rain has sprayed and washed us
And sun has dried us out and blackened us
Magpies and crows have pecked out our eyes
And torn off our beard and eyebrows ...

Luckily the poet was reprieved from this fate and survived intact!

Another legacy of the Middle Ages is the term *roman*, which by the seventeenth century had come to mean 'novel'. However, it originally meant a narrative translated from Latin into a Romance language (a language directly descended from Latin, such as French or Italian). *Le roman courtois*, of which the most famous example is *Le Roman de la rose*, was a story of courtly love. These origins are evident in the English meanings of the word 'romantic' which can be used to suggest affairs of the heart, to mean 'strikingly imaginative' as in a novel, or to refer specifically to the Romantic movement of the early nineteenth century.

La Renaissance and *l'humanisme* – the sixteenth century

In the sixteenth century, France, like the rest of Europe, experienced *la Renaissance* which literally meant a rebirth of interest in the values of ancient Greece. It also signified the spread of humanism, a new way of thinking that questioned established values, particularly those of the Church, and maintained the moral and intellectual worth of the individual.

François Rabelais (1494–1553) was a former monk, a doctor and a Greek scholar whose works of fiction are bursting with erudition, coarse humour and humanity. In five books about the giant Gargantua and his son Pantagruel, Rabelais' extravagant humour ridicules bigotry, superstition and religious dogma, while celebrating a respect for nature, and asserting the importance of personal experience in man's quest to understand himself and his world.

Today Rabelais is mainly remembered for the *bon vivant* aspect of his work as the English adjectives 'Rabelaisian' and 'gargantuan' testify. The first usually means 'ribald humour', while the second simply refers to the vast appetite of the giant who as a child was fed by the milk of 17,913 cows!

Pierre de Ronsard (1524–1585) and **Joachim du Bellay** (1522–1560) were members of a group of poets called *La Pléiade*. They were all classical scholars and humanists who shared a passion for etymology and who were committed to enhancing the beauty of the French language.

It is Ronsard's poignant sonnets which are remembered best today, as for example this *Sonnet pour Hélène* which finds an echo in Yeats' 'When you are old':

> *Quand vous serez bien vieille, au soir, à la chandelle,*
> *Assise auprès du feu, dévidant et filant,*
> *Direz, chantant mes vers, en vous émerveillant:*
> *'Ronsard me célébrait du temps que j'étais belle.'*

> When you are old and sitting by the fire, in the evening
> skeining and spinning in the candlelight,
> You will softly speak my verses and say,
> with wonder in your voice,
> 'Ronsard sang of my beauty in days gone by.'

The sentiment of the sonnet's concluding line has been taken up by generations of impatient lovers:

> *Cueillez dès aujourd'hui, les roses de la vie.*
> Pick life's roses now.

or, in the words of Robert Herrick: 'Gather ye rose-buds while ye may'!

'Je suis moy-mesme la matière de mon livre' ('I am myself the subject of my book') declares **Michel de Montaigne** (1533–1592) in the introduction to his *Essais* (Essays). Believing that each individual, however ordinary, *'porte en lui la forme entière de l'humaine condition'* ('represents the entire human condition'), he uses his own experiences to consider aspects of death, friendship, education, politics and religion.

Le classicisme and *le rationalisme* – the seventeenth century

In the seventeenth-century, often considered to be the golden age of French literature, Parisian literary salons were thriving, the first permanent theatres were established, writers received court patronage and the Académie Française, founded by Cardinal Richelieu, was the official arbiter of good taste and correct language (see p. 29). The questing and free-ranging spirit of the Renaissance had developed into a more focused desire to establish absolute truths by means of order and reason. In philosophy and science, which were still indistinguishable from each other, this meant pursuing a single, logical argument without, however, overtly challenging belief in God or the authority of the Church.

The Cartesian debate

The work of **René Descartes** (1596–1650) marks the beginning of modern French philosophy and of the rationalist tradition, still so strong in France today. In his best-known work, *Le Discours de la Méthode*, Descartes elaborates a deductive methodology for scientific and philosophical enquiry, beginning with the proof of his own existence: *'Je pense donc je suis.'* ('I think therefore I am.') His assertion of the dual nature of reality (mind and body) became the first tenet of Cartesianism, a school of philosophy which attempted to explain reality according to mechanical principles.

'I think therefore I am.'

An eloquent opponent of Cartesianism was **Blaise Pascal** (1623–1662), a brilliant scientist and mathematician who, incidentally, invented the calculator. In his *Pensées* (Thoughts), Pascal aims to persuade agnostics or sceptics to *parier* (make a wager) on belief in God because without such faith, life and suffering have no meaning. Pascal depicts the human condition as the ceaseless pursuit of *divertissements* (distracting activities) by which man avoids remaining still, living in the present and facing himself. In this perception, Pascal anticipates many modern writers, particularly Samuel Beckett (see p. 65).

Pascal is remembered above all for expressing man's humble but unique position in the universe:

'L'homme n'est qu'un roseau, le plus faible de la terre, mais c'est un roseau pensant.' ('Man is only a reed, the weakest thing in nature; but he is a thinking reed.')

Classical theatre

Because of the humanist interest in both Greek tragedy and Italian *commedia erudita*, in the seventeenth century French drama developed into the two separate genres of tragedy and comedy.

Tragic theatre observed conventions known as *les trois unités*, whereby the play should stick to a single event and its consequences occurring within one day and in one place. Such constraints heighten the power of the moral dilemmas featured by **Pierre Corneille** (1606–1684) whose heroes are torn between noble ideals and personal passion, but who finally achieve freedom of conscience and *la gloire* (glory) by acting with honour. In *Le Cid*, one of Corneille's best-loved plays, Rodrigue only becomes worthy of experiencing noble love by killing the father of Chimène, the woman he loves. There have been many startling modern productions of *Le Cid* since the Adonis-featured Gérard Philipe first played Rodrigue in 1951. The Irish director Declan Donnellan produced the play in English in 1986 and twelve years later brought a brilliant new French production to the 1998 Avignon festival, starring the young black actor William Nadylam.

The other great tragedian of the age was **Jean Racine** (1639–1699). His tragedies are concerned not with lofty ideals but with the exploration of character and emotion. His characters are the victims of their own passion which leads them inexorably to destruction. The 1997 production of *Phèdre* in London, translated by Ted Hughes and with Diana Rigg in the title role, testifies to Racine's continuing power and universal appeal.

Comédie in the seventeenth century was the comedy of manners, the humourous and often satirical depiction of contemporary life, perfected by Jean-Baptiste Poquelin, known as **Molière** (1622–1673). His genius lay in combining elements of farce and burlesque, the classical structure, linguistic refinement, and an acute portrayal of human weakness. The Church denounced what it perceived as an attack on religion (*Tartuffe* – the religious hypocrite) and morality (*Dom Juan* – the libertine), but Molière was protected by his patron Louis XIV. Molière's troupe subsequently joined forces with two other theatre groups and survives to this day as *la Comédie Française*.

Worldly wit and wisdom

Maxims, fables and letters were the respective genres of **La Rochefoucauld** (1613–1680), **La Fontaine** (1621–1695) and **Madame de Sévigné** (1626–1696) who were all *moralistes*, in the sense not of moralizing but of observing and reflecting on human nature.

La Rochefoucauld's sardonic *Sentences et maximes morales* reveal the underlying egoism of men's behaviour e.g. *'Dans l'adversité de nos meilleurs amis, nous trouvons toujours quelque chose qui ne nous déplaît pas.'* ('In the misfortune of our best friends, we always find something which is not displeasing to us.')

Madame de Sévigné's witticisms are similarly realist but sometimes kinder: *'Le coeur n'a pas de rides.'* ('The heart has no wrinkles.')

La Fontaine's early *Fables* were written to instruct but also to delight and entertain the young son of Louis XIV. Inspired by Aesop, La Fontaine wrote a total of 242 fables which, through allegories mainly featuring animals, reach sober and much-quoted conclusions such as:

Apprenez que tout flatteur
Vit aux dépens de celui qui l'écoute.

Know that all flatterers live at the expense of those who listen
to them.

Le Corbeau et le Renard, The Fox and the Crow

Le siècle des lumières (the Age of Enlightenment) – the eighteenth century

Eighteenth-century philosophy and literature were dominated by a
group of luminaries known as *les philosophes* whose ideas set
buzzing the predominantly feminine salons and the male cafés. It
was their works which fuelled a Europe-wide movement against
political and religious authority, culminating in France in the
Revolution of 1789. However, they did not advocate violent
change. What they shared was a hatred of fanaticism, religious or
political, and the belief that society, through the use of reason, could
be organized for the benefit of all. Their reasoning, unlike that of
Descartes, was inductive rather than deductive; that is, it was based
on experimentation and observation, and proceeded from the
particular to the general, rather than the other way round.

The intellectual giant of the eighteenth century was **Voltaire**
(1694–1778) who combined mastery of every literary form with
impassioned polemic against political and social injustice and
religious intolerance. Although he was aggressively anti-clerical,
Voltaire maintained a belief in God and in a universal morality
based on *le droit naturel* (natural law). He believed that an
individual is formed by his or her environment and experiences, as
exemplified in the ironic *conte philosophique* (philosophical tale),
Candide ou l'Optimiste. After progressing from false optimism –
'Tout est pour le mieux dans le meilleur des mondes possibles'
('Everything is for the best in the best of possible worlds') – to the
experience of evil and injustice, Candide finally takes stock of his
experiences and accepts what he has, deciding to *'cultiver son
jardin'* ('attend to his own garden').

Montesquieu (1689–1755) was France's first political theorist
who, by advocating the separation of executive, legislative and

judicial powers, influenced the drawing up of the American constitution. Like Voltaire, he thought man's nature was conditioned. He examined the interrelationship of environment (terrain and climate in particular), economics and culture, in an attempt to understand how societies develop and how human nature is conditioned. Like his seventeenth-century predecessors, Montesquieu was the master of one-line wisdom:

'*Si les triangles faisaient un dieu, ils lui donneraient trois côtés.*'
'If triangles created a god, they would give it three sides.'

Denis Diderot (1713–1784) was an atheist and materialist who dedicated most of his life to compiling *L'Encyclopédie*, an exhaustive inventory of human knowledge which was intended to undermine the superstition, ignorance and inequality of the political and religious establishment by informing and spiritually enlightening the reader. Despite the Church's condemnation and official opposition, Diderot toiled away, publishing all 28 volumes over a period of 21 years, although his collaborator d'Alembert withdrew after volume seven. The articles, 60,000 in total, were written by Diderot himself and a string of luminaries including Voltaire and Rousseau.

However, a relatively slim volume, *Le Contrat Social* (The Social Contract) by **Jean-Jacques Rousseau** (1712–1778) had a much more direct influence on revolutionary thinking. Pronouncing '*L'homme est né libre, et partout il est dans les fers*' ('Man was born free and everywhere he is in chains'), it fired the Revolution and inspired *La Déclaration des Droits de l'Homme* (see p. 15) which incorporates the fundamental principles of civil liberty and equal rights before the law.

Rousseau's ideas about child-centred education were equally influential and a direct attack on authoritarian teaching by rote. His *Emile ou de l'éducation* anticipated by nearly 200 years the radical changes in teaching methods which transformed state education in Britain and America in the 1960s, but which, however, had less impact in France (see p. 193). Rousseau's supreme confidence in his personal theories of child-rearing was unshaken by the fact that he was apparently unable to cope with his own offspring, whom he abandoned on the steps of a foundling hospital!

Romantic writers of the following century reveal many of Rousseau's characteristics – a love of nature, individualism, a sense of revolt against society, and an exasperating self-absorption.

Romantisme, réalisme, symbolisme – the nineteenth century

In the years between 1789 and the end of the nineteenth century, France experienced two revolutions, three republics, the restoration of the monarchy and two empires, as well as the scientific and technical advances which brought about the industrial revolution. It is not surprising that such material, political and social upheaval gave rise to conflicting world-views: on the one hand, individualism, subjectivity and spirituality; on the other hand, a supreme faith in science. From this polarization emerged the contrasting literary trends of *romantisme*, *réalisme* and *symbolisme*.

Science versus spirituality – two philosophers

Auguste Comte (1798–1857), who saw scientific discovery as the key to material progress and human happiness, developed his ideas into the theory known as positivism. He applied the scientific method not only to the natural world but to society, thus creating the new discipline of sociology which he believed could be used, like science, to predict the future. Comte's extreme confidence in the power of science was shared by later writers such as the literary critic and historian **Hippolyte Taine**, the sociologists **Emile Durkheim** and **Lucien Lévy-Bruhl** and the novelist **Emile Zola**.

The ideas of **Henri Bergson** (1859–1941), an ardent opponent of positivism, are largely disregarded in Britain and America, despite their lasting influence in France. Bergson used his knowledge of biology, physiology and psychology to counter the Darwinian concept of evolution with his own theory of *l'élan vital*, an innate vitality causing an organism to continually strive for perfection through innovation and change. Like the existentialists more than a century later, Bergson asserted individual freedom and creativity, believing that man creates his own moral values. The distinction he made between chronological time and time as a subjective experience is echoed and developed by both Proust and Beckett.

Le romantisme

Compared with the eighteenth-century *philosophes*, the Romantics were all colour, imagination and feeling. Nature, instead of providing data for classification, mirrored the Romantic individual's anguished emotions which found perfect expression in lyrical poetry. Perhaps the best-loved exponent of the genre was **Alphonse de Lamartine** (1790–1869) whose poems are renowned for their musicality. Although their poetry is less popular now than it was in the early part of the twentieth century, the Romantics still have a powerful hold on the popular imagination. The stormy relationship of Romantic poet **Alfred de Musset** (1810–1857) and the novelist, feminist and social reformer **George Sand** (1804–1876) is the subject of the 1999 film *Les Enfants du siècle* which stars Juliette Binoche and Benoît Magimel. Both writers flouted convention – Musset habitually dressed up to the nines as a dandy and Sand, who had adopted a man's name in order to get published, donned male attire and smoked in the street, for which she was fined.

Just as Rousseau was a sixties radical before his time, so **Gérard de Nerval** (1808–1855) anticipates not only the dissolute symbolist poets, but the 'Lucy in the Sky with Diamonds' generation of more than a century later. Nerval's drug-induced hallucinatory experiences run through his poetry which evokes an ideal world. The poor poet's fate in the material world was to hang himself from a Paris railing.

Although hardly read today, the Romantic novel has had a revival in other forms. *Les Trois Mousquetaires* (The Three Musketeers) by **Alexandre Dumas** (1802–1870) and *Notre-Dame de Paris* (The Hunchback of Notre-Dame) and *Les Misérables* by **Victor Hugo** (1802–1885) have all been the subject of countless films and, in the case of Hugo's novels, musicals. Would Hugo turn in his grave? Probably. Not only at Disney's cartoon version of *The Hunchback of Notre-Dame* but at the values of the consumer-driven society for whom it was produced. He believed man to be capable not only of material, but of spiritual progress and he fought tirelessly against social injustice. An outspoken opponent of the Second Empire, he was exiled to the Channel Isles for eighteen years.

Hugo's prodigious literary and artistic (see p. 74) output was fired by boundless creative, as well as sexual, energy, to which a succession of maids at his Guernsey home could testify. Despite his eccentric behaviour – such as regularly stripping off to wash on his roof top, and sending his fiancée a love letter containing a live bat – Hugo became a national hero. His street was named after him during his life-time; he received France's highest honour, *la Légion d'honneur* when he was only 23; 600,000 Parisians celebrated his eightieth birthday by parading under his window; and one million mourners attended his state funeral.

Le réalisme

While sharing some of the Romantics' preoccupations, some contemporary novelists like **Honoré de Balzac** (1799–1850) and **Stendhal** (1783–1842) wrote with precise attention to detail or with an objective tone, characteristics which were later associated with realism.

Balzac's monumental work *La Comédie humaine* (The Human Comedy) comprises a staggering total of 91 titles of which the best-known are probably *Le Père Goriot* and *Eugénie Grandet*. By describing an individual character's appearance, possessions and environment, Balzac evokes a particular animal, suggesting the half-concealed animal nature of the individual, and of social groups such as journalists, bureaucrats and financiers whom he depicts as packs of rapacious predators.

Stendhal shunned Romantic lyricism and overt emotion for an altogether more restrained and ironic style. With complete disregard for prevailing moral and social values, Julien Sorel, the hero of *Le Rouge et le Noir* (Scarlet and Black), seeks to follow the dictates of his heart through a series of carefully calculated acts of will, a form of self-realization that anticipates existentialist ideas of the twentieth century.

Realist author *par excellence*, **Gustave Flaubert** (1821–1880) conveys a spirit of scientific observation through adopting an objective viewpoint and through describing personal appearance and environment in telling detail. Flaubert was a master of style, expending enormous effort to find *le seul mot juste* (exactly the right word) and to create a rhythm in each sentence and paragraph.

Because of this, he took five years to complete his masterpiece *Madame Bovary*, the story of Emma Bovary, a provincial woman with romantic dreams, who is trapped in a mundane existence.

Whereas Flaubert had been principally concerned with the bourgeoisie, **Emile Zola** (1840–1902) wrote about the poor industrial workers of Northern France, sparing no grim detail of their miserable lives. For Zola, the novel was a kind of scientific experiment in which the influence of environment and heredity could be observed as the characters develop. To this end, he developed the twenty-volume Rougon-Macquart cycle which follows the fortunes of a poor working-class family and its descendents. The major novels of this cycle are *L'Assommoir* ('The Bar'), *Germinal* and *La Bête humaine* ('The Human Beast').

Zola was a committed socialist whose famous article *'J'accuse'*, written in defence of Dreyfus (see p. 16), earnt him a year in prison and the official disgrace of losing his *Légion d'honneur*.

Baudelaire and *les symbolistes*

Charles Baudelaire (1821–1867), and the symbolist poets who succeeded him, opposed realism by exploring the evocative and mystical power of language. Baudelaire's collection of poems entitled *Les Fleurs du Mal* (Flowers of Evil) describes the poet's emotional torment, torn between *le spleen*, meaning anxiety and physical and moral self-loathing, and a yearning for *l'idéal*, the world of beauty and the spirit. Baudelaire's classical style and evocative, elliptical use of language heighten the impact of his often sordid subject matter which caused him to be fined for indecency. His search for beauty in subjects shunned by earlier poets, and his vision of the world as a *'forêt de symboles'* ('forest of symbols') marked the beginning of modern poetry.

The symbolist poets, **Stéphane Mallarmé** (1842–1898), **Arthur Rimbaud** (1854–1891) and **Paul Verlaine** (1844–1896) used dream-like images, the sound of the words and layers of meaning to reveal an ideal world hidden behind everyday appearances. While the poetry of Mallarmé remains beautiful yet obscure to all but the truly determined reader, that of Rimbaud still conveys the passion of a brilliant and rebellious young man in quest of *'une alchimie poétique'* ('poetic alchemy'). Rimbaud's tempestuous love-affair with Verlaine ended when Verlaine shot and wounded him. Shortly after this incident, which earnt Verlaine two years in prison, Rimbaud wrote a prose poem entitled *Une saison en enfer* (A Season in Hell) in which he formulates his rejection of poetry. He was only nineteen when he abandoned literature to spend the rest of his short life as a gun-runner in North Africa.

The most accessible symbolist poems are those of Verlaine who aimed for '*la musique avant toute chose*' ('musicality above all'), which unfortunately is lost in translation!

Les sanglots longs	The long sobs
Des violons	Of the violins
De l'automne	Of autumn
Blessent mon cœur	Wound my heart
D'une langueur	With a monotonous
Monotone	Languor
Chanson d'automne	Autumn song

Self, politics and language – the twentieth century and beyond

Modern French fiction voices the many uncertainties of the twentieth century – the emotional and political issues arising from two world wars and the Occupation, as well as the question of identity in a period of rapid social and technological change. Not only was the confident vision of the nineteenth-century novel gone for ever, but by the 1960s, experimental writers were calling into question the novel itself. At this time too, France spawned a generation of cultural theorists whose preoccupation with language had a world-wide influence on the study of literature and culture. They were responsible for the words 'structuralist' and 'deconstructionist' slipping out of academic journals and into daily papers, even if most people had no idea what they meant. Although Alain Robbe-Grillet's arid 'new novels' are hardly read today, and French theories about language eventually became something of a stranglehold, they challenged literary conventions and accepted ideas and thus opened the door to the huge diversity of French writing today.

L'avant-garde

Although the expression *avant-garde* is sometimes used in a general sense to denote innovation in the arts, it is the name of a specific movement which was apparent in art and music before the First World War, and which found literary expression in poetry and in the violent satire and fantasy of **Alfred Jarry**'s (1873–1907) Ubu plays.

Guillaume Apollinaire (1880–1918) aimed to reflect the fragmentary and fleeting nature of experience captured by cubist painters. He freed poetry from formal constraints, using rhyming free verse, ignoring rules of grammar and punctuation and literally changing the shape of poetry by inventing *calligrammes* in which typography or the hand-written words of a poem form a picture on the page. Together with **Max Jacob** (1876–1944) and **Blaise Cendrars** (1887–1961), Apollinaire anticipated the irrationality and unfettered imagination of the surrealist movement whose name he coined.

The search for self

Marcel Proust (1871–1922) has had a legendary influence on modern literature, and his 4,000-page, eight-part series of novels, *A la Recherche du Temps perdu* (In Search of Lost Time), is the most revered work of fiction in the French language. 15,000 copies of the first volume, *Du côté de chez Swann* (Swann's Way) are still sold every year, 87 years after first publication.

'For a long time I went to bed early' the famous first sentence of Proust's masterpiece.

The novels mark a complete break with nineteenth-century realism, by exploring the subjective nature of time and consciousness. Only *la mémoire involontaire* (involuntary memory) triggered by the taste of a *madeleine* dipped in tea or by the smell of a flower, can recapture the past.

Proust's reputation as a difficult writer stems mainly from the absence of plot in his novels and the complexity of his elegantly constructed sentences. A strip-cartoon version of *Du côté de chez Swann*, which appeared in 1998 and attemped to make Proust more accessible to the general reader, was decried as sacrilegious by high-minded critics. They were less scathing about Raul Ruiz's 1999 film adaptation of Proust's final volume, *Le Temps retrouvé*, starring Catherine Deneuve and Emmanuelle Béart.

André Gide (1869–1951) was, like Proust, one of the first to question the concept of self in the novel. In *Les Caves du vatican*, for example, the hero commits a pointless murder which is *un acte gratuit* (a gratuitous act), a defining moment of spontaneous, unpremeditated, action that liberates him from the determining influences of his past. Gide's fiction reflects the personal conflicts he experienced as a homosexual brought up as a strict Protestant in the late nineteenth century. His *Journal* gives a fascinating insight into his beliefs and work and the Paris literary scene of the inter-war years.

Traditional realism

Of course, not all writers of this period were pushing back the boundaries of style or subject matter. Perhaps the best-loved novel of the early twentieth century is *Le Grand Meaulnes* by **Alain-Fournier** (1886–1914), a haunting tale of lost love. Many traditional novels, such as those of **François Mauriac** (1885–1970), powerfully convey the tensions of French bourgeois family life and evoke a strong sense of place. In Mauriac's *Le Mystère Frontenac* and *Thérèse Desqueyroux* you can almost smell the pine trees of his native *Landes* near Bordeaux. **Jean Giono** (1895–1970) is renowned for the affection with which he depicts the Midi and its peasants, most memorably in the trilogy *Colline, Un de Baumugnes* and *Regain*. He was also the author of *Le Hussard sur le toit*, which was successfully transposed to film as The Horseman on the Roof.

The author of lyrical, semi-autobiographical novels, **Sidonie-Gabrielle Colette** (1873–1954), was a much-loved figure, equally at ease at home with her cats, writing and gardening, or living it up in Parisian high society. The new fashion for 'emancipated' women early in the century – short hair and cloche hats – was named *la mode Claudine* after the heroine of many of Colette's novels.

Action and reflection

Many writers of the 1930s were deeply affected by the political events of the decade. **André Malraux** (1901–1976) was attracted to communism like many intellectuals of his generation. He wove into his novels, of which the best-known is *La Condition Humaine*, the experiences of his brilliant and idiosyncratic early career which included archeology, journalism and fighting in the Spanish Civil War, in the French war in Indo-China and in the Resistance during the Second World War. As Minister of Culture in de Gaulle's post-war government, he established *les maisons de la culture* (cultural centres) in major French towns.

The young and aristocratic **Antoine de St Exupéry** (1900–1944) was, like Malraux, an adventurer and a humanist. He was a daring pilot whose pioneering flights inspired his books such as *Vol de nuit* (Night Flight). However, he is best-known throughout the world for *Le Petit Prince* (The Little Prince) which has sold a total of 50 million copies in 102 languages or dialects including Latin, Basque and Esperanto.

Le surréalisme

André Breton (1896–1966) was the founder of surrealism which drew on Freud's view of the subconscious and asserted the power of the imagination and dreams as the route to knowledge. The juxtaposition of images, that at a rational level have no connection, is characteristic of surrealist poetry and evident in these lines from the collection *Capitale de la Douleur* (Capital of Pain) by **Paul Eluard** (1895–1952):

Ta chevelure d'oranges dans le vide du monde,
Dans le vide des vitres lourdes de silence
Et d'ombre où mes mains cherchent tous tes reflets

Your hair of oranges in the emptiness of the world,
In the emptiness of the window panes, heavy with silence
And shadow where my hands seek all your shimmering light

Louis Aragon (1897–1982), whose best-known collections are those dedicated to his wife Elsa Triolet, wrote movingly of love and war. In the late 1920s, all surrealist writers joined the Communist party but most became disenchanted with it. Aragon and Eluard were amongst the finest writers of the Resistance.

L'existentialisme

The popular image of existentialism is epitomized by the black clothes, long black hair and sexually-frank lyrics of singer Juliette Gréco who in the 1950s sang in the Left Bank cafés which were buzzing with intellectual debate. These were the cafés frequented by the formidable intellectual **Jean-Paul Sartre** (1905–1980), the principal exponent of existentialism in France. An atheist, Sartre believed that there are no absolute values beyond those which an individual creates himself. Many of his plays and novels, in particular *Les Chemins de la liberté* (Roads to Freedom) reflect Sartre's preoccupation with the conflict between political solidarity and the individual freedom that such solidarity is intended to protect.

The existentialist novels and philosophical works of **Simone de Beauvoir** (1908–1986), Sartre's companion of fifty-five years, were somewhat over-shadowed by the great man's work. However, certain critics claim that Sartre stole some of Simone's finest ideas. She is best known for her ground-breaking feminist work *Le Deuxième Sexe* (see p. 239) and for her three-volume autobiography. Her correspondence with her American lover, Nelson Algren, reveals a warm-hearted and passionate woman very different from her blue-stocking image.

Albert Camus (1913–1960) was part of the existentialist literary and philosophical circle, but he rejected the term itself and many of Sartre's ideas. In his first novel *L'Etranger* (The Outsider) and his philosophical work *Le Mythe de Sisyphe* (The Myth of Sisyphus)

Camus presents man's relationship to the world as *absurde*, meaningless and irrational, but it is a relationship that must be accepted and lived to the full. *La Peste* (The Plague) exemplifies Camus' belief in human solidarity as the way to combat the power of death. In contrast with Sartre's rather cold and cerebral novels, Camus' sparse but sensual style suggests an intense love of the physical world.

While **Jacques Prévert** (1900–1977) was not a member of the surrealist or existentialist movements, he was influenced by both. He was a master of popular song lyrics and cinema dialogue (see p. 107), as well as being a poet particularly popular with young people after the Second World War. He is still the best-known French poet, as all school children learn his deceptively simple poems and 550 schools are named after him. One of his best-loved poems, *Barbara*, is a reflection on the inhumanity of war. It begins with characteristic musicality:

Rappelle-toi Barbara
Il pleuvait sans cesse sur Brest ce jour-là
Et tu marchais souriante
Epanouie ravie ruisselante
Sous la pluie
Rappelle-toi Barbara

Remember Barbara
It rained and rained in Brest that day
And you walked smiling
Radiant, streaming-wet
In the rain
Remember Barbara

The French cultural review

A range of French intellectual journals offer the big names of literature, philosophy, politics, psychology and linguistics the chance to engage in intellectual combat. The two oldest titles are *Esprit*, a Catholic intellectual journal founded by the charismatic Jean Mounier before the Second World War, and *Les Temps Modernes* founded in 1945 by Jean-Paul Sartre and Simone de Beauvoir (see p. 62) as a forum for existentialist debate.

Cultural theorists

Le structuralisme

Structuralism grew from the ideas of the Swiss linguist **Ferdinand de Saussure** (1857–1913) who looked for meaning not in the historical origins of individual words or in the arbitrary relationship between a word and what it represents, but in language as a system, that is, in how words relate to each other. French intellectuals eagerly lifted this theoretical model from linguistics and applied it to just about everything you can think of.

While the anthropologist **Claude Lévi-Strauss** (1908–) was the first to show that all societies, whether 'primitive' or 'advanced', have similar structures, the trendy 1960s *intello*, **Roland Barthes** (1915–1980), subjected such everyday items as steak and chips and the Citroën 2CV to over-the-top structuralist analysis.

La déconstruction

Structuralism subsequently came under attack from intellectual heavy-weight Jacques Derrida (1930–) who claimed that the meaning of a text, or of anything else, is temporary and relative, simply an interpretation which inevitably suppresses countless other interpretations – hence the term *déconstruction* which suggests peeling away different layers of meaning. While Derrida is still a world-wide star in philosophy circles and cultural studies departments, he was voted 'the most overated' philosopher in a 1998 *Philosophers' Magazine* survey, no doubt reflecting the huge suspicion with which Anglo-Saxon philosophers view their continental colleagues. American scientist Alain Sokal was so incensed by the deconstructionists' tendency to relativize scientific method and discovery, that he wrote a spoof deconstructionist tract full of incomprehensible jargon and deliberate mistakes, then watched gleefully as French intellectuals lapped it up.

Psychoanalysis and language

Like Derrida, the Freudian psychoanalyst **Jacques Lacan** (1901–81) had a huge impact on literary criticism and on feminist theory as developed by **Luce Irigaray** and **Julia Kristeva** (see p. 240). In his notoriously impenetrable *Ecrits* (Writings) Lacan applied Saussure's ideas about language to the mind, claiming that the unconscious is structured in the same way as a language.

Le nouveau roman (The new novel)

Le nouveau roman was an experiment. Strongly influenced by *Nouvelle vague* cinema (see p. 148), novelists associated with *le nouveau roman* threw out traditional plot, character, chronology and narrative in an attempt to create their own reality, a reality which, however, was very different for each writer. **Alain Robbe-Grillet** (1922–) achieved a cinematographic effect in writing with his precise, impersonal and repetitive descriptions of objects, rooms and gestures. While this makes tedious reading, it is more successful transposed to film, as in *L'Année dernière à Marienbad* (Last Year in Marienbad) (see p. 149). **Claude Simon** (1913–) and **Michel Butor** (1926–) experimented with the presentation of time and space, while **Nathalie Sarraute** (1900–99) and **Marguerite Duras** (1914–1996) achieved psychological subtlety without traditional characterization. Like Robbe-Grillet, Duras also wrote for the cinema, notably *Hiroshima mon amour* (see p. 149). The best-known and most-read of this group of novelists, Duras was a war-time friend of François Mitterrand and the subject of a best-selling biography in 1998. Duras won the prestigious Prix Goncourt in 1984 for her novel *L'Amant* (The Lover), one of her finest works.

Le théâtre de l'absurde (The theatre of the absurd)

Samuel Beckett (1906–1989) changed the course of twentieth-century European theatre with his first play *En attendant Godot* (Waiting for Godot). Beckett was Irish and a gifted linguist who made his life in Paris and wrote most of his plays in both French and English. In Beckett's plays, characterization and plot are dispensed with. Instead, the gestures and speech of the characters construct a bleak metaphor of the human condition in which the stage becomes an almost bare waiting-room for death. The language and the visual imagery convey, touchingly, ironically and sometimes brutally, man's futile attempts to accept or avoid the reality of time passing and his hopeless situation. So Winnie in *Oh les beaux jours* (Happy Days), first played in France by Madeleine Renaud and in England by Peggy Ashcroft, finds herself up to her waist in sand, able only to occupy herself with her parasol and the contents of her handbag.

At the end of the play, when the sand reaches her neck, she still addresses the pathetic Willie, her husband, with painful optimism.

Other influential writers of *l'absurde*, the Roumanian **Eugène Ionesco** (1912–1994) and the Russian **Arthur Adamov** (1908–1970), like Beckett, spoke and wrote French as foreigners, which inevitably heightened their perception of communication, and of its absence, which is the subject of their plays. Ionesco made his name in the theatre with his first play *La Cantatrice chauve* (The Bald Prima Donna), which he called *une antipièce* (an anti-play).

La création collective and director's theatre

This was a completely different kind of theatre, produced by cooperatives who devised their own plays. In the late 1960s, **Jérôme Savary**'s Grand Magic Circus was an anarchic, exhuberant and provocative blend of street theatre and circus. On the other hand, **Ariane Mnouchkine** and her Théâtre du Soleil pioneered a more studied and political, but equally spectacular form of theatre, in particular the productions of *1789* and *1793* in which the actors addressed the unseated audience who gathered around them, drawn in to playing the role of the pre- and post-Revolutionary crowd.

From this period onwards in French theatre, the director has been a more important figure than the actors or the writer. However, the acclaimed playwright **Bernard-Marie Koltès** (1948–1989) constitutes something of an exception to this trend. He is known throughout the world for his play *Dans la solitude des champs de coton* (In the loneliness of the cotton fields), the dialogue of a drug dealer and his client, which has played to packed houses in 125 countries. The play was directed by one of France's top directors, Patrice Chéreau. France's foreign directors include Britons Peter Brook and Deborah Warner who are an established part of the French theatre scene.

Fragmentation (1970s–present)

New philosophers and new moralists

Amongst those who took issue with the intellectuals of 1968 were *les nouveaux philosophes* (the new philosophers) who emerged in the 1970s to attack Marxism, and reject political *engagement* while championing human rights. **Bernard-Henri Lévy, Alain**

Finkielkraut and **André Glucksmann** were, unlike their predecessors, determinedly *médiatiques*, that is they wrote about the part played by the media in contemporary consciousness, while at the same time making full use of it to reach their public.

The philosophers currently fêted by the media, but scorned by some fellow philosophers, are *les nouveaux moralistes* (the new moralists), **Luc Ferry** and **André Comte-Sponville** who are concerned to make philosophy as accessible as possible. In the tradition of French *moralistes* throughout the centuries, they address the enduring question of how to conduct our lives. Comte-Sponville has had a string of best-sellers including *Petit Traité des grandes vertus* (A small treatise on great virtues).

The newer novel

The *nouveau roman* of the 1960s has left a legacy of experimentation with language and style, as for example in the novels of **Philippe Sollers** (1936–) author of *Femmes* (Women) and **Georges Perec** (1936–1982), author of *La Vie mode d'emploi* (Life, a User's Manual). Perec revelled in weaving word games into his extraordinarily varied and ambitious works. He even wrote a whole novel – *La Disparition* (The Disappearance) – without the letter 'e'.

The 1970s saw a return to story-telling in a classical narrative style. One of the most inventive writers of this period is **Michel Tournier** (1924–) who uses ancient myths and other well-known stories to examine recent history and current values. In *Le Roi des Aulnes* (The Erl King), Tournier evokes the horrors of the Second World War through the story of an ogre. *Vendredi ou les limbes du Pacifique* is a re-telling of the Robinson Crusoe story, but in this version it is Friday who teaches Crusoe about life.

Foreign fiction

In their reading tastes, as in every other cultural domain, the French are very open to, and interested in, other countries' idioms. Unlike insular Anglo-Saxons, the French are keen readers of contemporary novels in translation. In fact, translated fiction and non-fiction account for a third of French book sales, but only 3 per cent of sales in Britain.

A plethora of new, young talent includes many women writers such as **Marie Darrieussecq** (1968–) whose phenomenally successful first novel, *Truismes* (Pig Tales) has been translated into 34 languages. The book has been France's most successful first novel since **Françoise Sagan** (1935–) took the Parisian literary world by storm, forty years earlier, with *Bonjour Tristesse*, a frank and unsentimental tale of first love. Darrieussecq's style is less realist and more scary – the heroine of *Truismes* switches between pig and human form, finally settling down with a ravenous wolfman.

Another publishing sensation of the late 1990s was **Michel Houellebecq** (1958–) whose best-sellers include *Extension du domaine de la lutte* (Whatever), and *Les Particules élémentaires* (Elementary Particles). At first he was fêted by the Left for attacking the ills of consumer society. However, in his second book he set about denouncing sacrosanct leftist ideals and promptly fell out with fellow members of the modish literary review *Perpendiculaire*, much to the delight of Parisian literary editors thirsting for an intellectual skirmish.

Alongside such 'serious' fiction, the last twenty years have seen a growth in *romans de terroir*, big-selling novels of rural life. *L'Ecole de Brive* (the Brive School) is so-called not just because Brive, at the heart of rural Corrèze, epitomizes country values, but because the first authors were snapped up by publishers at the annual *Foire du livre de Brive*, the town's book fair. Popular authors include **Michel Peyramaure** whose *Le Beau monde* ('High Society') recounts a young peasant woman's adventures in the Paris of 1880, and **Christian Signol** whose *La Rivière Espérance* ('River of Hope') was adapted for television.

By contrast, the ever-popular crime novel or *polar* has won over authors of other genres such as **Daniel Pennac**. There are now 46 crime collections which published over 800 titles in 1998, twice as many as in 1994. One publisher, *Editions de la voûte* has even pioneered selling short detective novels in self-service dispensers at *métro* stations. Favourite titles are **Pennac**'s *La fée carabine* available in translation as *Fairy Gunmother*, **Didier Daeninckx**'s *Meurtres pour mémoire* (Murder in memoriam) and **Jean Echenoz**'s *Lac* (Lake).

Le Prix Goncourt

This is France's most prestigious literary prize. The ten-member Académie des Goncourt, which chooses the annual prize winner, was created at the bequest of nineteenth-century writer Edmond Goncourt. With his brother Jules and other literary friends, he conceived the prize to be part of the nation's heritage. Winning *le Goncourt* guarantees huge sales and makes any writer the toast of the chattering classes – at least for a year.

If you are new to French literature, try these in French or English for good, interesting writing.

Le Grand Meaulnes (1913), Alain-Fournier
Thérèse Desqueyroux (1927), François Mauriac
La Maison de Claudine (My Mother's House) (1900), Colette
Paroles (1946) – poetry collection, Jacques Prévert
L'Etranger (The Outsider) (1942), Albert Camus
Oh les Beaux Jours (Happy Days) (1963) – play, Samuel Beckett
L'Amant (The Lover) (1984), Marguerite Duras
Le Roi des Aulnes (The Erl King) (1970), Michel Tournier
Truismes (Pig Tales) (1997), Marie Darrieussecq
Lac (Lake) (1989), Jean Echenoz

VOCABULARY

la langue de molière *language of Molière*
l'auteur *author*
l'écrivain (m.) *writer*
le romancier *novelist*
le poète *poet*
le/la dramaturge *dramatist*
écrire *to write*
rédiger *to compose/draft*
l'œuvre (f.) *the work/s*
raconter *to tell*
décrire *to describe*
représenter *to portray*
évoquer *to evoke*

citer *to quote*
l'ouvrage (m.) *work*
les oeuvres complètes (f.) *complete work*
le roman *novel*
le récit *short story*
le conte *tale, story*
la pièce de théâtre *play*
le recueil de poèmes *poetry collection*
la strophe *stanza*
le vers *line*
les vers *verse*
la citation *quotation*
l'extrait (m.) *extract*
le résumé *summary*
les personnages (m.) *characters*

les idées (f.) *ideas*
l'intrigue (f.) *plot*
l'action (f.) *plot*
le dénouement *outcome*
la signification *meaning*
l'engagement (m.) *commitment*

l'édition (f.) *publishing*
publier *to publish*
la parution *publication*
décerner un prix *to award a prize*
le Dépot légal *collection of every book
    published in France since 1537*

Taking it further

Places
La Comédie Française, 2 rue de Richelieu, Paris; tel. 01 44 58 14 00
Houses of Victor Hugo:
  6 Place des Vosges, Paris 75004; tel. 01 42 72 10 16
  Hauteville House, St Peter Port, Guernsey; tel. 01481 721911
Café de Flore and **Les Deux Magots**, Boulevard St-Germain-des-
  Prés, Paris – left-bank cafés frequented by Sartre, de Beauvoir and
  other existentialist writers
Café de Phares, La Bastille, Paris: venue for regular philosophical
  debates; for details of other *cafés philo* contact l'Association
  Philos; tel. 01 43 87 88 67
Shakespeare and Co, 37 rue de la Bûcherie, Paris 75005; tel. 01 43
  26 96 50: in its former premises in rue de l'Odéon this English-
  language bookshop was frequented by the likes of Hemingway,
  Erza Pound and James Joyce in the 1920s, and became the hub of
  English-speaking Parisian literary life. Now it is a mecca for back-
  packing Anglo-Saxon intellectuals.
Musée Marcel Proust, 4 rue du Docteur Proust, 28120 Illiers-
  Combray, tel. 02 37 24 30 97
Avignon theatre festival, Palais des Papes; tel. 04 90 27 50 71 –
  annual (July) festival of theatre, dance, music and street performances

Books
France, Peter, **The New Oxford companion to French literature
  in French** (Oxford: OUP, 1995)
Dictionnaire des grands écrivains de la langue française (Paris:
  Dictionnaires Le Robert, 2000)
Thurman, Judith, **Secrets of the Flesh: A life of Colette** (London:
  Bloomsbury, 1999)
Beauvoir, Simone de, **Beloved Chicago Man: Letters to Nelson
  Algren 1947–1964** (London: Gollancz, 1998) – fascinating
  insight into de Beauvoir's literary friends

Botton, Alain de, **How Proust can change your life** (London: Picador, 1997)

Bowie, Malcolm, **Proust among the stars** (London: HarperCollins, 1998)

Heuet, Stéphane, **Combray** (Paris: De court, 1998) – strip-cartoon version of vol. I of **A la Recherche du Temps perdu**

Le Bulletin Marcel Proust and other publications (Société des Amis de Marcel Proust et des Amis de Combray, 4 rue du Docteur Proust, 28120 Illiers-Combray, tel. 02 37 24 30 97; **http//webperso.alma-net.net/proust**)

Robinson, Dave and Garrett, Chris, **Introducing Descartes** (London: Icon/Totem, 1998)

Thody, Philip and Read, Howard, **Introducing Sartre** (London: Icon/Totem, 1998)

Cobley, Paul and Jansz, Litza, **Introducing Semiotics** (London: Icon/Totem, 1997) – includes Saussure, Lévi-Strauss, Barthes and American structuralists

Horrocks, Chris and Jevtic, Zoran, **Introducing Foucault** (London: Icon/Totem, 1997)

Sturrock, John, **The word from Paris** (London: Verso 1998 – low-down on French intellectuals

Journals

Le Magazine littéraire, 40 rue des Saint-Pères, 75007 Paris; tel. 01 45 44 14 51; **www. magazine.litteraire. com**

Le Matricule des anges, BP 225, 34004 Montpellier Cedex 1

La Quinzaine littéraire, 135 rue Saint-Martin, 75194 Paris; tel. 01 48 87 75 41; **www.quinzaine-litteraire.presse.fr**

Les Temps modernes, 4 rue Férou, 75006 Paris; tel. 01 43 29 08 47

Esprit, 212 rue Saint-Martin, 75003 Paris; tel. 01 48 04 08 33; **www.esprit.presse.fr**

La Nouvelle Revue française, 5 rue Sébastien-Bottin; 75007 Paris; tel. 01 49 54 42 00

CD-Rom

Saint-Exupéry, Antoine de, **Le Petit Prince** (Paris: Gallimard, 1998)

Websites

Gallimard: **www.saint-exupery.org.**

4 | ART AND ARCHITECTURE

Wherever you go in France, the country's artistic heritage is very much in evidence. France does have her share of ugly urban sprawl and unlovely out-of-town hypermarkets, but these are eclipsed by her wealth of beautifully restored and maintained historic buildings which, together with striking new architecture and works of art, are part of the fabric of everyday life.

Since the seventeenth century, when the Académies of painting and sculpture, and architecture were founded, architecture and the visual arts have been a central concern of the French state. Today, the Ministry of Culture receives one per cent of the national budget, and a healthy proportion of this is devoted to art and architecture. The ministry is housed in the elegant seventeenth-century Palais-Royal, alongside two of the nation's highest institutions, the Conseil Constitutionnel and the Conseil d'Etat (see p. 189), exemplifying the belief of culture minister Catherine Trautmann, that *'la culture est au cœur de notre système démocratique'* ('culture is at the heart of our democratic system'). This sentiment echoes the aims of her predecessors who include de Gaulle's post-war minister André Malraux and Mitterrand's innovative and daring minister, Jack Lang, both of whom wanted to enrich the lives of ordinary citizens.

Painting and sculpture

France has had an important role throughout the history of western art which began with the cave painters of the Dordogne, long before their land became a nation. From the Renaissance onwards French kings invited the finest European painters to decorate their palaces, and Paris became the centre of nearly all important artistic developments, whether the artists concerned were French or not.

It was only in the nineteenth century that French painters formed a distinctively French movement that was far more influential than the Flemish, German and Italian schools of previous centuries. The impressionists and their successors radically altered the direction of European art, attracting even more foreign artists to Paris. *L'Ecole de Paris* describes not an artistic movement but the group of young foreign artists who converged on Paris in the early years of the twentieth century.

The seventeenth and eighteenth centuries

While the most influential period of French painting was undoubtedly from the 1860s to the 1930s, certain earlier French painters rank amongst the finest in the world. The seventeenth century produced **Nicolas Poussin** (1594–1665), famed for his classical, pastoral scenes, and **Claude le Lorrain** (1600–1682), the creator of cool, green, idealized landscapes.

In the eighteenth century, **Antoine Watteau** (1684–1721) broke with classical restraint by creating the genre of *fête galante* – the nostalgic and dreamy depiction of aristocrats decked up as shepherds and shepherdesses. However, his best-known work is *Gilles*, a pierrot who fixes the observer with his enigmatic gaze. Watteau's successors were **François Boucher** (1703–1770), a protégé of Madame de Pompadour whom he immortalised on canvas, and **Jean Honoré Fragonard** (1732–1806), famed for his light-as-thistledown depictions of care-free aristocrats at play in picturesque settings (e.g. *La Balançoire* – The Swing).

In reaction to these fripperies, **Jacques-Louis David** (1748–1825) adopted a more austere, neo-classical style which found favour first with Louis XVI, subsequently with Robespierre and finally with Napoléon whom David represented in many heroic poses.

The hallmark of David's pupil, **Jean Auguste Dominique Ingres** (1780–1867), was an extremely precise and sensitive style which made him very much in demand as a portraitist of nineteenth-century bourgeois dignitaries seeking immortality in oils. He also painted fellow artists and musicians and is well-known for the creamy contours of his monumental nudes as in *Le Bain turc*. Ingres influenced later painters as diverse as Degas, Matisse and Picasso.

Les romantiques

In art as in literature (see p. 55), the Romantic style was a complete break away from the restraint epitomized by David and Ingres. The Romantic painter par excellence was **Eugène Delacroix** (1798–1863) whose canvases depicted scenes of passion and high drama, exaggerated gestures and plentiful half-clad bodies: *La Mort de Sardanapale* (The Death of Sardanapalus) and *La Liberté guidant le peuple* (Liberty on the Barricades) which featured the first known image of Marianne leading the 1830 revolution.

The maverick writer **Victor Hugo** (1802–1885) (see p. 55–56) who was, perhaps understandably, less well-known as an artist, took Romantic experimentation to extremes by painting craggy châteaux and melancholy ruins with anything he could lay his hands on, such as gouache mixed with charcoal, toothpaste, coffee grounds, soot and saliva – and this was before he dabbled in the occult and allegedly conjured up spirits to guide his drawing!

But Hugo did not seek the acceptance of the art establishment nor to have his works included at the Salon, the annual official Paris art exhibition which exhibited hundreds and sometimes thousands of paintings and sculptures. This body, which determined the taste of the day, considered only grand subjects drawn from antiquity or mythology and which displayed a particular finesse of execution, to be worthy of the term 'art'.

Auguste Rodin (1840–1917)

Famed in particular for his sculptures *Le Penseur* (The Thinker) and *Les Bourgeois de Calais*, Rodin combined Romantic sensibility with exceptional technical expertise.

Les réalistes

Gustave Courbet (1819–1877) was one of the first to challenge the art establishment with his unsentimental landscapes and naturalistic nudes which earnt him what was then the insulting title of *réaliste*. Nonetheless, Courbet was hugely influential on later painters such as Cézanne. Like Courbet, **François Millet** (1814–1875) was also vilified as vulgar and shocking, particularly for his peasant paintings such as *Les Cribleuses de blé* (The Gleaners).

Les impressionnistes

Less than ten years later, the impressionists went much further. Not only did they reject the idealized treatment of historical subject matter, preferring a direct approach to everyday scenes and objects, but they aimed through their use of the three primary colours, white canvas and visibly distinct brush strokes, to capture the light and movement of nature. Many of these artists executed their landscape paintings outdoors which gave their canvases more immediacy than those of the old masters who had painted in the studio from sketches.

Edouard Manet (1832–1883), who was in the vanguard of this new movement, had two of his most famous works, *Le Déjeuner sur l'herbe* and *l'Olympia*, rejected by the Salon of 1863. In both paintings a naked woman, painted without classical ornamentation or Romantic gestures, simply looks out of the canvas directly at the observer. In the next few years, other young painters, who admired and were influenced by Manet and Courbet, were systematically refused inclusion in the Salon show. As a result, in 1874 these *refusés* set up their own exhibition, which brought to the public the works of Monet, Renoir, Degas, Cézanne, Pissarro, Sisley, Guillaumin and Berthe Morisot, Manet's sister-in-law. Six further exhibitions followed, including the works of painters sometimes designated as post-impressionist – Gaughin, Seurat and Signac.

It was **Claude Monet**'s (1840–1926) painting of a boat in a misty, red dawn – *Impression, soleil levant* – at the first such exhibition that caused a journalist to dismiss the group as merely *'impressionniste'*. However, the young artists defiantly adopted the pejorative term, little suspecting that in time it would become synonymous with respectability, nor that over a century later, far from shocking polite society, their works would grace a thousand birthday cards (or birth cards, as does Berthe Morisot's ubiquitous *Le Berceau* – (Cradle).

Although many impressionist painters died in poverty, their talent unrecognized, Monet at 60 was hailed as one of France's greatest living painters and was awarded the *Légion d'honneur* which he refused. He was sufficiently well-off to buy the house at Giverny whose garden provided him with the material for his vast series of *Nymphéas* (Water-lilies). The changed colours of his later water-lily canvases testify to Monet's failing sight due to cataracts.

While Monet is renowned for his representation of light and movement, Renoir for his pleasing figures, Degas for capturing the fleeting gestures of dancers, Sisley for his delicate landscapes and Pissarro for his bird's-eye views of Paris, the styles of all of these artists changed in time and many developed away from impressionism.

Les post-impressionnistes

Paul Cézanne (1839–1906) who was interested in more than the impressionist concern with visual appearance, wanted to capture simultaneously every essential aspect of a thing, person or landscape. He declared, *'Avec une pomme, je veux étonner Paris!'* ('I want to amaze Paris with an apple!'). This he did with richly-coloured still-lifes, often incorporating different points of view and geometric shapes, anticipating fauvist and cubist painting of the twentieth century. When painting figurative works, Cézanne was famously impatient with fidgety sitters and even ordered his wife to pose like an apple. Perhaps he solved the problem by letting his models lounge around, as in his famous series of bathing nudes. Here the figures are distorted, in the same way as his landscapes, to achieve what Cézanne termed his *motif* or unifying vision.

Georges Seurat (1859–1891) developed *pointillisme*, the painstaking method of applying small dots of separate colour which when viewed at the correct distance were meant to fuse, creating a colour of greater purity and intensity. The result, as for example in *Une baignade à Asnières*, is a patterned monumentality and emotional stillness quite at odds with Seurat's short and turbulent life.

By contrast, the works of **Vincent Van Gogh** (1853–90) are so full of emotion that his broad, distinct brush strokes seem to leap off the canvas. Van Gogh was Dutch, but was so dazzled by the work of the impressionists that he soon abandoned the sombre tones of his early paintings and moved to Provence for its light and colour, making his life in France. His correspondence with his brother Théo in Paris reveals his discoveries, his solitude and periods of despair as well as manic activity (he produced his last seventy paintings in the two months before he committed suicide at the age of 37). Although Van Gogh only sold one painting in his life-time and gave portraits to his sitters because he could not afford to pay them, his paintings now command the world's top prices. *Le Portrait du Docteur Gachet* which sold at Christie's New York in 1990 for $82.5m is still the world's most valuable painting, followed by Renoir's *Le Moulin de la Galette* ($78.1m in 1990) and Van Gogh's haunting self-portrait *L'Artiste sans barbe* ($71m in 1998). But perhaps his best-known paintings are of *Les Tournesols* (Sunflowers), the flowers which accompanied his coffin.

Initially influenced by the impressionists, **Paul Gauguin** (1848–1903) developed a powerful, almost two-dimensional style, painting Breton women and landscapes. Captivated by the primitive art and glowing colours of the tropics whilst on a visit to Panama and Martinique, he broke his links with Paris, abandoning his comfortable life as a stockbroker, his family and friends in order to settle in Tahiti. Here he painted many exotic paintings such as *Nave Nave Mahana* (Days of Delight) which depicts a dignified, idyllic life, ironically at a time when the syphilitic Gauguin was becoming increasingly isolated and impoverished.

Henri de Toulouse-Lautrec (1864–1901)

Toulouse-Lautrec's paintings and lithographs vividly depict the world of Paris music hall and brothels in the late nineteenth century. His advertising posters were produced as lithographs and were a perfect medium for the curving lines and two-dimensional nature of Art Nouveau design (see p. 91). A century later, Charles Aznavour played the part of Toulouse-Lautrec in a musical celebrating the artist's brief and intense life.

Les symbolistes

Although symbolism was primarily a literary movement (see p. 57–58), several important French painters such as **Odilon Redon** (1840–1916) and **Gustave Moreau** (1826–98) explored the imagery of myths and dreams. They were influenced by the English Pre-Raphaelites, who, much in vogue at the time (Edward Burne-Jones received the *Légion d'honneur*), are hardly known in France today. Moreau was an inspiring teacher whose students included Matisse, Dufy and Braque.

Le nabis

This short-lived movement which began in 1888 arose in reaction to extravagant symbolist imagery. The two best-known painters of this school, **Edouard Vuillard** (1868–1940) and **Pierre Bonnard** (1867–1947) painted informal, intimate domestic scenes in soft, vibrant colour. For the rest of his life, Bonnard continued to document his home life with his wife Marthe who appears in many of his paintings – putting on her black stockings, sitting beside a red-check table cloth and, most luminously, in the bath of *La Grande Baignoire, nu*. Bonnet declared *'Je voudrais arriver devant les jeunes peintres de l'an 2000 avec des ailes de papillon'* ('I would like to reach the young painters of the year 2000 on butterfly wings'). Anyone seeing his glowing canvases would agree that he has done just that.

Les fauves

Fauve (wild beast), like *impressionniste*, was an unflattering term coined by an art critic to describe the early works of Matisse, Rouault, Derain, Dufy, Vlaminck and Braque. These painters only exhibited together between 1905 and 1907, but what they shared, which earnt them the label *fauve*, was a boldness of execution, colour and composition. **Henri Matisse** (1869–1954) was the *fauve* who made the greatest impact on later French painting. He was greatly influenced by Gauguin and also Cézanne whose *Trois baigneuses* (Three Bathers) he studied every morning before starting work. Having grown up in Picardy amongst the silk weavers and Jacquard looms of the textile industry, Matisse retained a love of flat decorative designs which frequently feature on the shawls and draperies of his models and which also influenced the layout of a whole canvas. Drawn by the light of the south of France, he settled there, producing vibrantly colourful landscapes and interiors such as *Le Bonheur de vivre*, lyrical nudes including *La Danse*, engravings, sculptures and the collages of *Jazz*. In later life, his style became less representational and revealed even more powerfully his love of simple line, colour, shape and space. Cézanne claimed to be a very ordinary person but his life was a ceaseless quest. As an old man he said, *'Si je vivais plus longtemps, je pourrais peindre'* ('If I lived longer, then I could paint').

Les cubistes

The young Spanish painter **Pablo Picasso** (1881–1973) settled in the south of France before the First World War, at the same time as other foreign artists (Modigliani, Chagall, Brancusi, Foujita ...) were flocking to Paris. Between 1901 and 1905 he produced the well-known paintings of his *époques bleue et rose* (blue and pink periods). However, it was his subsequent cubist work that had a profound impact on European art.

Cubism, of which Picasso's *Les Demoiselles d'Avignon* is often hailed as the first example, sprang from Picasso and **Georges Braque**'s (1882–1963) desire to capture the three-dimensional nature of things, without letting the observer forget that the canvas is two-dimensional. They achieved this by using several viewpoints simultaneously and by breaking up an object before rearranging its constituent parts: in Picasso's words – *'Auparavant ... un tableau était une somme d'additions. Chez moi, un tableau est une somme de destructions'* ('In the past ... a painting was the sum of its parts. But my painting is the sum of what has been destroyed'). The cubists, who included **Juan Gris** (1887–1927), **Fernand Léger** (1881–1955) and **Robert Delaunay** (1885–1941), were not aiming simply to create the illusion of reality; they were concerned with the tension between the artefact and what it represents. What was already implicit in impressionist, and later in *fauve*, paintings was now made explicit – that a work of art has a reality independent of what it represents. In fact it may not be representational at all, as in the later work of Delaunay. In his early works, Delaunay's vibrant colours appear as segments of recognizable objects such as the Eiffel Tower (in his *Tour Eiffel* series), but later they form completely abstract, lyrical compositions.

Collage was another cubist innovation. Picasso and Braque stuck wood, leather, card and string to their canvases; Picasso incorporated these materials in his sculptures too, even creating *Tête de taureau* (Bull's Head) out of a bicycle seat and handlebars, contributing to the emergence of a new kind of sculpture that was assembled rather than modelled or carved.

But is it art? – Dada

Sculpture took an even more radical turn with **Marcel Duchamp** (1887–1968). He abandoned cubist painting after the success of his famous *Nude descending a staircase, no.2* and joined the 'anti-art' Dada group whose provocative, sometimes jokey works e.g. Duchamp's moustachioed *Mona Lisa*, were designed to challenge all preconceptions about art. What shocked the art world most were Duchamp's 'ready-mades', such as a perfectly normal iron bottle rack which he offered up as an *objet d'art*, and a urinal which he entitled *Fontaine* (Fountain) and signed with the punning pseudonym 'Rose Sélavy' (*C'est la vie*). After a decade or so of such playful experiments, which were to influence the pop art of the 1960s, Duchamp gave up art altogether and devoted himself to his other passion – chess!

Les surréalistes

By 1920 Dada had been superseded by surrealism, a literary as much as an artistic movement (see p. 61–62) which gave vivid expression to the unconscious. While Paris was the home of surrealism, the movement's most famous artists were foreigners who had converged there: the Spaniard Salvador Dali, the Belgian René Magritte, the German Max Ernst, and the American Man Ray. The Italian sculptor Alberto Giacometti was part of the group before creating the elongated and emaciated figures for which he later became well known. At this time, Picasso painted his surrealist masterpiece *Guernica*, inspired by the horrors of the Spanish Civil War.

Up to the present

After the Second World War, Paris did not regain its previously undisputed dominance of artistic taste. It was New York, not Paris that became the home of abstract expressionism in the 1940s and pop art in the '50s and '60s. However, although France did not produce new movements to equal the influence of impressionism or cubism, she continued to nurture the distinct paths of many French and foreign artists – the long and constantly innovative career of Picasso, the passionate *abstraction lyrique* of the Russian painter **Nicholas de Staël** (1914–1955), the *art brut* (primitive or child-like style) of **Jean Dubuffet** (1901–1985) and the *nouveau réalisme* of sculptors such as **César Baldaccini** (1921–1998) whose use of commercial objects as rubbish rather than as icons, was something of an antidote to pop art. The son of poor Italian immigrants in Marseille, César as he became known, began scavenging rubbish dumps for scrap material because he could not afford clay. In 1960 he created a *succès de scandale* with the first of his *Compressions* – sculptures made of crushed cars and other scrap metal. César is one of France's best-known modern artists, particularly because a cast of his thumb (*Pouce*), a giant metal version of which graces La Défense in Paris, was used as the model for the French cinéma awards, *Les Césars*.

Jean Tinguely (1927–1991) too, used an assortment of discarded materials for his extraordinary sculptures. Unsuspecting visitors to the Forest of Fontainebleau may suddenly see a huge mirrored tongue glinting through the trees, or they may hear the clanking 'brain' machinery of Tinguely's 22-metre-high *Cyclop*. For this fascinating, walk-in construction Tinguely enlisted the help of 15 fellow artists, including that of his French-American wife Niki de Saint Phalle (1930–). Her multicoloured, voluptuous sculptures also feature in other collaborative works such as Tinguely and de Saint Phalle's *Fontaine de Stravinski* on the Right Bank of the Seine in Paris.

The haunting sculptures of French-born **Louise Bourgeois** (1911–) were largely ignored for most of her long life until she won world-wide acclaim with her exhibition at the Museum of Modern Art in New York in 1982. Her works include sinister giant spiders and stitched fabric torsos, sometimes headless, sometimes shockingly elegant, wearing the flimsy garments and treasures of the artist's past.

Georges Mathieu (1921–) and **Pierre Soulages** (1919–) are probably the best-known of present-day French painters – Mathieu for his abstract paintings created in public, and Soulages for his black canvases textured by slashes and stripes, a seemingly paradoxical expression of his fascination with light. Soulages explains *'ce qui m'intéresse, ce n'est pas le noir en lui-même mais ce que la lumière réfléchie par cette couleur provoque en nous'* ('What interests me is not black in itself but what the light reflected by this colour stirs in us'). Given this, it is perhaps less surprising that Soulages' recent work includes the stained glass windows of the Gothic Abbaye de Ste-Foy in Conques.

Amongst a younger generation of artists are **Christian Boltanski** (1944–) whose works often incorporate memorabilia such as old photographs and biscuit tins, and **Daniel Buren** (1938–) whose striped, column-like blocks complement the classical columns of the courtyard of the Palais-Royal in Paris.

Architecture

For well over a century, France has led the world in conservation and the restoration of historic buildings. In the nineteenth century, the zealous architect, Viollet-le-Duc, set about restoring to their former glory many medieval buildings which had suffered damage or neglect, although sometimes with unnatural results, as he frequently ripped out the fine decoration of later periods. Greater caution was enforced in 1913 with the introduction of preservation orders. These have been given to over 1,000 historical, functional or eccentric buildings including Rouen's ornate railway station, Le Corbusier's Salvation Army Hostel in the rue Cantagruel in Paris, and another pre-war Parisian institution – the brothel at 32-34 rue Blondel, which closed in 1947 along with 1,400 such establishments throughout France.

In the 1960s, culture minister André Malraux introduced legislation to permit the conversion of old buildings for modern uses and to attract new businesses to old areas in order to keep them alive as communities rather than as open-air museums. This adventurous attitude to the past is matched by the flair and daring of France's modern architecture.

Operation clean-up

Restoration work includes cleaning which has transformed Paris in recent years. Many historic facades and streets have been spruced up, not without a touch of French ingenuity: strategically-placed, electrically-charged metal rods deter hapless pigeons from disfiguring Notre-Dame with their droppings; and teams of council workers driving *motocrottes* (a sort of pooper scooper scooter!) clear the pavements of dog dirt.

Roman remains

Most of France's fine Roman remains are in Provence which was relatively unscathed by later invasions or by the urban developments experienced by northern cities. Particularly well-preserved are the Roman temple and amphitheatre in Nîmes and the theatre and triumphal arch in Orange.

Churches

The golden age for French church building was the period from the eleventh to the fifteenth century. It was a time of relative political stability, economic growth and most importantly, strong Christian faith.

Romanesque

The term *roman* or *romanesque*, describes the style of architecture that became current in Europe at the end of the tenth century. While French romanesque shared some features of classical architecture – round arches and heavy vaults for example – the style varied throughout the country, according to local building materials, the individual tastes of patrons and other regional influences. An austere, undecorated form of romanesque developed in the north and found its way to England thanks to the Norman invader Guillaume le Conquérant (William the Conqueror). In Provence, where the Roman influence was strongest, the churches have domes and aisle-less naves. But further west and north, the romanesque style features more sculptured decoration, sometimes twin towers and sometimes the influence of Moorish Spain, as in the decoration of Notre-Dame in Le Puy and in Poitiers' Notre-Dame-la-Grande. Burgundy has some of France's finest romanesque architecture including St-Philibert at Tournus, the basilica of Ste-Madelaine in Vézélay and the abbey of Fontenay. It was the reforming zeal of the Benedictine order of Cluny in Burgundy that brought not only Christianity but romanesque architecture to many parts of Europe. Sadly, once the largest church in Europe, Cluny was one of many to be ransacked in the Revolution.

Gothic

Les marbres grecs regardent en dedans, mais les beaux gothiques ont toujours l'air d'aveugles qui cherchent.

Greek marbles look inwards, but beautiful Gothic churches always seem like blind people searching.

André Malraux (1901–1976)
Les Noyers de l'Altenburg

Europe's first Gothic cathedrals appeared in the Ile de France in the late twelfth century and set the style for the rest of Europe. Their pointed arches, flying buttresses, ribbed vaulting, slender columns and delicate, stained glass windows (including round 'rose' windows) displayed not only French artistry but a mastery of revolutionary engineering skills. These cathedrals epitomized the intellectual confidence of Paris as a centre of learning, as well as a

The fine Gothic cathedral of Bayeux.

humbler striving after the divine. The whole building represented heaven with, as its gateway, the main doorway which was frequently decorated with a tympanum depicting the Last Judgement.

Chartres cathedral, which was completed in 1250, has been described as the mind of the middle ages. It is the finest representative of what is known as early Gothic, and has what is probably the most stunning collection of medieval stained-glass windows in the world.

By the fourteenth century, the Gothic style had become even more delicate with ever higher clerestory windows and ever taller naves. At Beauvais, the builders over-reached themselves and the cathedral's 46 metre-high ceiling came crashing down. Not surprisingly, it was customary at the time for prayers to be said before the scaffolding was removed! Today the 41-metre-high roof of Amiens cathedral makes this the country's tallest nave.

The style of fifteenth-century churches is often termed flamboyant Gothic as *flamboyant* (flaming) refers to elaborate flame-shaped columns, visible in parts of the cathedrals of Strasbourg, Sens, Limoges and Albi.

Gothic features	
l'arc brisé (m.)	pointed arch
l'ogive (f.)	diagonal rib
la voûte en ogive	rib vault
l'arc-boutant (m.)	flying buttress
le vitrail	stained-glass window
la nef	nave
la chapelle	chapel
le choeur	chancel
le déambulatoire	ambulatory
la tour	tower
la flèche	spire

Châteaux forts

Until the mid-fifteenth century most of France was controlled by local lords vying for power and also by the English who at different periods owned large chunks of French territory and who engaged France in the long and bloody Hundred Years War (see p. 10). Consequently, noble homes and garrisons were fortresses, often perched atop craggy vantage points – as for example Château Gaillard at Les Andelys, built by the English king Richard the Lionheart (Richard Coeur de Lion) in the thirteenth century.

Whole towns, such as the beautiful Aigues-Mortes in the Camargue and Carcassonne in the Languedoc, were fortified too. But very few of these fortified castles or towns survived intact during subsequent royal campaigns to destroy the nobles' power.

However, parts of over 300 *bastide* towns and villages can be seen in the area south of Périgord. Both the French and the English built these sturdy towns which, with their grid-like layout, are the thirteenth-century ancestors of twentieth-century new towns.

Châteaux

The châteaux of the Loire vividly exemplify the changes that France experienced between the early fifteenth and mid-sixteenth centuries. Whereas Château Chinon was a medieval fortress, the later castles were built as royal hunting lodges and their lavish decoration testifies to the king's increased power and confidence. While Italian decoration at Amboise shows the influence of Charles VIII's Italian campaigns, Chambord, built by François I in 1533, is a full-blown example of Renaissance art and architecture.

From this period right through until the nineteenth century, the royal châteaux reflected not only the current fashions of the rest of Europe, but also the king's personal taste. For this reason French architecture and decoration is often designated by the name of the king. While in the sixteenth century *le style François I* of the Château de Fontainebleau set the trend for Florentine exuberance, *le style Louis XIV* of the seventeenth century combined varying degrees of baroque theatricality and classical restraint.

One of the finest examples of classicism is the austerely elegant Château de Maisons at Maisons-Laffitte near Paris. It was built in 1642 by François Mansart who gave his name to the mansard roof. However, it was the magnificent Château at Vaux-le Vicomte, owned by court financier Nicolas Fouquet, that provoked Louis XIV's jealousy. Enraged that one of his subjects should have a more splendid residence tham himself, Louis called for Fouquet's arrest and poached his architect Le Vau and the brilliant garden designer Le Nôtre, to create the Château and gardens of Versailles. In their splendour and their design these were a physical expression of the king's power – the king's bedroom was placed at the centre of the palace on the axis that determined the layout of both the house and the formal gardens.

Modern architecture

Le Corbusier (1887–1965), whose real name was Charles-Edouard Jeanneret, was one of the greatest architects of the twentieth century. Declaring *'la maison est une machine à habiter'* ('the house is a machine for living in'), he pioneered a new functionalism, exploiting concrete and glass in his early, angular and airy buildings such as the Villa Savoye in Poissy and the austere block of flats or *unité d'habitation* in Marseille which – unlike later cheapskate copies throughout the West – incorporated shops, a gym plus running track, and even a school. By contrast, Le Corbusier's later works in the 1950s, such as La Tourette monastery near Evreux and the Chapelle de Ronchamp south of Nancy, have softer, lyrical contours.

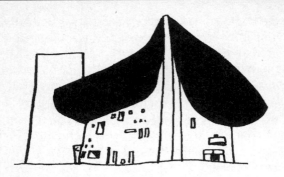

La Chapelle de Ronchamp by Le Corbuiser.

Since the 1960s, Paris in particular has benefited from a series of ambitious architectural projects which have become known as *les grands projets* or *les grands travaux* and which were initiated by the presidents of the day. Although these enterprises were undeniably statements of national pride, in the tradition of le Château de Versailles or la Tour Eiffel, they were also fired by a desire to enliven the urban landscape and to enhance the life of ordinary people with works of artistic excellence. Significantly, France sought the best of foreign architects for many of these schemes. The Centre Pompidou, whose colourful, exposed pipes caused controversy in the late 1970s, was designed by British architect **Richard Rogers** (1933–), and the Italian **Renzo Piano** (1937–). A favourite with the French, Rogers was also snapped up for the new Bordeaux courts of justice. To mark the bicentenary of the French Revolution, François Mitterrand commissioned la Grande Arche de la Défense designed by Danish architect **Otto von Spreckelsen** (1929–1987) to be the *pièce de résistance* of the La Défense plate-glass office and shopping complex. The 105 metre-high Arche itself houses 35 storeys of offices. In the same year, the startlingly beautiful Pyramide du Louvre was created by the Chinese-born architect **Ieoh Ming Pei** (1917–).

It was not until the 1980s and '90s that French architects again made their mark on world architecture. The most highly-acclaimed is **Jean Nouvel** (1945–) whose graceful, glass and steel urban buildings create a sense of light and purity. His most famous buildings are the Institut du Monde Arabe in Paris and the Palais des Congrès in Tours. **Dominique Perrault**'s (1953–) most recent claim to fame or infamy has been as the creator of François Mitterrand's last, and much-maligned, *grand projet*, la Bibliothèque nationale de France which was beset with technical teething problems. The library's four book-shaped towers dominate the Seine opposite another piece of striking municipal architecture, Le Palais Omnisports at Bercy, designed by **Bernard Zehrfuss** (1911–1996). Further north, the smart complex of La Villette is graced with **Adrien Fainsilber**'s (1932–) Cité des sciences et de l'industrie and **Christian Portzamparc**'s (1944–) Cité de la musique (see p. 110).

Local features

The delightful variety of French building styles reflects the huge diversity of local materials and the different climatic conditions throughout the country. Here are just a few local features to look out for.

Le Nord

Being a clay region with little stone, the north is characterized by red brick houses, sometimes nestling in squat terraces, sometimes standing shoulder to shoulder as taller, elegant town houses. Like bricks, the tiles are usually clay-fired pantiles or *tuiles flamandes*. A strip of black tar often covers the base of a house as protection against damp and mud. Some houses are now painted white, which would have been quite impossible before the closure of the mines put an end to blackening air pollution.

La Normandie

While tall coastal town houses have slate wall coverings and slate roofs as protection against wet winds, the lower, half-timbered houses further inland have a stone base and steeply-pitched roofs covered with flat tiles or thatch. In July some thatched roofs even sprout a row of cheerful yellow irises – presumably planted by the thatcher.

La Bretagne

Slate and granite are the dominant materials here. Sometimes the rosy tone of houses built in freestone *granit rose* (pink granite), half-timbered facades, or the white walls of tidy modern *pavillons* (detached houses) relieve the general grey.

La Loire

Le tuffeau, a soft, white variety of limestone, is what gives local houses their luminous appearance. Sometimes limestone and brick are used together to give a chequer-board effect.

La Vendée

Brightly-painted fishermen's cottages on the Vendée coast still echo the soft blues and orange browns of the traditional fishing boats, *les dundées*, which were finally replaced by motor boats fifty years ago.

Le Limousin

This region is rich in different rocks used for building (granite, red sandstone, gneiss) and in schist, a grey stone which easily separates into sheets and is, like slate, an ideal roofing material. The rusty-coloured village of Collanges-la-Rouge in Corrèze, apart from its lichen-covered slate roofs, is built entirely of red sandstone.

Le Pays Basque

Colourful, half-timbered Basque houses feature red or greenish-blue, geometrically-arranged timbers. These houses usually face the sunrise and the finer weather. West-facing houses on the opposite side of the road may well have white-washed sandstone facades, better suited to withstand westerly rain and wind.

La Provence

The warm tones of provençal houses come from the mortar of earth used to set limestone blocks as well as from the ochre wash that is painted over finished walls. Ochre, which is sand coloured by iron oxide, was one of the first pigments used in painting, as France's wealth of prehistoric paintings testify. The country's largest ochre quarry used to be at Roussillon in the Vaucluse.

Viewed from above, shallow provençal roofs make a patchwork of terracotta shades, varying from pale pink to dark brown according to the age, or the type of clay used in the *tuiles canal* (Roman or curved tiles).

La Côte d'Azur

Traditional houses were built in the local limestone evident in the white *calanque*s or rocky inlets between Marseille and Cassis, or in the old yellowy red volcanic rock of Esterel inland from Nice. As limestone was porous, it was covered in sand and chalk and painted with an ochre wash. In the Alpes-Maritimes, houses were painted in the sharp pinks and yellows favoured by Piedmontese immigrants from over the Italian border.

Alsace

The stone walls of some half-timbered Alsatian houses are still coloured in traditional pale green, pink, blue (in Catholic areas such as Kochesberg) or ox red (on Protestant families' houses). The steep roofs have flat, moulded red tiles.

Paris

Many of the distinctive features of present-day Paris date from the nineteenth century when the town-planning pioneer and Préfet de la Seine, Baron Haussmann, master-minded the renovation of the city centre. Below ground he laid 1,300 miles of sewers, and above ground 85 miles of new streets, including wide boulevards lined with well-proportioned buildings. As early as 1783, building regulations had stipulated that the width of the road should determine the acceptable height of new buildings. This was the time of the characteristic, six-storey Paris building, immortalized a century later in the snowy roof-top scenes of Parisian painter Gustave Caillebotte (1848-1894).

French decorative art and design

Art Nouveau

In the late nineteenth, and early twentieth, century, the Art Nouveau movement embraced the decorative design of many aspects of the environment, the facades of buildings, street lamps, *métro* stations, early advertising posters, glassware and ceramics. Strongly influenced by the English arts and crafts movement pioneered by William Morris, and by French symbolism, Art Nouveau was typified by curving, asymetrical lines and stylised natural forms such as flowers and leaves. Nancy became the flourishing centre of the movement in France. Here, **Emile Gallé** (1846–1904) inspired a school of designers who brought art to industrial production, creating hundreds of thousands of beautiful *objets*, in particular the Nancy tulip-shaped glass vase.

Art Deco

Art Deco which superseded Art Nouveau after the First World War was equally stylised but more geometric. Flowers lost their delicate, flowing tendrils to become tight, symetrical rosebuds. Perfectly-formed, neoclassical nudes adorned facades, lampstands, radiators ... Art Deco was a style for every corner of public buildings or private homes. Since the movement was intimately linked with fashion design, Paris was its centre.

In the 1920s, **René Lalique** (1860–1945), who had previously produced luminous, Art Nouveau jewellery, created a vast range of elegant Art Deco glass and crystal-ware including lamps, clocks, vases, Coty perfume bottles.

Design today

After Art Deco's decline, eclipsed by cubism and German and American functionalism, it was not until the 1980s that French contemporary design again caught the world's imagination.

France's design superstar is **Philippe Starck** (1949–), famed for his transformation of the President's offices in the Elysée Palace, as well as for projects as diverse as a toothbrush for Fluocaril, a Nîmes bus stop, chairs, lights, factories and hotels world-wide.

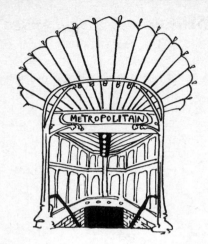

VOCABULARY

les arts plastiques *plastic arts: sculpture and painting*
le/la peintre *painter*
le sculpteur *sculptor*
peindre *to paint*
sculpter *to sculpt/to carve*
dessiner *to draw*
esquisser *to sketch*
la peinture *painting*
la sculpture *sculpture*
la céramique *ceramics*
le dessin *drawing*
l'esquisse (f.) *sketch*
le croquis *rough sketch*
la toile *canvas*
le tableau *painting*
le portrait en pied *full-length portrait*
la nature morte *still life*
le paysage *landscape*

le/la paysagiste *landscape painter*
l'exposition (f.) *exhibition*
le vernissage *preview*
exposer *to exhibit*
le mouvement *movement*
l'art figuratif *figurative art*
l'art abstrait *abstract art*
les restes (m.) *remains*
construire *to build*
l'attique (m.) *small upper storey introduced in 16th century*
la maison à collombages *half-timbered house*
le calcaire *limestone*
le grès *sandstone*
la pierre de taille *free stone*
l'ardoise (f.) *slate*
les enduits (m.) *coating*
le mortier *mortar*
la couverture *roofing*

Taking it further

Museums and art collections

Le Musée Ingres, Montauban, Le Palais Episcopal, tel. 05 63 22 12 91
– 4000 paintings of the nineteenth-century portraitist

La fondation Claude Monet (Monet's house), Giverny, Gasny, tel. 02 32 51 28 21

Renoir's house, Les Collettes, Cagnes sur Mer, near Nice, tel. 04 93 20 61 07

Le Musée d'Orsay, 62 rue de Lille, Paris 75343 – best collection of impressionist paintings in the world, plus all twentieth-century schools

Le Musée Henri de Toulouse-Lautrec, Palais de la Berbie, Albi, tel. 05 63 49 48 70

Le Musée de l'Ecole de Nancy, 36–38 rue de Sergent Blandan, Nancy, tel. 03 83 40 14 86 – Art Nouveau furniture, fabrics, jewellery and glassware

Le Musée Matisse, 164 avenue des Arènes de Cimiez, Nice, tel. 04 93 81 08 08

Le Musée Picasso, Hôtel de Salé, 5 rue de Thorigny, Paris, tel. 01 42 71 25 21

Le Musée Picasso, Château Grimaldi, Antibes, tel. 04 92 90 54 20

La Fondation Maeght, St Paul-de-Vence – modern art collection including Miró and Chagall

Le Musée d'Art Contemporain, Promenade des Arts, Nice, tel. 04 93 62 61 – Andy Warhol, Jean Tinguely, Niki de Saint Phalle, César and Yves Klein etc.

Places

Gothic cathedrals: Ile de France: Paris (Notre-Dame), Laon, Reims, Amiens, Beauvais, Chartres; Normandy: Bayeux, Coutances, Rouen; Southern France: Narbonne, Perpignan, Béziers, Carcassonne, Rodez

Bastide towns: Cordes, Lauzerte, Montaubon, Montflanquin, Monségur

Paris sewers: entrance in front of 93, quai d'Orsay Paris 75007, tel. 01 47 05 10 29

Art Nouveau: *métro* stations designed by Hector Guimard (many still bear old green arches bearing the full name, *métropolitain*); superb Art Nouveau facades – 29 avenue de Rapp, Paris 75005 (designed by Jules Lavirotte), 14 rue la Fontaine, Paris 75016 (designed by Guimard)

La Fondation Le Corbusier, Villas de Roche and Jeanneret, 8–10 Square du Docteur Blanche, Paris 75016 – Le Corbusier documentation centre in two Paris houses built by the architect in the 1920s

Auberge de la Colombe d'Or, St Paul-de-Vence – a haven for painters such as Picasso, Léger, Cocteau, writers and film stars

Le Cyclop (Forêt de Fontainebleau), Office de Tourisme, Milly-la-Forêt, tel. 01 64 98 83 17

Information

Ministère de la Culture et de la Communication, 3 rue de Valois 75042, Paris; tel. 01 40 15 80 00; **www.culture.fr** (in Fr and Eng)

La direction du Patrimoine, 3 rue de Valois 75042, Paris; tel. 01 40 15 80 00

Le Centre National des Arts Plastiques (CNAP) 27 avenue de l'Opéra, 75001 Paris; tel. 01 40 15 73 00

Books

Tocqueville, Aude Grouard de, **Guide Tocqueville des musées de France** (Paris: Minerva, 1997) – beautifully-illustrated, town-by-town guide to museums

Raeburn, Michael, **Architecture of the western world** (London: Macdonald, 1988)

Breuille, Jean-Philippe (ed.) **Dictionnaire de la peinture française**, Larousse Essentiels (Paris: Larousse, 1989)

Breuille, Jean-Philippe (ed.) **l'Impressionisme et la peinture de plein air**, Larousse Essentiels (Paris: Larousse, 1992)

Spurling, Hilary, **The Unknown Matisse** (1869–1908) – Vol 1 (London: Hamilton, 1998)

Everett, Peter, **Matisse's War** (London: Vintage, 1997) – novel based on Matisse's life during the German Occupation when his wife and daughter were imprisoned

Magazines

Le Journal des Arts, 23 Avenue Villemain, Paris 75014, tel. 01 45 43 82 60; **http://www.artindex.tm.fr** – fortnightly magazine of the fine art world

CD-Rom

Le Musée du Louvre, les collections, Montparnasse multimédia; www.montparnasse.net – 400 of the Louvre's exhibits

5 | MUSIC AND DANCE

The French love music. Every summer, foreign holiday-makers are delighted to discover a music festival somewhere near them – and where there is music there is usually song, dance or drama too. For centuries these arts have been intimately linked in France. They have come together in the French flair for spectacle, be it in ballet, opera and operetta, the sequined reviews of the *Folies Bergères*, modern-day musicals, street theatre, or in the dazzling *son et lumière* of Jean-Michel Jarre. Even where these forms have not combined, as in France's more intimate tradition of popular song and folksong, and in her purely instrumental music, there has been a striking cross-fertilization with other arts – poetry in particular, but also painting, for example in the music of Debussy and Ravel.

Another factor that has influenced the French musical heritage is France's historical role as a cultural centre and *terre d'accueil* (land of welcome) – many foreign musicians have made Paris their home and have left a lasting mark on French music. In addition, ever since the Revolution, which put an end to the King's rigid control of musical taste, the French have revelled in the exotic and the new. Much nineteenth-century French music reveals a passion for Spanish themes, while in the twentieth century, France opened its arms to American jazz. Only in pop music was foreign influence considered to be excessive – a legal quota for French music on the radio was introduced in 1994 – and this was as much an economic decision as an artistic one. Today French pop is thriving. Its extraordinary diversity is due in no small measure to the inventiveness of performers who are second and third generation immigrants from France's former black African and North African colonies. French rap is only one example of France's ability to embrace a foreign idiom and make it distinctively French.

Early music and song

From the nineteenth century onwards, the French have led the world in early music research. The musicologist, Vincent d'Indy (1851–1931) is mainly remembered today for his *Symphonie sur un chant montagnard français*, the first serious work of western music to be based entirely on an old folk tune. However, he was also one of the first (later followed by Saint-Saëns, Berlioz and Messiaen) to incorporate in his compositions the pure melodies of medieval Gregorian chant. By the late twentieth-century, Gregorian chant was being played on cassette and CD by a wide secular audience seeking release from the stresses of modern life. Among its best-known performers are the monks of the Abbey of Solesmes in la Sarthe in southern Normandy.

Polyphony, the combination of melodies for several voices, succeeded Gregorian chant and was first sung in the soaring Gothic cathedrals of northern France. Introduced by twelfth-century French religious composers Léonin and Pérotin, polyphony was subsequently adopted by secular composers throughout Europe. By the sixteenth-century, it was part of the light, airy and vivacious style considered typical of French Renaissance song.

During the centuries when medieval monks were singing plain chant and subsequently polyphony, France's *troubadours* and *trouvères* (see p. 46) were performing in France's noble households. Their poetic songs influenced the development of lyric poetry throughout Europe and initiated France's particularly rich tradition of popular song, perhaps best known to the world through twentieth-century singer-songwriters such as Charles Trénet, Georges Brassens or Jacques Brel (see p. 107).

The birth of ballet and opera

Dance was an essential skill for any noble man or woman and an important court activity. In the sixteenth century, favourite dances were the slow and stately *pavane* followed by the lively *gaillarde* whose distinctive rhythms made their mark on the instrumental music of the time and that of centuries later, as in Ravel's *Pavane pour une infante défunte*.

Opéra-ballet star, Louis XIV.

Seventeenth-century dance and music, like all the arts, were subject to the clearly-defined rules of classicism (see literature pp. 49–51). Not for the French the excesses of the new Italian opera. The court preferred dignified dances and elegant songs which soon became combined in the ancestor of modern ballet, the *ballet de cour*, a sumptuous court entertainment executed with the enthusiastic participation of the king. Contemporary artists captured the young Louis XIV posturing in golden tunic and plumed headdress as the Sun King, to modern eyes the epitome of high camp, perhaps the distant ancestor of the twentieth-century Bluebell girls. However, the master of the *ballet de cour* was **Jean-Baptiste Lully** (1632–87), an ambitious and ruthless Florentine musician and dancer who, from humble beginnings as a cook cum violinist (a not unusual combination at the time), had worked his way up to become Louis XIV's court composer. Lully collaborated with the writer Molière to produce a series of *comédies ballet* – full-length dramas incorporating music and dance (e.g. *le Bourgeois Gentilhomme*), before he broke away to create the new form of *tragédie lyrique* and the beginning of French opera. The best-known of his thirteen tragic operas is *Armide*. Lully's death was caused by over-zealous conducting (in those days performed by beating with a staff) – he stubbed his toe, which went septic, and later died of septicaemia.

While the works of **François Couperin** (1668–1733) spread the use of the harpsichord throughout Europe, it was another gifted harpsichordist, the brilliant composer and musical theorist, **Jean-Philippe Rameau** (1683–1764) who influenced the course of

French opera. It was only late in life that Rameau began to produce his vast output of tragic operas including *Hippolyte et Aricie* and *Castor et Pollux* in which he sought through music to evoke the inner nature of his characters.

The German **Christoph Willibald Gluck** (1714–87), who achieved his greatest successes in Paris, was a kind of bridge between the opera of Lully and Rameau and that of the nineteenth-century Romantics. He dispensed with arias and dances that were not directly relevant to the plot, and was the first to use the favourite Romantic device of *leitmotif* – a recurring melody that denotes a character or an idea.

Music and Revolution

The direct impact of the 1789 revolution on music was a wealth of Revolutionary and counter-Revolutionary songs, including in 1792 the *Carmagnole*, the song of the *sans-culottes*, and of course, the *Marseillaise* (see pp. 171–172).

The Revolution also meant a democratization of music, an end to musicians' reliance on patronage and to the dominance of the royal taste for French opera. Orchestral music came into favour and musicians formed their own orchestras to enable their works to be heard by a wider audience; there was no limit on size, some orchestras reaching a thousand members. Although, initially, the Théâtre de l'Opéra in Paris was closed because it symbolised aristocratic privilege, it was reopened for the presentation of pro-revolutionary works. Gradually, about sixty theatres sprang up in Paris, at last allowing the people to acquire a taste for Italian opera.

But most importantly, the ideas and attitudes which brought about France's political revolutions of 1789, 1830 and 1848 led to the desire for greater artistic freedom and the birth of Romanticism.

Romantics and post-Romantics

French Romantic music was dominated by **Hector Berlioz** (1803–1869), a composer of expansive, colourful music who wrote many vast works with large ensembles, both orchestral and choral. Influenced by Beethoven and by lesser-known French Revolutionary and Napoleonic composers, Berlioz could command a grand style, but also, in the manner of his contemporary, the poet Baudelaire (see p. 57), he evoked extreme emotions of ecstacy or despair. Berlioz' *Symphonie fantastique* is one of his best-loved works. But his Requiem, *La Grande Messe des morts*, is the most powerful. Berlioz has been a particular favourite in Britain where his complete works were first recorded with the conductor Colin Davis.

Hector Berlioz – a favourite of the British.

In complete contrast with the large-scale orchestra, the piano was the preferred instrument of some Romantic composers. *'Mon piano, c'est ma parole, c'est ma vie ... C'est là qu'ont été tous mes désirs, tous mes rêves, toutes mes joies et toutes mes douleurs.'* ('My piano is my word, my life ... with it I have experienced all my desires, all my dreams, all my joys and all my sorrows.'), wrote **Franz Liszt** (1811–1886). Although Liszt was Hungarian he was a central figure in the Parisian musical and intellectual scene of the early nineteenth century, strongly influenced by Berlioz, and the writers George Sand, Alfred de Musset and Victor Hugo. His friend, **Frédéric Chopin** (1810–1849) the son of a French émigré in Poland, like Liszt, made Paris his cultural home. Chopin is best-known for his *Etudes*, *Nocturnes*, *Ballades* and *Polonaises*. He was particularly influenced by the Romantic painter Eugène Delacroix, and the writer George Sand with whom he had a nine-year-long stormy relationship.

The versatile and fluent composer, **Saint-Saëns** (1835–1921), a contemporary of the Romantics, was influenced by Berlioz, but frequently displayed the restraint and balance of classicism, particularly in his early symphonies. Unfortunately, Saint-Saëns did not manifest these qualities in his dealings with fellow musicians who frequently fell foul of his nasty temper. He did not hide his dislike for Franck and Wagner or for Debussy, whose work he persistently denigrated. Nonetheless, his violin and piano concertos are brilliant vehicles for virtuosity, while his best-known orchestral work, *Le Carnaval des animaux*, (Carnival of the Animals) contains skilful writing for solo instruments, for example, the cello solo *Le Cygne* (The Swan).

By contrast, the composer and organist **Gabriel Fauré** (1845–1924) who was a pupil of Saint-Saëns and also a traditionalist, was extremely respectful of other musicians' work. Although he is considered to be the true founder of French chamber music, Fauré's best-loved composition is probably the haunting 'Pie Jesu' of his *Requiem*, written following the death of his parents. Compared with the challenging works of many of Fauré's contemporaries, Fauré's subtle organization and delicate melodies have made him a favourite for restful listening. Sadly, he became deaf at the end of his life.

Nineteenth-century opera and operetta

While Italian opera was immensely popular at this time, **Georges Bizet's** (1838-1875) *Carmen*, based on Prosper Merimée's tale of jealousy and murder, never fails to stir the most frosty of northern temperaments. It was the great triumph of Bizet's short life (1838–75) and was probably the most-performed opera of the nineteenth century. Embodying the Romantic taste for sensuality, dramatic passion and an exotic setting, it even won over Wagner-loving Germans and caused the philosopher Nietzsche to declare *'Il faut méditerraniser la musique'* (We must mediterraneanize music'). A very different work is Bizet's delightful piano suite *Jeux d'enfants*.

Other composers of serious opera include **Charles Gounod** (1818–1893) who is best-known for his opera based on Goethe's *Faust* and for his setting of *Ave Maria*, and the sometimes syrupy composer **Jules Massenet** (1842–1912) dubbed 'Mademoiselle

Wagner' by his contemporaries, who is principally renowned for his opera *Manon*.

However, the genre that took Paris by storm, and that brought long knickers and can-can to the world, was operetta, the precursor of the modern musical. The Bouffes-Parisiens, a small theatre near the Champs-Elysées, was the venue for **Jacques Offenbach's** (1819–1880) rousing productions of *Orphée aux enfers* (Orpheus in the Underworld), *Les Contes d'Hoffmann* (Tales of Hoffmann), *La Belle Hélène* and *La Vie parisienne*.

Musical impressionists

Even during his lifetime, **Claude Debussy** (1862–1918) was recognized as having changed the course of European music. He shocked the musical establishment by challenging all established rules of composition, declaring, *'Il n'y a pas de théories, il suffit d'entendre. Le plaisir est la règle.'* (There are no theories, hearing is enough. Pleasure is the rule.'). His audiences either adored or hated his piano and orchestral works in which he created a new evocative musical language that shared the same spirit as symbolist poetry (see pp. 57–58), impressionist painting (see pp. 75–76) and contemporary dance (see below). Debussy's *Prélude à l'après-midi d'un faune* from which Nijinsky later created a ballet, was inspired by a poem of Mallarmé, and his opera *Pelléas et Mélisande* was based on Maeterlinck's play of the same name. His symphonic poem, *La Mer* captures not only the colours, sounds and mood of the sea, but evokes a fluid, dreamlike state of consciousness in which material and psychic worlds merge.

From his Basque mother, **Maurice Ravel** (1875–1937) inherited an affinity with Spanish music which was very popular in France at this time. The Spanish influence is particularly clear in his yawningly familiar *Boléro*, in his innovative short opera *L'Heure Espagnole*, in *Rhapsodie Espagnole* and in his last work *Don Quichotte à Dulcinée*. He also collaborated with many of his contemporaries, composing the music for *L'Enfant et les Sortilèges*, a delightful play based on a fairy-tale by Colette (see p. 61), and working with Diaghilev to create the ballet *Daphnis et Chloé* starring Nijinsky.

Les Ballets Russes

French ballet developed separately from opera in the eighteenth century, took root in Russia in the nineteenth century, and was brought back to Paris in 1909 in an experimental and exotic form. The Ballets Russes of impressario **Serge Diaghilev** (1872–1929) and his star dancer and choreographer, **Vaslav Nijinsky**, (1889–1950) caused a sensation far beyond the world of dance. Their innovative ballets, created with the music of Debussy and Ravel, shocked the public, but Nijinsky's ballet to the music of Stravinsky's *Sacre du Printemps* caused a riot at its Paris première and was renamed by critics as *Le Massacre du Printemps*!

After Diaghilev's death in 1929, the artists of the Ballets Russes dispersed. However, the Russian influence continued in America with the choreographer George Balanchine whose school of classical dance became today's New York City Ballet.

Satie and *le Groupe des Six*

In 1917, the ballet *Parade* written by Jean Cocteau for the Ballets Russes, featuring sets by Picasso and the music of **Eric Satie** (1866–1927), introduced a complete change of style. Satie's clarity, precision and humour were an implicit rejection of dreamy impressionism, and inspired a new generation of composers. Despite the wealth earned from his success, Satie lived in one room for thirty years and spent his money on quantities of umbrellas and clothes (all unused) and drink, which caused his death by cirrhosis of the liver. His best-loved compositions are *Trois Gymnopédies* and *Trois Gnossiennes* for piano.

The so-called *groupe des Six* were six young friends Auric, Durey, Honegger, Tailleferre, Poulenc and Milhaud who were all influenced by Satie and Jean Cocteau, and who briefly produced some collaborative works. Like many French musicians before them, their compositions were intimately linked with the works of contemporary artists. **Georges Auric** (1899–1983), for example, was particularly close to surrealist writers and cubist painters and also provided many scores for the films of René Clair, Jean

Cocteau, Max Ophuls and John Huston. **Francis Poulenc** (1899–1963), the most enduring of *Les Six*, brilliantly captured the brittle, irreverent mood of France during the inter-war years. Sometimes brash and gimmicky, as in *Le Bal Masqué* which features whip-crack, whistle and woodwind belching, Poulenc also wrote sensitive songs from the poems of Guillaume Apollinaire and Paul Eluard, and in his later works such as *le Dialogue des Carmélites* and *Stabat Mater* displayed an austere spirituality.

Messiaen and his legacy

The organist and composer **Olivier Messiaen** (1908–1992) who experimented with rhythm, oriental forms and electro-acoustic music, was the spiritual guide of the present generation of French composers, even though his pupils took his technical innovations in the very different direction of *la musique concrète* (concrete music). Messiaen was one of the first composers to make use of *les ondes Martenot*, an electronic keyboard instrument which in the 1920s was the precursor of the electronic synthesiser. The twin sources of Messiaen's inspiration were his Catholic faith, which informed *Vingt regards sur l'enfant Jésus*, and his love of birdsong. He meticulously transcribed the songs of hundreds of different birds and transposed these into a form mostly unrecognizable to ornithologists, but which constituted a new musical language, as in his *Catalogue des oiseaux*.

Pierre Schaeffer (1910–1995), not only a musician, but also an engineer, was well-qualified to invent *la musique concrète* – the completely new form of recorded and synthesized music, which incorporated human sounds such as cries, groans and laughter. In 1953 he created an *opéra concret* with the choreographer Maurice Béjart (see below).

Pierre Boulez (1925–), who studied under Messiaen, is renowned in particular for his early compositions using the 12-tone scale such as *Le Marteau sans maître* and *Pli selon pli*. He is an outspoken theorist and composer, and a conductor of boundless energy who during the 1970s was simultaneously chief conductor of the BBC Symphony Orchestra in London and the New York Philharmonic. He founded France's world-famous electro-acoustic music research institute (l'Institut de recherches et de coordination acoustique l'IRCAM), collaborated in the creation of the Paris music and research centre (la Cité de la Musique), and performs with his own Ensemble InterContemporain. Boulez has frequently collaborated with the Greek musician **Yannis Xenakis** (1922–), a naturalized Frenchman who combines the skills of architect, mathematician and musician. His powerful electro-acoustic works *Metastasis, Prolytope* and *Nomos Gamma* have been performed throughout the world.

Modern dance

The creative, libertarian genius of **Maurice Béjart** (1927–) has been the guiding light of French dance for the last forty years. His mastery of stagecraft, and the spectacular, yet controlled sensuality of his choreography, which remains faithful to classical ballet technique, have brought dance to a wide audience and contributed to France's reputation as the dance centre of the world. Béjart founded the Béjart Ballet Lausanne in Switzerland and he is also director of Rudra, an experimental dance school and workshop.

The Ballet de Lyon is France's most famous modern dance company. While it tours extensively, its home is Jean Nouvel's strikingly modern Opéra de Lyon, one of the finest dance theatres in the world.

Today, France's best-known ambassador for French dance, outside France, is the star ballerina Sylvie Guillem who left the company of l'Opéra de Paris for London's Royal Ballet. Reputed to be the world's best-paid ballerina, she commands world-wide admiration – Rudolf Nureyev, whose homosexuality was no secret, even said that she was the only woman he could think of marrying!

Twentieth-century song

The extraordinary voice of **Edith Piaf** (1915–1963) immediately brings to mind the world of French cabaret in the 1930s, '40s and '50s. A contemporary of the urbane charmer **Tino Rossi** (1907–1983), Piaf won the hearts of the French public with her direct style and her bitter-sweet, often painfully hopeful or nostalgic love songs. Two of her best-loved songs, *'La Vie en Rose'* and *'Non, je ne regrette rien'*, are instantly recognizable throughout the world.

Charles Trénet (1913–) is another icon of French song, a poetic lyricist and singer remembered today in particular for the idyllic world captured in *'La Mer'*. His all-time hit *'Douce France'*, which was particularly moving for the generation who experienced the Occupation, was recorded in a new version in the 1980s by the *beur* singer Rachid Tara and his group Carte de Séjour.

> *Douce France*
> *Cher pays de mon enfance*
> *Bercé de tendre insouciance*
> *Je t'ai gardé dans mon cœur*
> *Mon village*
> *Au clocher, aux maisons sages*
> *Où les enfants de mon âge*
> *Ont partagé mon bonheur*
> *Oui je t'aime*
> *Dans la joie ou la douleur ...*

Sweet France
Dear land of my childhood
Tenderly brought up to have no cares
I have kept you in my heart
My village
With the church steeple, the modest houses
Where children of my age
Shared my happiness
Yes, I love you
In joy or pain ...

In the 1950s, a new generation of younger singers continued the melodic and romantic tradition of Trénet but incorporated something of the big-band jazz style of Ella Fitzgerald and Frank Sinatra. The diminutive **Charles Aznavour** (1924–), who as a young man wrote many songs for Edith Piaf and learnt to perform in the cabarets of Pigalle and Montparnasse, remains immensely popular on both sides of the Atlantic thanks to English versions of many of his songs. In 1997, EMI France issued a 30-CD box of his complete works and in 1999, Aznavour's 1974 hit *'She'* was again in the charts, this time sung by Elvis Costello as the theme tune for the film *Notting Hill*.

Claude Nougaro (1929–) was the French singer to most closely make jazz rhythms his own, notably in *'La Java'*. **Gilbert Bécaud** (1927–), on the other hand, made his mark as a more middle-of-the-road entertainer renowned for his dynamic stage presence and in particular for *'Et maintenant'*. The style of **Barbara** (1930–1997) was more subtle. She often accompanied her songs on the piano and created the much-loved, lilting ballad *'Ma plus belle histoire d'amour'* and the powerful *'L'Aigle Noir'*.

A parallel trend in French music of the 1950s was that of the more overtly political or anarchic *chanteurs à texte* such as **Juliette Gréco** (1927–), **Léo Ferré** (1916–1993), **Georges Brassens** (1921–1981) and **Jacques Brel** (1929-78). Nicknamed *la muse de Saint-Germain-des-Prés* (see p. 62), Gréco set to music many poems of Raymond Queneau (*'Si tu t'imagines'*), Jacques Prévert and even Sartre (*'Rue des Blancs-Manteaux'*), capturing the libertarian and hopeful spirit of post-war Parisian intellectuals.

The shaggy grey hair of Léo Ferré was still a familiar sight on stage at the Paris music hall, l'Olympia, in the early 1990s. The songs *Jolie môme* and *Merde à Vauban* earned him early notoriety and his poetic lyrics continued to express, sometimes tenderly, sometimes aggressively, his personal brand of anarchism.

An equally anti-establishment figure but with a more understated style was singer-poet Georges Brassens, a modern-day *troubadour* from Sète who often accompanied himself on the classical guitar. The sexual frankness and social criticism contained in his lyrics caused several of his songs, including *'Le Gorille'*, to be banned from French radio. Other favourites are *'Chanson pour l'Auvergnat'* and *'Les Copains d'abord'*. Although often linked with Brassens, the style of Belgian-born Jacques Brel was more effusive and he often gave his lyrics the big-band treatment. His songs were poetic (*'Le Plat pays'*), impassioned (*'Ne me quitte pas'*) and satirical (*'Les Bourgeois'*).

French rock, rap, *raï* ...

While the quintessentially French tradition of *chanson à texte* is still alive in contemporary singers **Jean-Jacques Goldman**

(1951–) and **Hubert-Félix Thiefaine** (1948–), French modern popular music has many different forms.

Le king of French rock and pop is **Johnny Halliday** (1943–) who slicked back his hair, discarded his own name (Jean-Philippe Smet) for being too Gallic, and in the '50s was one of the first to unashamedly ape American singers. There is undoubtedly nobody like him – and he's still rocking. Halliday is virtually unknown outside France but he commands adulation at home. In 1998 at 55, he pulled in the crowds, including President Jacques Chirac and France's political and cultural elite, to three sell-out performances at the 80,000-seat Stade de France.

Long-derided by Anglo-Saxons, today's French pop has gone far beyond 1990s lookalikes of English boy bands. A plethora of young female artists includes the well-established **Patricia Kaas** and the relatively recent **Zazie**. In forms as diverse as soul, reggae, rap and techno, French music is travelling – soul singers **Les Nubians** have a considerable following in the United States, while French rap (**MC Solaar** and **Doc Gynéco**) and techno (**Daft Punk** and **Air**) have crossed the Channel. Much of this explosive new talent comes from *beur* culture (see p. 247), as well as from second and third generation black African immigrants. It is the voice of the *cités*, the grim urban ghettoes, but also that of distant roots in Algerian *raï* music (as performed by singer **Faudel**), and in congo rhythms (captured by the Sarcelles group **Racines**). The dance form of the *cités* is energetic and skilful break-dancing (*le hip-hop*), which has its own dance festival at the prestigious music venue la Cité de la musique. Pop's cross-cultural heritage is clear too in Celtic rock band **Matmatah** and the Breton rap band **Manau**. Far from marginal, these hybrid forms express the defiant spirit and exuberance that have been an integral part of French popular culture through the ages. MC Solaar was awarded the *Grande médaille de la chanson française* from the Académie Française, and nothing could better prove the French establishment's pride in its young musicians.

VOCABULARY

la **musique sacrée** *religious music*
la **musique profane** *secular music*
le/la **compositeur/-trice** *composer*
le **chef d'orchestre** *conductor*
le/la **soliste** *soloist*
le **choeur** *church choir/chorus*
la **chorale** *choir*
le **chanteur/la cantatrice** *singer/opera singer*
exécuter un morceau au violon *to play a piece on the violin*
interpréter *to perform*
l'**interprète (m.f.)** *performer*
le/la **mélomane** *music lover*
inspirer *to inspire*
influencer *to influence*
l'**oeuvre (f.)** *work*
le **style** *style*
le **chant** *song*
la **voix** *voice*
la **tragédie lyrique** *musical tragedy*

la **symphonie** *symphony*
le **mouvement** *movement*
la **sonate** *sonata*
le **poème symphonique** *symphonic poem*
la **vitesse** *tempo*
le **contrepoint** *counterpoint*
la **musique de chambre** *chamber music*
le **sérialisme** *serialism*
la **musique sérielle** *serial music*
le **bal musette** *popular dance with accordeon*
le **café-concert** *café music*
les **variétés** *music hall*
le **chanteur engagé** *politically-committed singer*
contestataire *anti-establishment*
le **chansonnier** *popular singer of satirical lyrics*
le **rappeur** *rap singer*
le **métissage** *hybridization (of musical cultures)*
le **clip** *promotional video*

Taking it further

Books

The New Oxford Companion to Music (Oxford: OUP, 1983)

Duneton, Claude, **Histoire de la chanson française**, 2 volumes (Paris: Seuil, 1998) – history of song to 1860

Authelain, G, **La Chanson dans tous ses états** (Fondettes: Van de Velde, 1988)

Cairns, **David Berlioz: Servitude and greatness** (London: Penguin, 1999)

Acocella, Joan (ed.), **The Diary of Vaslav Nijinsky**: unexpurgated edition, (London: Allen Lane, 1999)

Boulez, Pierre, **Boulez on Music today** (London: Faber, 1971)

Venues

Cité de la musique, 209 avenue Jean-Jaurès, Paris 75019,
   tel. 01 44 84 45 00 – music school, concert hall, research centre
L'Opéra de Paris Bastille, 120 rue de Lyon, Paris 75012,
   tel. 01 44 73 13 00
L'Olympia, 28 boulevard des Capucines, Paris 75009,
   tel. 01 47 42 25 49
Le Palais Omnisports de Paris-Bercy, 8 boulevard de Bercy,
   Paris 75012 – vast arena for international pop
L'Opéra Garnier, Place de l'Opéra, Paris 75009, tel. 01 44 73 13 99
   – home of the Opéra de Paris ballet company
Le Théâtre de la Ville, 2 Place du Chatelet, Paris 75004,
   tel. 01 42 74 22 77 – modern dance and classical music

Information

Le Musée de la musique, Cité de la musique, 221 avenue Jean-
   Jaurès, Paris 75019; tel. 01 44 84 46 00
The French Music Bureau (for info on French pop music), The
   French Embassy, 23 Cromwell Road, London SW7 2EL,
   tel. 020 7838 2043
Le Musée Edith Piaf, 5 rue Crespin-du-Gast, Paris 75011, tel. 01
   43 55 52 72

Film

Tous les matins du monde dir. Alain Corneau – based on the true
story of the daughters of Monsieur de Sainte-Colombe, a virtuoso
viola player, and of their brilliant young music teacher Marin
Marais played by Guillaume Depardieu.

Main music festivals

Aix en Provence (July); Ambronay (Sept); Antibes – Jazz festival
(July); Auvers sur Oise (May); Beaune (July); Bourges – Le
Printemps de Bourges (April) – French pop; Cannes – Jazz festival
(Feb); la Chaise-Dieu (Sept); Chartres – organ festival (July to Sept);
Comminges (July and August); Evian (May); Ile de France (Sept and

Oct); Le Mans – Europa Jazz Festival (April); Lorient – Interceltic festival (August); Noirlac (July and August); Orange (July and August); Prades – Festival Pablo Casals (July and August); La Rochelle – les Francopholies – French rock etc; Montpellier and Radio France (July and August); La Roque d'Antheron (July and August); Sablé sur Sarthe (August); Saint-Denis (June and July); Strasbourg (June and July); Sully sur Loire (June and July); Saint-Chartier (July); Vienne – Jazz festival (July).

For contact numbers for these and for many more annual music events, contact The French Embassy Cultural Service, 23 Cromwell Road, London SW7 2EL, tel. 0207 838 2055; or the French Government Tourist Office, 178 Piccadilly, London W1V OAL, tel. 0906 8244 123, fax 0207 493 65 94

6 | TRADITIONS AND FESTIVALS

The French year is packed with traditional festivals including twelve public holidays. Many of these are religious festivals and saints' days which take place at the time of much earlier, pre-Christian festivities. A host of other national and local festivals commemorate key events in French history. The fact that festivals are still so enthusiastically celebrated today is partly because France is a predominantly Catholic country which has for centuries embraced religious ritual and still recognizes each day of the year as the festival of a particular saint. An equally important factor is France's rural past, evident in a wealth of country sayings and in traditions related to activities of the agricultural year. Until the mid-twentieth century, 25 per cent of the French population still lived off the land, leading a way of life that had changed little over the centuries and in which local folklore and festivals played an important part. Even national celebrations still vary enormously from region to region and from town to town, showing that festivals are an important expression of local identity.

The fundamental reason for the survival of France's many celebrations is the fact that in France a serious respect for the country's heritage goes hand in hand with an irrepressible urge to cast all seriousness aside and enjoy the present moment to the full, whether to the deafening pop music of the firemen's ball on 14th July or at a slap-up family lunch following the serious rituals of *Toussaint* (All Saints).

The guardian of these festivals, the person who ensures that they are fixed in the national memory, is the humble *facteur* (postman). Every January he chooses, buys and delivers to French households *l'almanach des Postes*, a calendar which lists every national festival and saint's day. In return he receives *les étrennes* (New Year's gift), a tip, modest or generous according to the means and inclination of the householder.

Janvier (January)

Le vent dominant au jour de l'an existe moitié de l'an.

The prevailing wind on New Year's day stays the same for half the year.

Bonne Année! (Happy New Year!)

Le jour de l'an (New Year's Day) is a public holiday, a day for visiting friends and relatives. *Les cartes de nouvelle année* (New Year's cards) are much more common than Christmas cards. Within the family, children often receive *les étrennes* (gifts of money) and New Year gifts which, although usually smaller than Christmas presents, are given more widely.

La fête des rois (the festival of the three kings)

This is epiphany, the celebration of the day when, according to tradition, the three kings visited the baby Jesus. Traditionally falling on 6th January, Epiphany is now celebrated on the first Sunday in January. The delicious *galette des rois*, a large cake or pie made from pastry and *fourrée à la frangipane* (filled with almond paste) graces the dinner table. The custom is for the youngest member of the family to hide under the table and call out the order in which people should be served with *galette*. Everybody tucks in, but not too enthusiatically in case their helping contains a tiny gold-coated china ornament known as *le baigneur* or *la fève* (broad bean) which has been hidden in *la galette*. While today's *baigneurs* may be cartoon characters such as Astérix or Bart Simpson, in the past a golden Louis was sometimes hidden, just as a silver sixpence used to be put in English Christmas pudding. The person who has *le baigneur* is promptly crowned and toasted with white wine: *'Vive le roi!'*, after which 'the king' drinks to cries of *'Le roi boit!'*

While many families still make their own *galette*, many others nip to the *pâtisserie* to buy this delicacy which, whether it is made with *pâte feuilletée* (flaky pastry) in Paris, *briochée* (made with enriched bread) in the south-west and in Lyon, or shaped like a crown in Provence and called *un royaume* (a kingdom), always indicates that the new year is well and truly underway.

Une Galette des Rois

400g puff pastry
80g melted butter
2 eggs
6 tablespoons of sugar
8 tablespoons of ground almonds
1 baigneur (small china figure)

1. Mix sugar, ground almonds butter and egg yolk.
2. Line a flan dish with pastry.
3. Add the mixture to the lined dish — pop in the 'baigneur'.
4. Cover the mixture with pastry.
5. Decorate with any left over pastry, and brush with egg yolk.
6. Cook in the oven for 30 minutes at 230°C or regulo 7.

Février (February)

Neige de février, une poule l'emporte aux pieds.
February snow sticks to the chicken's feet.

La chandeleur (Candelmas, 2nd February)

In France *la chandeleur* is just as much a pancake day as *mardi gras* at the beginning of Lent.

Like many religious festivals, Candelmas celebrating Jesus' presentation to the temple and Mary's purification 40 days after the birth, occurred at the time of an old Celtic winter festival celebrating fire and light. In the church festival, people walked in procession holding lit candles (*les chandelles*) which were later carefully stored away in the family cupboard and only brought out and lit again to request God's help in times of crisis. *Les crêpes* (pancakes) like candles, were made of precious ingredients, and in the same way were used to guard against illness and misery – even thirty years ago it was still customary to lay out the first *crêpe* of Candelmas day on top of the linen cupboard.

Le carnaval

Carnaval, said to originate from the Italian *carne levare* (omitting meat – for Lent), is a time for processions, dressing up and generally leaving everyday worries behind.

In early times in France, as in many other European countries, the end of winter and the fertility of the Earth were celebrated with music and colourful disguises. These celebrations subsequently became part of the Church festivities on the Sunday, Monday and Tuesday before *le carême* (Lent). In France they are *les jours gras* (fat days) culminating in *le mardi gras* (Shrove Tuesday) when people used to stoke themselves up with fatty soups and meats to cope with the lean times of Lent. Today's revellers prefer *crêpes*, *beignets* (doughnuts) or *gaufres* (waffles).

The noise, jostling crowds and sometimes over-the-top high spirits of *carnaval* have as much to do with ancient fertility celebrations as with the preparation for Lent. One hazard of *carnaval* is getting drenched or coated with unpleasant substances such as flour, soot, mud, wine dregs, or even, in Dunkerque, with kippers!

The largest and most famous festival is the *Carnaval de Nice* which lasts for twelve days. An enormous model, *Sa Majesté Carnaval*, leads a procession of floats which are piled high with flowers, ammunition for the ensuing *bataille des fleurs* (battle of flowers). At *mardi gras*, *Sa Majesté Carnaval* is burnt, against a background of spectacular fireworks. In the nineteenth century, onlookers were showered with dried plaster, until in 1892 the first confetti was made by cutting up paper used in the local silk worm industry.

Children usually have two weeks' school holiday at *carnaval* time to enable them to make the most of the festivities – but some in the south and east of the country prefer to zoom off to the mountains with their families for *le ski*.

Mars (March)

Tel mars, tel août!
August will be like March!

Avril (April)

En avril, ne te découvre pas d'un fil.
In April, do not take off a single thread.

Poisson d'avril! (April Fool!)

1st April is a day for practical jokes, particularly in school where children try to pin a *poisson* (paper fish) to a victim's back. This tradition of a *journée du rire* (day of laughter) goes back to ancient Greece and festivities in honour of the god of laughter, and subsequently of Aphrodite who was not only the goddess of love but, being born in the waves, was the protectress of fish.

Les rameaux (Palm Sunday)

On *le dimanche des rameaux* which celebrates Christ's entry into Jerusalem, people take twigs to be blessed by the priest during Mass. The twigs are always from non-deciduous trees so they will stay green throughout the coming year. In Paris and the north these twigs are picked from *le buis* (box tree), in Brittany and south of the

Loire from *le laurier* (laurel), in Alsace and Lorraine from *le houx* (holly) or *le sapin* (pine) and in the Mediterranean from, of course, *le palmier* (palm tree). Afterwards, the twigs may be put on family tombs in the cemetery or taken back to the house where, in the past they would have been fastened to a crucifix.

Joyeuses Pâques! (Happy Easter!)

Eggs, a symbol of life and completeness, have been at the centre of spring-time celebrations since Roman times and even earlier. In twelfth-century France, eggs were blessed at the Easter Mass and distributed by the king, and by the fifteenth century the tradition of offering eggs as gifts was established. Subsequently eggs were decorated and often painted red, the colour of the resurrection.

Many regions have their own egg-rich recipes. In Savoie *la soupe dorée* (golden soup) is an Easter delicacy, while in Vendée *l'alise pacaude* is a delicious orange-flavoured bread – but anyone tempted to taste it before Easter morning will find it stuffed with toads!

After having rung the Gloria on *le jeudi saint* (Holy week Thursday), church bells are silent until *la veillée de Pâques* (Easter Saturday night). Tradition has it that *les cloches de Pâques* (the Easter bells) fly off to Rome to dine with the Pope, or even to take confession, before returning on the Saturday night full of chocolate eggs and sweets which they scatter into children's gardens or in their homes. While this story may stretch the imagination even further than the idea of a globe-trotting Easter bunny, who is, in legend at least, a living creature, it seems that chocolate has a universal power to suspend disbelief.

Mai (May)

En mai fais ce qui te plaît.
In May do what you like.

Le 1er mai

May is a very busy month for national festivals, starting off with *la fête du travail* (Labour Day) and *la fête du muguet* (festival of the lily of the valley) which harks back to earlier May-time festivities when young men went out searching, either for May blossom to present to favourite girls, or brambles for bad-tempered ones. Since the eighteenth century, people have given sprigs of *muguet* to friends and relatives as a good-luck charm. Some regions have une *fête du muguet* with *une reine du muguet* (queen of the lily of the valley) and a procession with floats. On this day anyone is allowed to sell in the street *le muguet* from their garden, and not that cheaply at 6 francs a stem.

La fête du travail is marked by trade union marches in large towns. In Paris, trade unionists parade with their banners from la Place de la Bastille, symbol of the Revolution, to la Place de la Nation. From 1947 this date has been a public, paid holiday which in four years out of seven favours a long weekend or enables the French worker to *faire le pont*, that is, to take a day's leave before or after the 1st, to make an even longer weekend!

The end of the Second World War in Europe is celebrated on 8th May when the schools are closed all day. On that evening or on the following Sunday, there are remembrance ceremonies at the local *monuments aux morts* (war memorials). This Sunday is also the *fête de Jeanne d'Arc* who is commemorated principally in the towns associated with her: Orléans, Reims, Compiègne and Rouen. In recent years on this day, Orléans has become the scene of confrontations between the extreme right-wing Front National, for whom Jeanne d'Arc is a nationalist symbol, and anti-FN demonstrators.

La fête des mères (Mother's day)

In France this festival, which takes place on the last Sunday in May, is rooted in a bit of social engineering that followed the First World War. In 1920, in an attempt to compensate for the terrible loss of life during the war and to boost France's diminishing birthrate, the Minister of the Interior introduced *la journée nationale des mères de famille nombreuse* (the national day of mothers of large families) together with funds to reward large, and therefore deserving, families. In celebrations at the Trocadéro, 7,000 people witnessed a hitherto unknown but fecund Madame Marcelle Comblet-Sue receiving *la médaille d'or de la famille française* (the gold medal of the French family) for having given birth to thirteen little French citizens. Although the patriotic associations of motherhood were finally dropped, and since 1950 the festival has been *la fête des mères*, a private rather than a public celebration, the French state has continued to encourage large families by offering them generous benefits (see p. 201).

Juin

En juin le temps qu'il fait le trois sera le temps du mois.
In June the weather on the third will last for the whole month.

La fête des pères (Father's day)

Falling two or three weeks later than *la fête des mères*, an equivalent day for fathers has been celebrated in France only since 1968. A recently created *fête des grand-mères* (Grandmothers' festival) in March has almost fizzled out. After all, the French have plenty of festivals without observing new ones created to line the pockets of greetings card manufacturers.

La fête de la musique

Wherever you go on 21st June, music is in the air. Since 1982 when Jack Lang, President Mitterrand's innovative Minister of Culture, introduced this festival, the summer solstice has been an occasion for music and dancing in public parks and gardens and in the street, where professional and amateur musicians perform all types of music completely free of charge.

Juillet

Année de groseilles, année de bouteilles!
A good year for red-currants is a good year for bottles of wine!

La fête nationale

The 14th July is a mixture of pomp and ceremony and letting your hair down. The tricolore flag adorns all public buildings, and processions of brass bands, *les pompiers* and local organizations, not forgetting *Monsieur* or *Madame le maire*, parade through the streets. In the evening, the sounds of *le bal populaire* (local dance) drift from the local fire-station, while fireworks light up the sky. The whole of France is celebrating the 1789 storming of the Bastille, and drinking to the republican values of *liberté*, *égalité* and *fraternité*.

In Paris, the traditional parade is a more serious affair with military bands, displays of tanks and rockets, and jet aircraft roaring overhead. The Parisian 14th July fireworks are the most impressive display of the year. The French have long excelled at public firework displays, having no equivalent of the small-scale, back-garden variety enjoyed in England on November 5th. However, on 14th July, children can freely buy *les pétards* (firecrackers) which they let off all day long and all over the place, annoying many adults and terrorizing pets. Although fireworks first graced the wedding of Louis XIII and Anne of Austria, it was not until 1730 that a pyrotechnic Italian family, the Ruggieri brothers, settled in Paris and founded a firework dynasty. It was their expertise that enabled Napoléon to repeatedly dazzle the populace on his birthday, his marriage, his coronation and after each of his military victories ...

Août (August)

Après le 15 août, lève la pierre; la fraîcheur est dessous.
After 15th August, if you pick up a stone, it will be damp underneath.

L'Assomption

Woe to foreign holiday-makers who turn up at the *hypermarché* or hope to change their currency on *le 15 août*! France has shut up shop to celebrate the Assumption – when the Virgin Mary passed from earthly to eternal life. It is also a time for *la bénédiction des bateaux* when, in ceremonies in many French ports, a priest blesses the boats and throws flowers onto the water in memory of past generations of sailors.

Septembre

En septembre, se coupe ce qui pend.
In September, everything that hangs is cut.

Les journées du patrimoine

This relatively new festival on the third weekend of September was introduced to celebrate France's rich cultural heritage. It is a chance for the French Joe Soap to get a look inside l'Assemblée Nationale, le Palais de l'Elysée (President's residence), l'Hôtel Matignon (Prime Minister's residence) and many other national and local government buildings. The public also has free access to many historic sites.

Octobre

Octobre ensoleillé, décembre emmitouflé.
A sunny October means a well-wrapped up December.

Halloween

Halloween has only recently become popular in France. Its supporters claim that this festival on All Hallows Eve has impeccable Celtic credentials, while its detractors object to its American origins. However, being the night before the more sombre festival of *Toussaint* it is an opportunity for light-hearted celebration, so it is not surprising that on 31st October pumpkins, ghosts and ghouls are now almost as evident here as they are in America and Britain.

Novembre

A la Sainte Catherine, tout bois prend racine.
Plant a tree on Saint Catherine's day and it will take root.

La Toussaint

La Toussaint (All Saints Day) on 1st November and *le jour des morts* (remembrance of the dead) on 2nd November are treated as one *fête*. Church services commemorate the dead on 1st November which is a public holiday and a busy time at cemeteries where flower sellers at the gates sell over-priced chrysanthemums for people to put on the graves of dead friends and family. Consequently, at any time of year, chrysanthemums are definitely not the right flowers with which to thank a French host for their hospitality!

La Toussaint is a big family festival and because many Parisians make a mass exodus from Paris to reach their home towns, the closest weekend to 1st November is generally regarded as *le weekend le plus meurtrier* (the deadliest weekend) on the French roads.

Le 11 novembre

This is another solemn day, the anniversary of the day in 1918 when France and Germany signed an armistice at Compiègne, thus bringing an end to the First World War. In 1920, the body of an unknown soldier was buried under the Arc de Triomphe and a flame was lit to commemorate the one and a half million Frenchmen who died in the war. Every year on this day the flame named *la flamme du souvenir* is rekindled by the President, and throughout France wreathes are placed on local *monuments aux morts*. Just as the British Legion sells poppies to raise money for disabled veterans and their families, so French school children sell stickers of *bleuets* (cornflowers), because the French military uniform was blue.

La Sainte-Catherine

This important medieval festival celebrates Sainte Catherine of Alexandria, a virgin martyr believed to be a mystical bride of Christ. Catherine was seen as the protectress of young girls and her help was invoked by them in their search for a husband. On 25th November, twenty-five-year-old unmarried women known as *catherinettes* wore fanciful bonnets decorated with green and yellow and often took part in a competition resembling an Easter bonnet parade. Because of this association with sewing, the date has long been *la fête de la couture* and an important day for Paris fashion houses. Today it is still quite common for groups of young women to make a bonnet for a twenty-five-year-old single friend. Because of her learning and wisdom Sainte Catherine is the patron saint of schools, lawyers and philosophers. But because she was tortured with a hideously ingenious device made of wheels and rotating knives, she is also the chosen saint of wheelwrights, millers, grinders – and barbers!

Décembre

Noël au balcon, Pâques aux tisons.
Christmas on the balcony means sitting round the fire at Easter.

La Sainte-Barbe

Nothing to do with beards, this festival on 4th December is the annual knees-up of *les sapeurs-pompiers* (firemen) whose patron saint is Sainte Barbe. Like Sainte Catherine, this third-century saint suffered unspeakable tortures on account of her Christian beliefs. She was finally decapitated by her father who was promptly struck by lightning and burnt on the spot. Because of this Sainte Barbe was often invoked as protection against fires caused by lightning:*Quand le tonnerre tombera, Sainte Barbe me retiendra* (When lightning falls, Sainte Barbe will save me).

La Saint-Nicolas

Saint Nicolas was a Turkish bishop who was persecuted for his faith and died on 6th December 343. Some of his remains found their way to Lorraine and, consequently, it is mainly in the north and east of France that this Germanic festival is still celebrated on 6th December. Gruesome legend has it that three orphans who lost their way were captured by a butcher who cut them into pieces and put them in his salted-meat barrel. Then Saint Nicolas happened by, asking for shelter. He made straight for the meat barrel and ordered

the children to wake up. Out they hopped, happy and well. Because of this and other interventions on behalf of young people, Saint Nicolas became the patron saint of children who still put out their shoes for him to fill with presents on the eve of 6th December. It is customary to leave a carrot and some hay or sugar for Saint Nicolas' donkey. In some north-eastern towns, a Saint Nicolas look-alike, complete with bishop's outfit and cross, parades through the crowds distributing sweets. Sometimes he is accompanied by le Père Fouettard (Black Peter) his devilish acolyte, who carries a whip or a cane supposedly to punish children who have been naughty.

Joyeux Noël! (Happy Christmas!)

Entre le bœuf et l'âne gris   Between the ox and the grey donkey
Dors, dors le petit fils ...   Sleep, sleep little son ...

So begins the Christmas song known to all French children. The French do not have a tradition of carols equivalent to that of America and Britain, but they do decorate their homes in much the same way – the *sapin de Noël* (Christmas tree) has been a common decoration since the end of the nineteenth century. *La crèche* (the crib scene) is another family tradition going back to the seventeenth century and the reign of Louis XIV when even the poorest families had one in their homes. In Provence, the crib became an art form with *les santons*, painted clay and china models, representing not only the holy family and shepherds, but the characters of a whole village.

Father Christmas, who developed in England and America from a number of different mythical figures, including Saint Nicholas, only made his appearance in France as *le père Noël* at the beginning of the twentieth century. The old man with the red robes, fake beard and *hotte d'osier* (wicker basket) instead of a sack, is now well-established, but only fifty years ago he still outraged die-hard Catholics. In 1951, the Archbishop of Toulouse denounced *le père Noël* as a cunning device to take the religion out of Christmas; and his colleague the Bishop of Dijon disturbed the spirit of peace and goodwill in his locality by burning an effigy of *le père Noël* on the church steps.

Happily, *le père Noël* still visits every child's house on Christmas Eve, and in the manner of Saint Nicholas fills their shoes with presents. However, in recent years French children have adopted the Anglo-Saxon habit of leaving out Christmas stockings as well. Christmas Eve is a more important celebration than Christmas day as this is when many people attend *la messe de minuit* (Midnight Mass), traditionally returning home for a very indigestible meal, *le réveillon*. Nowadays many families prefer to eat before the Mass. The principle components of the traditional menu are *les huîtres* (oysters), *la dinde* (turkey) and *la bûche de Noël* (chocolate log) which everyone sleeps off in time for exchanging presents on Christmas morning and before tucking in to *le repas de Noël* (Christmas lunch), a mercifully lighter meal.

The delicious *bûche de Noël* is a descendent of the real thing. For centuries, on Christmas Eve a special log was chosen to burn all night and, in some regions, even until epiphany on 6th January.

As there is no equivalent of Boxing Day, France is back to work on 26th December, to the relief of 37 per cent of the population who, in a recent survey, confessed to experiencing end-of-year-festivity blues, partly brought on by pretending to be enjoying themselves! Unsociable Anglo-Saxons can take comfort from knowing that even the French, sometimes, find it all a bit too much.

La Saint-Sylvestre

New Year's Eve is the *fête* of Saint Sylvestre and the time for kissing under *le gui* (the mistletoe) to ensure happiness in the coming year. The Celts attributed many healing and mystical properties to mistletoe which was ceremoniously cut down at this time of year, hence the saying: *Au gui, l'an neuf* (With mistletoe the New Year). Apart from this, the French see in the new year with white wine, another *réveillon* often in a restaurant, and *un concert d'avertisseurs* – that is, much honking of car horns.

Some regional celebrations

French local festivals are so many and so varied that it would take a whole book to do them justice. While many are religious or historical, others are distinctly quirky such as *le Championnat des cracheurs de cerises* at Francescas in Lot-et-Garonne (cherry spitting contest), *le Championnat de lancer de bérets* at Berzème in Ardèche (beret-throwing competition) or the *fête des andouilles et des cornichons* at Bèze in Bourgogne where gastronomes may regale themselves with strong sausage and gherkins. Here are a few of the largest local festivals.

Brittany

Le Festival InterCeltique

This festival is a more formal and certainly much larger event than the many local *festou-noz* (night feasts) which attract good-time Bretons in the summer months. For ten days every August, a quarter of a million people come from all the Celtic countries to join in Breton *gavottes* or to sing along to the *bombard* (like an oboe), the *biniou* (Breton bagpipe) or the *telenn* (Breton harp) which has enjoyed a revival thanks to the popular Breton folksinger Alain Stivell.

Les pardons

Breton *pardons* were ritualized pilgrimages or church processions in memory of a local saint. Many *pardons* have been revived and feature the colourfully embroidered banners of local parishes carried by men and women wearing traditional costume including *les coiffes bretonnes* (perilously tall, lace head-dresses). One of the most famous and largest *pardons* is that of Sainte-Anne d'Auray on 26th July when as many as 100,000 pilgrims have been known to gather in prayer with lighted candles and torches.

Provence

Le pèlerinage et la fête des gitans (gypsy pilgrimage and festival)

Every year on 24th and 25th May thousands of gypsies from all over the world come to the town of les Saintes-Maries-de-la-Mer in the Camargue in the south of France. According to local legend, after the crucifixion, Marie-Jacobé (Christ's aunt) and Marie-Salomé (the mother of James and John) together with their black servant Sara known as *l'Egyptienne*, fled from Palestine in a boat and finally landed on the site of this town where they built an altar, thus bringing Christianity to Provence. In the centuries-old ceremony commemorating the three women, Camargue herdsmen on white horses escort first the statue of Sara, the patron saint of gypsies, and on the following day the statues of the two Maries, down to the sea where the priest and the participating crowds wade into the water. The two Maries are set down in a little boat to bob about on the waves. After a blessing, everyone returns in their dripping clothes to the church where the statues are set back in place to wait for next year's moment of glory.

Les corridas et courses de taureaux (Bullfights and bullraces)

In the south of France at Nîmes, Béziers, Arles, Fréjus, and Gers Mont-de-Marsan there are many bull-fights and bull-chases in the summer months. The Roman arenas of Arles and Nîmes obviously lend themselves to this sport which has come under increasing criticism in recent years. Bull-chasing does not involve the bull being put to death, instead, daring and foolhardy young men attempt to remove a rosette from between the bull's horns. Those who are less exhibitionist but equally reckless can risk being trampled underfoot in *un lâcher de vachettes*, when young cows are released to stampede through the narrow streets.

Le Nord

Les géants

Throughout the summer, many towns of northern France have local festivals featuring *les géants*, huge models of historical or legendary figures. There are more than twenty *géants* in the area around Dunkerque, including Jehan de Calais, a fourteenth-century pirate, and his wife Constance; the Flemish Reuze Papa and Reuze Maman of Cassel; and Kopierre of Aniche who in real life was an unusually tall drummer in the army of Napoleon III. The most famous, oldest and largest giant is Gayant who is paraded through the streets of Douai with his wife and giant children every July.

Family celebrations

While national festivals are often a time for family get-togethers, a key family event is an even more important occasion for celebration.

Le baptême (christening): More than half of French babies are baptised in church and it is still customary to distribute *les dragées* (sugared almonds) to local children when the ceremony is over. *Un cornet de dragées* (a paper cone of sugared almonds) is given to invitees and posted to those unable to attend.

La communion solennelle (official communion): This is an important landmark for children in Catholic families, although less picturesque than in the past when girls were adorned with metres of white gauze and boys were spruced up in suits or sailor outfits. Children take their *communion privée* (first communion) at around the age of nine, and then at 13 they may take *la communion solennelle* with their parents. It is a time for a big family meal, often in a restaurant, when gifts such as *un chapelet* (rosary), crucifix or bible are given.

Le mariage: In France a civil ceremony is obligatory and this takes place at *la mairie* where the mayor officiates. If the couple are not going on to a church ceremony, the wedding rings are exchanged outside *la mairie*. The following lengthy *repas de noces* (wedding meal) features *une pièce montée*, a tiered sponge cake.

Les obsèques (funeral): Although the tradition of *un cortège funèbre* (a funeral procession) is no longer widespread, it is still customary for mourners to sign a book of condolences outside the church after the ceremony. *L'enterrement* (burial) together with a shiny marble headstone is still generally chosen instead of *l'incinération* (cremation), despite the fact that it is about 10,000 francs more expensive.

Bonne fête!: As every day of the year is a saint's day in the Catholic Church, a person with the name of a saint celebrates on the same day. It is their *fête* – a mini-birthday when they may receive cards and presents. Until 1993, nearly every one in France had a saint's day because if children were christened they had to have a saint's name. However, as other names are now permitted, some children have to be content with a *Joyeux anniversaire!* (Happy Birthday!).

VOCABULARY

le jour férié *public holiday*
la fête légale " "
les fêtes de fin d'année *Christmas and New Year*
fêter *to celebrate*
faire la fête " "
la réjouissance *festivity*
défiler *to parade*
arroser au champagne *celebrate with champagne*
boire à la santé de *to drink the health of*
porter un toast à *to toast*
klaxonner *to sound the horn*
le faire-part *announcement of birth, marriage or death*
se fiancer *to get engaged*

les fiançailles (f.) *engagement*
épouser qqn. *to marry someone*
se marier avec qqn. " "
la mariée *bride*
le marié *groom*
le témoin du marié *best man*
la demoiselle d'honneur *bridesmaid*
les invités *guests*
l'alliance (f.) *wedding ring*
la lune de miel *honeymoon*
l'anniversaire de mariage (m.) *wedding anniversary*
les noces (f.) d'argent *silver wedding*
les noces (f.) d'or *golden wedding*
le parrain *godfather*
la marraine *godmother*
les pompes funèbres (f.) *funeral directors*
être en deuil *to be in mourning*

Taking it further

Events

Festival InterCeltique (first Friday to second Sunday of August), Office du tourisme de Pays de Lorient, Place Jules-Ferry, 56100 Lorient, tel. 02 97 21 07 84

Quinzaine Celtique (June/July), Office du tourisme, place du Commerce, Nantes, tel. 02 40 20 60 00

Festival Cornouaille (July), Office du tourisme, place de la Résistance, Quimper, tel. 02 98 53 04 05

Carnaval de Nice (February), Office du tourisme, 5 promenade des Anglais, tel. 04 92 12 48 00

Gypsy pilgrimage (end of May), Office du tourisme, 5 ave Van Gogh, les Saintes-Maries-de-la-Mer, tel. 04 90 97 82 55

Bull-fighting Feria, Mont-de-Marsan (third week of July), Office du tourisme, 6 place du Général Leclerc, tel. 05 58 05 87 37 – top French and Spanish bull-fighters, plus *la course landaise* (bull vaulting!)

For details of the many other regional and national festivals contact the **French Government Tourist Office**, 178 Piccadilly, London W1V OAL, tel. 0906 8244 123, fax. 020 7493 6594

French Tourist Office, 444 Madison Avenue, New York 100022, tel. 212 838 7800

French Tourist Bureau, BNP Building, 12th floor, 12 Castlereagh Street, Sydney, NSW 2000, Australia, tel. (2) 231 52 44

French Tourist Office events website: **franceguide.com**

Books

Martin, Philippe-Henri, **Les Jours de Fête** (Paris: Arléa/le Seuil, 1995)

Baume, Renaud de la, **Le guide familier des fêtes de France** (Paris: La Boétie, 1981)

7 | FOOD AND FASHION

Food and drink

'Il faut vivre pour manger et non pas manger pour vivre' ('One should live to eat and not eat to live') declares many a French gourmet, misquoting Molière with impunity. In fact, the seventeenth-century playwright advised the opposite, but such caution has always been out of place in France where eating is much more than a physical necessity. Given the tantalizing tastes and textures of France's vast array of local produce and beautifully-prepared regional dishes, eating in France has long been a sensual delight, an opportunity for conviviality, and a powerful expression of regional and national identity. But the last thirty years have seen changes in French food and eating habits that exemplify, perhaps more than any other aspect of French culture, the country's struggle to embrace modern life without losing her essential character.

Les repas (meals)

The French are renowned for spending a long time at the table. Sunday lunch or any special occasion is an unhurried affair when no trouble is spared to produce the very best home cooking, to choose the finest wines, and to set the table as beautifully as possible. A celebration meal is likely to comprise: *hors-d'oeuvre*, fish, meat and a vegetable, salad, a mouth-watering selection of cheeses, and dessert (often bought from the local *pâtisserie*) polished off with coffee and liqueur.

Day to day, however, working households do not linger over *le déjeuner* (lunch) which used to be the main meal of the day. Things have changed since Simenon declared his ideal woman to be Madame Maigret, his famous Parisian detective's stay-at-home wife who devoted whole mornings, if not days, to the careful preparation of slowly simmering stews. Today's workers often grab a *baguette* sandwich or a pastry for lunch. Others are lucky enough to have a staff canteen where they can wolf down four appetizing courses that are generally of a far higher standard than what is served up to Anglo-Saxon workers.

A weekday *dîner* (evening meal) will take about thirty minutes to prepare and at least once a week it will be a *surgelé* (frozen product) – French frozen food companies have won the public's trust by engaging the skills of top French chefs such as Michel Guérard. However, the French are still attached to their *quatre ou cinq plats* (four or five courses) even though each course may be quite simple: a starter such as grated carrots or tomato salad, grilled meat or fish served with a vegetable and often followed by salad, cheese and a dessert of yoghurt or fruit.

Le petit-déjeuner (breakfast) has never been a big meal in France. Even early-rising agricultural workers used to skimp on breakfast and had a bigger *casse-croûte* (snack) mid-morning. But now that evening dinner is generally the main meal of the day, the French are spending longer over breakfast, in fact four times as long as forty years ago when they took only five minutes to gulp down their bowl of *café noir* (black coffee), *café au lait* (white coffee) or *chocolat chaud* (hot chocolate) with *tartines* (bread and butter with jam) or *croissants*. Today, this is often supplemented with fruit juice, cereals, yoghurt or eggs. Nowadays, about one in seven French people have even adopted the Anglo-Saxon habit of drinking tea for breakfast.

Croissants

First introduced to France from Austria by Queen Marie-Antoinette, these familiar crescent-shaped pastries were allegedly baked to celebrate the defeat of the Turkish army which had lain siege to Vienna in 1683. Their shape commemorates the crescent moon (*croissant*) which appears on the Turkish flag. Today, in some parts of France, a very curved *croissant* denotes the use of margarine, while a straighter shape confirms the genuine article – *un croissant pur beurre* (pure butter croissant).)

Le goûter (tea), consisting of a *pain au chocolat* or bread with either butter and jam, or a slab of chocolate, is routinely eaten by children between 4 and 5 p.m. It is intended to keep them going till the evening meal at 7 or 8 p.m. as few French families cook separately to cater for hungry or picky children.

Today's top dishes

Once, the country's favourite dishes were *pot-au-feu*, a tasty beef stew with carrots, leeks and turnips, *gigot* (leg of lamb) cooked to leave the inside meat slightly pink, and *blanquette de veau* (veal in white sauce). But for several years, and despite the scare of *la vache folle* (mad cow disease), the most popular dish both at home and in restaurants has been *le steak-frites* (steak and chips). This would certainly not do, however, for a special occasion when one of France's superb regional dishes would be chosen instead.

Couscous is another favourite, particularly amongst 15 to 19 year olds who prefer this North African, semolina-based dish even to hamburgers. The assimilation of *couscous* into the French national diet reflects France's colonial links with the Maghreb and the country's large North African population. French chauvinism about food sometimes gives way to the French love of exoticism, particularly if an exotic dish comes from a former French territory. Thus *le méchoui*, a whole lamb roasted on a spit in the North African manner, has become a common feature of summer-time festivities. The spicy food of Vietnam, also a former colony, is sometimes cooked at home, but it is most often eaten in Vietnamese restaurants which are as common as Chinese restaurants are in Britain and America. However, the Anglo-Saxon habit of takeaway food and TV dinners has not really caught on with the French for whom sitting around the table to eat home-cooked food remains a sacrosanct ritual.

The basics

Le pain (bread)

Bread has a central place in French life, as many everyday expressions prove, for example:

bon comme le pain	good as bread
long comme un jour sans pain	long as a day without bread

avoir du pain sur la planche	to have a lot of bread on one's plate i.e. to have a lot to do
faire passer le goût du pain	to deprive someone of the taste of bread i.e. to kill someone
c'est pain bénit	it's blessed bread i.e. a godsend

Today, bread is freely available to accompany restaurant meals and is the cheapest food, as it has been for centuries. In the past, a good harvest and the availability of bread meant the difference between life and death for the majority of French people, the peasants working the land. Bread represented basic human dignity, and shortages sparked off many popular uprisings, including the French Revolution. King Louis XVI's Austrian wife Marie-Antoinette famously dismissed the people's needs, urging them to eat *brioche*, not cake as Anglo-Saxon legend has it. *Brioche* then, as now, was an enriched bread more like a bun, far more expensive than the scarcest loaf.

'If the French people have no more bread, let them eat brioche.'

In a long-time Catholic country, bread must, even at an unconscious level, evoke the bread of communion. Today, just as they have for centuries, many people still score the sign of the cross on the underside of a loaf before cutting it.

A couple of stereotypes

Just as the French collective noun for the supposedly roast-beef-guzzling Brits is *les rosbifs*, so the British term for their neighbours, 'the frogs', derives from a one-time belief that *les cuisses de grenouille* (frogs legs, or thighs!) formed the French person's staple diet. In fact, this expensive delicacy rarely appears on French menus. Usually eaten as an *hors d'oeuvre*, *les cuisses de grenouille* are the back legs of a special breed of small green, edible frog.

Escargots (snails), too, are far from everyday fare. There are two edible varieties which, to ensure that they are safe for eating, are reared in *escargotières* on a special diet of vine leaves. They are exported around the world canned or frozen, the easiest way to try them. Fresh snails, on the other hand, require hours of preparation, which is reflected in restaurant prices.

Baguette

The familiar long, light-textured *baguette* did not appear in Parisian *boulangeries* until the nineteenth-century. Before this, all French bread was round (the word *boulanger* derived from the picard word for 'round', *boulenc*). The new shape was probably adopted in order to maximise the area of golden crust; in fact the crust was considered such a delicacy that gentlemen would save a piece as a tasty morcel to present to their ladies.

Even though nowadays the French eat much less bread than in the past, it is still the common accompaniment for every course apart from dessert. *Baguette* sandwiches, which were once simple café fare filled with ham, camembert or saucisson, have taken on a new lease of life with exotic fillings, sold from *points-chauds* (hot bread or pastry bars) and eaten *sur le pouce* (on the go) – France's perfect gift to the international snacking culture.

For years, bread lovers have been lamenting a deterioration in the quality of the cherished *baguette*, hastened by industrial baking methods and, in some supermarkets, by the use of partially-frozen dough. Even more anathema to purists is the widespread sale of English-style, sliced and packaged white loaves. However, these are mainly reserved for toast and *croque-monsieur* (toasted ham and cheese). Fortunately, French hypermarkets and supermarkets account for only about a sixth of bread and *croissant* sales as many French people still make daily trips to their local independent *boulangerie artisanale*, before or after work, in order to buy the tastiest bread.

According to bread experts, a good loaf should charm all the senses: it must smell of good flour; its crust must be golden and resonant when tapped with the finger; its inside must be creamy white, fine-textured and springy, but with plenty of air holes.

One final test of an excellent baguette: scratch the inside with your thumb, and if the crumbs don't fall off ... that *boulangerie* is worth a detour!

Le fromage (cheese)

France's 350 varieties of cheese are another source of national pride. So it is not surprising that feelings run deep over an EU directive which requires stringent testing for listeria in those soft cheeses traditionally made *au lait cru* (with unpasteurized milk) such as camembert, brie, Pont l'Eveque and many lesser-known regional varieties. The smallest trace of listeria found in a random sample does not necessarily constitute a health risk, but is nonetheless enough for the cheese to be recalled amidst adverse publicity devastating for the small producer.

French cheese lovers, who consume 80 per cent of all the unpasteurized cheese produced in Europe, consider the use of pasteurized milk in traditional soft cheeses to be a bland-tasting affront to the sophisticated French palate.

Le vin et l'eau (wine and water)

For the French, an empty wine bottle is *un cadavre* (a corpse) suggesting that wine is the life blood of the nation. While France is the world's top wine producer and exporter, the importance of wine in the home market is clear from the amply-stocked wine shelves of even small supermarkets and from the *caves* (cellars) that continue to be built in modern houses and blocks of flats.

Although wine remains a vital part of the economy and French culture, drinking habits have changed. Even though the French are still among Europe's biggest wine drinkers (only surpassed in consumption per head by Portugal), they now drink half as much wine as thirty years ago. The government hopes to cut this further and so reduce France's high level of alcohol-related illnesses and accidents (see pp. 196–197).

Nowadays, few French people drink *vin de table* (table wine) with every meal and many prefer to drink better quality wines and to keep these for social occasions. On the other hand, every lunch and dinner table will have a bottle of mineral water and often even tap water. The mineral water habit is confirmed by the countless brands of *or blanc* (white gold), so-named not because of the purity of its minerals but because of the fortune made by the bottlers! Health fanatics can even peruse a mineral water guide which analyses the constituents of 90 different brands, and advises on their suitability for many complaints.

Reflecting and also contributing to the gradual change in drinking patterns was the EEC's decision to chop subsidies to uneconomic producers of poor quality wines. In the 1980s, this had a drastic effect on the vine growers of the Languedoc whose grapes were mainly used for coarse *vins de table* (table wines), at one time the cheap staple drink of the French working man. The producers of such wines were forced to replant their vineyards with better vines, thus upgrading their wines, or to diversify into other fruit or vegetables. So from being the most frequently drunk French wines, *vins de table* now form only about a sixth of the total produced. On the other hand, top quality wines worthy of the classification *appellation d'origine contrôlée* (see box) constitute nearly half of all French wines, a far higher proportion than thirty years ago.

Wine classifications

Appellation d'origine controlée (AOC)
This designates a very high quality wine from a particular vineyard in a strictly-defined area; for a wine to retain the AOC label, the proportion of alcohol, the production level and nature of the soil must remain the same.

The finest and most expensive AOC wines are known by their property of origin (*Château* or *Domaine*). They are further graded into: *grand cru*, the best, then *premier*, *deuxième*, *troisième cru* etc.

Vin délimité de qualité supérieure (VDQS)
This second category is for good local wines which have passed strict quality controls.

Vins de pays and vins de coupage
These table wines are either local wines or blended, mixed-origin wines which do not qualify for the above classifications. They must have a minimum alcohol content of 9.5°.

L'apéro (l'apéritif)

Dinner guests in France are always offered an *apéritif* before their meal, together with *amuse-gueules* (salty nuts or biscuits). *Apéritif* time is also the moment to share a drink with friends, whether eating together or not. The most popular *apéritifs* used to be *kir*, made with sparkling white wine and *cassis* (blackcurrant liqueur), *porto* (port) and *pastis* or *pernod,* cloudy aniseed-flavoured spirits particularly common in the south of France. However *le Scotch* has taken over as today's sophisticated *apéro*, and the French down more of the fiery Scottish spirit than either the British or the Americans.

Le digestif

There is no shortage of French liqueurs and cognacs with which to round off a meal. Some, such as the Norman apple brandy Calvados, are traditionally supped as an aid to digestion between courses, hence its nickname *le trou normand* (the Norman gap). Contrary to what Anglo-Saxons might think, France's top-selling Cognac abroad, Courvoisier, is less popular in France. It seems that

French advertisers are experts at peddling the gallic image. In the 1980s they were equally successsful at shifting the Piat d'Or wines which were shunned by the French.

Restaurants and chefs

The world has been in awe of French cooking ever since the nineteenth century when the great chefs, who before the Revolution had worked in noble households, opened *restaurants*. Here, the newly-empowered bourgeoisie could flaunt their wealth and their taste for the intricate dishes of *haute cuisine*, previously reserved for the aristocracy. The renown of French chefs spread far beyond France and some of the greatest, such as **Marie Antoine Carême** (1784–1833) were engaged to cook for the Prince Regent and the Czar.

However, the French chef who revolutionized restaurant practice throughout the world was **Georges Auguste Escoffier** (1847–1935). He simplified recipes and speeded up the cooking process through a strict division of labour in the kitchen, and the hierarchy of posts still used in catering today. He managed many restaurants including that of the new Paris Ritz where he created his delicious dessert *pêche melba* in honour of the famous soprano, Dame Nellie Melba.

le Guide Michelin

France's famous restaurant bible was first published in 1900 as a free gift distributed by the Michelin tyre company. The aim of this first edition was not to turn its gourmet customers into lookalikes of the company's rotund logo, but to boost tyre sales by encouraging drivers to burn rubber in search of a restaurant that *vaut le détour* (is worth a detour).

It was not until the 1970s that smart hotels and restaurants abandoned Escoffier's style of cooking in favour of *la nouvelle cuisine*. This used only fresh ingredients, cut out rich sauces, drastically reduced cooking times, and was frequently served in artistically-displayed, but meagre, portions. One of the pioneers of this simpler, but equally sophisticated, style of cooking was **Paul Bocuse** (1926–) who renewed the old tradition of chefs owning their own restaurants. Since the 1980s, however, *nouvelle cuisine* has given way to the rediscovery of hearty regional dishes – *la cuisine du terroir* – much to the delight of hungry diners.

A French cookery teacher, Richard Filippi, revolutionized the diet of Mir spacecraft astronauts who were previously reliant on nutritious, but mushy concoctions in tubes. M. Filippi devised a surgically sterile way of preparing French cuisine in tins, thus enabling the astronauts to sample the delights of quail in Madeira sauce and swordfish provençale.

The restaurant habit

Because of France's profusion of small family-run restaurants which, for the last century, have offered delicious meals at reasonable prices and welcomed children rather than endured them, eating out has been a frequent pleasure for many French families. However, in the last decade the steady spread of restaurant chains and their unimaginative but cheap menus have put many small family restaurants out of business. The might of chains such as Buffalo Grill, Hippopotamus, Bistro Romain and Leon de Bruxelles, is particularly evident in Paris where their 144 branches swiftly serve an unchanging three-course menu to thousands of people every day. No self-respecting French person would choose a wild-west style diner for their daughter's first communion meal, or for a sophisticated *dîner à deux* (dinner for two), but independent restaurants need to hold on to day-to-day trade in order to survive.

Where the French eat out	
Type of restaurant	**% of total spent on meals out**
Fast-food outlets	27
Sandwich bars	26
Grill restaurants	11
Pizzerias	10
Traditional restaurants	6
Brasseries (café-bars)	3
Fish restaurants	3

Fashion

Part of France's reputation for elegant and sophisticated design rests on her fashion industry. Despite losing ground to New York and Milan in the 1970s, despite repeated claims that extravagant *haute couture* is out of touch with modern life, Paris is still the heart of the fashion world, as she has been for over a century. Ever since the designer **Paul Poiret** (1879–1944) freed women from the constraints of the corset, Parisian couturiers have set trends that have radically changed women's appearance.

It was, however, an Englishman, **Charles Worth** (1825–95), who founded the first Parisian *haute couture* fashion house in 1858. Ten years later *Le syndicat de la couture parisienne* was established to prevent designs being plagiarized. Subsequently the Ministry of Industry regulated the use of the term *haute couture* which today can be used only by design houses employing a minimum of 20 production workers and presenting at least 50 original, handmade, and therefore phenomenally expensive, outfits each season. The 23 or so houses which meet these requirements produce four *prêt-à-porter* (ready-to-wear) shows a year, in addition to their spring and autumn *haute couture* ranges. Many of them are in or near the rue du Faubourg St-Honoré and Avenue Montaigne.

French *haute couture* is big business, even though the couturiers' made-to-measure outfits are bought by only 2,000 or so fabulously wealthy women and represent only a small part of the fashion houses' turnover. The *haute couture* shows fill newspaper columns and promote the names which sell all the ready-to-wear collections and all the spin-offs – perfumes, jewellery, bags. Few fashion houses are independent: Dior, Givenchy and Christian Lacroix are part of the luxury goods group LVMH (Louis Vuitton Moët Hennessy) owned by French business tycoon Bernard Arnault; Yves Saint Laurent and Nina Ricci are owned by the Sanofi group. In the cut-throat world of top fashion, many designers have been shunted out of the houses to which they gave their names.

French fashion pioneers

1920 and '30s

Like the ladies for whom her clothes were designed, **Coco Chanel** (1883–1971) was super-rich (she died at the Ritz Hotel in Paris where she had lived for 37 years). In 1916, a time when women were still wearing elaborate dresses, Chanel introduced women's suits and well-cut frocks whose simple lines epitomized not only classic good taste but women's greater social freedom if not political freedom, (French women did not win the vote until 1944!). Such was Chanel's fame and influence that her healthy, bronzed appearance after a holiday in the south of France in 1925 reversed the fashion for lily-white skin. Henceforth, instead of suggesting the rigours and deprivations of rural life, a sun tan was the mark of expensive glamour, an image exploited by l'Oréal in 1935 when it launched the first mass-market sun lotion, Ambre Solaire.

The elegant Coco Chanel.

Chanel is also remembered for her puzzling advice *'Montrer les cuisses, oui ... mais les genoux, jamais!'* ('Show your thighs, yes ... but your knees, never!')

1940s

In 1947, **Christian Dior**'s (1905–1957) first collection lifted the spirits of the post-war world. His New Look, featuring longer, fuller skirts and nipped-in waists, captured an expansive, hopeful mood, even if the ordinary woman was still restricted by ration cards and unable to buy the metres of fabric required.

1950s

Although the legacy of the New Look was the ubiquitous gathered skirt, 1950s sophisticates opted for the shorter, elegant designs of **Hubert de Givenchy** (1927–) for whom the stylish Jackie Kennedy and film star Audrey Hepburn were walking advertisements.

1960s

After **André Courrèges** (1923–) launched the mini-skirt in 1965, clothes became leaner and much shorter, designed for a younger, more hedonistic generation. It was in this spirit that **Paco Rabanne** (1934–) created sci-fi-style dresses, influenced perhaps by his belief in astral travel (he claims to have murdered Tutankhamen in one of his former lives!). Unfortunately, his plastic and chain-metal outfits (even one made of forks and spoons) did not translate into comfortable high-street designs, unlike the geometric jersey dresses of **Pierre Cardin** (1922–) which were copied throughout the world.

1970s and '80s

Whereas Chanel is said to have given women their freedom, **Yves Saint Laurent** (1936–) is famed for having given them power. It was YSL who created the *tailleur-pantalon* (trouser-suit) and made it acceptable in the boardroom, even before his big-shoulder jackets and pencil skirts set the 1980s power dressing trend. One of his most famous clients is Catherine Deneuve. YSL was the first of the fashion houses to launch a men's collection, the ready-to-wear *Rive Gauche pour hommes*.

The most colourful designer of this period was undoubtedly **Christian Lacroix** (1951–) who produced showy, bright and beaded outfits for the Jean Patou house, before creating his own fashion house in 1987.

1990 onwards

By 1990, several daring younger designers, dubbed *enfants terribles*, were hitting the big time with provocative, theatrical collections. **Jean-Paul Gaultier** (1952–), known to British television viewers in the 1980s as co-presenter of *Eurotrash* and as the man who tried to get men to wear skirts, became a household name when he launched underwear as outerwear, notably Madonna's cone-shaped bra. In 1999 his *haute couture*, ready-to-wear and perfume business hitched up with an unlikely partner, the luxury goods firm Hermès famed for its silk scarves worn by the Queen.

While **Thierry Mugler**'s (1946–) particular brand of glamorous vampishness looks a million dollars on models like Jerry Hall, the understated designs of *prêt-à-porter* designer, **Agnès b** (1942–), are favourites with film stars and high-street shoppers alike. There are over a hundred Agnès b shops worldwide, including 50 in Japan. Now France's 43rd richest person, Agnès b also owns the modern art Galerie du jour as well as a film production company.

In fashion as in other art forms, Paris attracts foreign talent. A clutch of British designers incudes couturier **John Galliano** (1939–) who stirred up the formerly staid house of Dior with his extravagant and irreverent designs, **Alexander McQueen** (1969–), the flashy showman of Givenchy, and **Stella McCartney** (1971–), daughter of ex-Beatle Paul, at fashion house Chloé. The Chanel collections are the creation of German couturier **Karl Lagerfeld** (1938–).

VOCABULARY

la toque *chef's hat; also used as 'star' in gastronomic ratings*
les plats mijotés *slowly-simmering dishes*
le grignotage *snacking*
grignoter *to nibble, to snack*
l'en-cas (m.) *snack*
les surgelés (m.) *frozen food*
la restauration rapide *fast food*
les plats à emporter (m.) take-away dishes
la semaine du goût *annual, week-long, cookery event (chefs in schools, food tastings, exhibitions etc.)*

l'Alliance Végétarienne *French vegetarian body*
l'eau minérale gazeuse (f.) *sparkling mineral water*
l'eau minérale plate (f.) *still mineral water*
déguster *to taste, to savour*
la dégustation *wine-tasting*
le nez *nose, aroma*
le grand cru *great wine or vintage*
le tonneau *barrel*
le cep *vine stock*
le cépage *type of wine*
boisé *woody*

gouleyant *very drinkable*
chaleureux *warms the throat after swallowing*
long/court *long/short – according to number of seconds before aroma disappears after swallowing.* Grand cru *aroma lingers for at least 12 seconds!*

l'eau de vie *brandy*
le défilé *fashion show*
le couturier *designer*
la maison de couture *fashion house*
la griffe *couturier's label*

Taking it further

Places

Le Musée de la Mode et du Costume, Palais Galliera, 10 avenue Pierre 1er de la Serbie, 75116 Paris; tel. 01 47 20 85 23

Books

Robuchon, Joël, **Larousse Gastronomique** (Paris: Larousse, 1996) – definitive guide to all aspects of food and wine plus recipes
Larousse de la cuisine (Paris: Larousse-Bordas, 1997) – step-by-step French recipes
Le Guide du buveur d'eau (Paris: Solar, 1997)
Le Guide Hachette des Vins (Paris: Hachette, 1999) – annual, serious and comprehensive wine guide
Encyclopédie touristique des vins de France (Paris: Hachette, 1999) – beautifully illustrated guide to wine and wine regions

Films

Prêt-à-porter (Ready-to-wear), Robert Altman, 1994

8 | CINEMA, MEDIA AND SCIENCE

Cinema

The cinema was born in France and remains a national passion. Even in these days of videos and DVD, France has the most cinemas and cinema-goers in Europe; half of the adult population goes to the cinema at least once a year. For the French, cinema is an art with the same status as theatre or literature, and as such it receives generous state support. Ten per cent of the price of every cinema ticket goes towards funding new films, and state encouragement of co-productions involving film companies and television networks also helps to get new films off the ground. Another reason why low-budget films are not elbowed out by Hollywood blockbusters is the fragmentation of film production and distribution in France. The country's biggest distributors – Gaumont, Pathé and the Union Générale Cinématographique – control only a fifth of French cinemas.

French films have a reputation for being subtle, thought-provoking and stylish, or introspective, slow and boring, depending on your taste. While this stereotype stems from the *Nouvelle vague* (New Wave) period in the 1950s and '60s, there remains something quintessentially French about even today's very different big-budget productions or lower-key social realist films. This quality is a sense of the director's personal vision, a vision that frequently captures the rational, the romantic or the stylish elements of the French character.

While French and American film styles have often been poles apart, since the 1940s American cinema has exerted a fascination over French *cinéphiles* (film lovers) who have earned a reputation as the intellectuals of the cinema world. It was French critics who coined the term *film noir*, for 1940s Hollywood crime films. The term was borrowed from the *Série-Noire* detective novels which were French translations of American thrillers by Dashiell Hammett and Raymond Chandler.

Early cinema pioneers

The brothers **Auguste** and **Louis Lumière** patented the first camera to successfully project a moving image onto a screen in 1895. In the same year, Louis produced his film of Lyon factory workers leaving the brothers' photographic materials factory in Lyon, *La Sortie des usines Lumière*. It was the first documentary film to be publicly screened, and was just eleven minutes long.

'Je n'ai pas inventé le cinéma mais je l'ai industrialisé', declared **Charles Pathé** who made a fortune from developing and renting out films. He founded the news film company Pathé-Journal whose crowing cockerel became known to cinema-goers world-wide.

Léon Gaumont, another early film producer, opened many Gaumont cinemas including le Gaumont-Palace in Paris which, with 3,400 seats, was the biggest cinema in the world.

The inventive and tireless **Georges Méliès** (he was his own producer, director, stage-manager, editor, distributor and actor) made over 500 silent films designed to entertain and enchant. A former magician and illusionist, Méliès was the first to develop *le trucage* or effects such as slow motion, time-lapse photography and colour-tinting of the film strip.

French cinema landmarks

1930s

Freed from the constraints and conventions of silent film, French cinema flourished with the advent of sound at the end of the 1920s. Directors developed the style of poetic realism evident in Marcel Carné's *Le Jour se lève*, (Daybreak) and *Quai des Brumes* (Port of Shadows) featuring Jean Gabin; in René Clair's musical, *Sous les toits de Paris*, (Under the roofs of Paris); and in *l'Atalante*, the last work of the radical and passionate Jean Vigo who died from tuberculosis at the age of 29.

Jean Renoir, the son of impressionist painter Auguste Renoir, sold off some of his famous father's paintings to finance his first films. These lyrical chronicles of working-class life reveal the social and political commitment which informs Renoir's masterpiece, *La Grande Illusion* – an anti-war film that affirms the soldiers' common humanity irrespective of nationality or race.

Post-war

In 1945, Marcel Carné and script-writer Jacques Prévert created one of French cinema's greatest films, *Les Enfants du paradis* (Children of Paradise), starring Jean-Louis Barrault and Madeleine Renaud. A year later Jean Cocteau made *La Belle et la Bête*, a symbolic version of *Beauty and the Beast*. His later *Orphée* is a powerful and surrealist retelling of the Greek myth of Orpheus. Both films featured Cocteau's lover Jean Marais. Jean Renoir, who moved to America during the Occupation, made his later films there, including *French Cancan*, the story of the Moulin Rouge starring Jean Gabin and Edith Piaf (see p. 105).

Nouvelle vague

It was the young Françoise Giroud, now a renowned journalist, who gave the name *Nouvelle vague* to the films of a group of young directors in the late 1950s. Many were critics writing for the new cinema journal *Cahiers du Cinéma* which is still the most-respected film magazine read by cinema buffs world-wide. These directors, although influenced by Hollywood cinema, rejected the impersonal style of the big studios together with costume dramas, lavish sets and famous stars. Instead, they focused on personal relationships and emotional development; their films became known as *films d'auteur* because they expressed the director's own artistic and philosophical vision. Some of these low-budget productions, and in particular those of Jean-Luc Godard, were shot in the streets with a hand-held camera in order to achieve a fresh, naturalistic style that looked improvised and unedited.

Nouvelle vague who's who

Claude Chabrol (1930–): jowly, bespectacled and pipe-smoking pioneer, director of the first *Nouvelle vague* feature, *Le Beau Serge* (Handsome Serge). In the '70s Chabrol continued to make powerful, Hitchcock-influenced, suspense films such as *Le Boucher* (The Butcher) and *Les Noces Rouges* (Blood Wedding) starring his wife Stéphane Audran.

Agnès Varda (1928–): one of the earliest *Nouvelle vague* directors, she shocked middle-class France with her attack on conventional family values in the 1965 film *Le Bonheur* (Happiness).

Alain Resnais (1922–): stunned cinema audiences with his study of war, love and memory, *Hiroshima mon amour* scripted by Marguerite Duras (see p. 65). His later *L'Année dernière à Marienbad* (Last year in Marienbad), based on the novel of the same name by Alain Robbe-Grillet (see p. 65), was filmed as a poetic stream of consciousness, defying norms of chronology or characterization. Although seen as the archetypal French intellectual film-maker whose slow and evocative films have not been a success with Anglo-Saxon audiences, Resnais is an anglophile and ardent admirer of that most English of playwrights Alan Ayckbourn whose work he regularly sees in Scarborough. Resnais' 1998 film *On connaît la chanson* (The Same Old Song) is a dark musical comedy and homage to another of Resnais' favourites, the late Dennis Potter.

François Truffaut (1932–84): died-young director whose *Les quatre-cent coups* (400 Blows) sensitively chronicles the adventures of a young delinquent played by one of Truffaut's favourite actors, Jean-Pierre Léaud. Truffaut's best-loved film is *Jules et Jim*, starring Jeanne Moreau as the pivotal character in a finely-acted love triangle. His greatest commercial success was his Oscar-winning *La Nuit Américaine* (Day for Night), a film within a film starring an adult Jean-Pierre Léaud with Jacqueline Bisset.

Jean-Luc Godard (1932–): intense-looking *auteur* with black-frame specs and dishevelled appearance. Godard epitomized the rebellious spirit of *Nouvelle vague*, notably in *A bout de souffle* (Breathless) starring Jean-Paul Belmondo and American actress Jean Seburg, *Le Mépris* (Contempt) starring Brigitte Bardot and Michel Piccoli, and *Pierrot le fou*, an ironic hybrid of gangster film, musical and thriller starring Jean-Paul Belmondo.

Louis Malle (1932–1995): the director of *Nouvelle vague* film *Zazie dans le métro* went on to explore uncomfortable subjects in a frank and compassionate way. *Souffle au coeur* is about an incestuous mother-son relationship, while *Lacombe Lucien* and *Au revoir les enfants* examine the issues of collaboration and Jewish persecution in occupied France. Malle made several films in America including *Atlantic City* with touching performances from Susan Sarandon and Burt Lancaster.

Jacques Demy (1931–90): best-known for his delightful musical *Les Parapluies de Cherbourg* (The Umbrellas of Cherbourg) which stars an all-singing, all-dancing Catherine Deneuve, and for *Les Demoiselles de Rochefort* (The Young Women of Rochefort), choreographed by Gene Kelly who made one of his last dancing performances in this film.

Eric Rohmer (1920–): a former schoolteacher, famed in particular for the six films of his *Contes moraux* (Moral tales) series beginning with *Ma nuit chez Maud* (My Night at Maud's) and finishing with *L'Amour, l'après-midi* (Love in the Afternoon) which, despite their racy titles, show sexual desire thwarted by emotional angst. Rohmer's films, throughout his career, display a fine understanding of people, particularly women, who are decades younger than himself. In 1999, at the age of 79 he made *Conte d'Automne* (Autumn Tale), a characteristically subdued and lightly humorous talk-piece about a middle-aged woman who finds a man for her widowed friend through a lonely hearts ad.

Femmes fatales

Brigitte Bardot (1934–) shot to fame as a 1950s sex symbol in Roger Vadim's *Et Dieu créa la femme* (And God Created Woman). For post-war youth, in France and beyond, she epitomized sexual freedom and a rejection of rigid social mores. After making 45 films, she retired from the cinema at the age of 40 to devote her life to animal protection. Many French people were happy for her to be the sexy face of France, even the official face of Marianne (see p. 170). However, Bardot's popularity has slipped in recent years, not only because her commitment to stray dogs and baby seals is seen as somewhat cranky, but because of her offensive remarks about Muslim religious practices and her connections with the right-wing, racist party le Front National.

The best-known French actress outside France and Bardot's successor as Marianne, **Catherine Deneuve** (1943–) has starred in nearly 90 films and continues to work with most of France's major directors. She shot to fame for her early role as a bored housewife turned prostitute in Spanish director Luis Bunuel's *Belle de jour*, and for her part in Truffaut's *Le Dernier Métro* (The Last Metro). Often nicknamed 'the iceberg' because of her cool beauty and aloofness, Deneuve has consistently chosen varied and difficult roles.

From *Nouvelle vague* to the present

Since the 1970s, French cinema has diversified, offering many superb films which all bear the unmistakable stamp of their director. Enthusiasts will be able to watch most of these films in subtitled versions on video (see Taking it further).

Films focusing on relationships

Such films are the direct descendants of *Nouvelle vague*. One of the most gifted of contemporary film-makers, **Bertrand Tavernier** (1941–), is particularly interested in documenting the relationships between parents and children, the old and the young, as in *l'Horloger de St Paul* (The Watchmaker of St Paul's) set in

Tavernier's native Lyon, *Autour de minuit* (Round Midnight) about the Paris jazz scene and *Daddy nostalgie* (These Foolish Things) starring Jane Birkin and Dirk Bogarde.

The films of **André Téchiné** (1943–) are renowned for their lyrical blend of ideas and emotion. *Ma saison préférée* (My Favourite Season) starring Catherine Deneuve and Daniel Auteuil is a study of intense family relationships, while *Alice et Martin* starring Juliette Binoche and Alexis Loret examines the relationships surrounding a case of patricide.

Claude Sautet (1924–) is relatively well-known to Anglo-Saxon audiences for the subtle psychology of *Un coeur en hiver* (A Heart in Winter) in which Emmanuelle Béart plays a musician who is finally won over, only to be rejected by an unfeeling Daniel Auteuil.

The marvellous 1998 film *La Vie rêvée des anges* directed by **Erick Zonca** (1956–) is also in this tradition of documenting inner change. But it is more social realist, compassionately and unsentimentally following the paths of two ordinary girls struggling in dead-end jobs in Lille.

Amongst other unromantic depictions of modern France is **SandrineVeysset's** (1967–) *Y aura-t-il de la neige à Noël?* (Will there be Snow at Christmas?). The film gives a bleak picture of rural Provence where the lot of women is particularly tough.

Another female director is **Catherine Breillat** (1947–) whose 1999 film *Romance* is anything but romantic. Although the French are quite used to nudity on screen, Breillat shocked audiences with her brutally frank depiction of the impassive heroine's sexual encounters. Probably the most sexually-explicit art film ever made, it deliberately raises questions about the boundaries between art and life.

Historical dramas

Dramatic and action-packed literary or historical films are part of a very different trend, an attempt to capture wider international audiences. Particularly successful was the 1991 film version of Edmond Rostand's play *Cyrano de Bergerac*, directed by **Jean-Paul Rappeneau** (1932–) and starring Gérard Depardieu. *Le Hussard sur le toit* (The Horseman on the Roof), Rappeneau's retelling of Jean Giono's novel, recreates the grim atmosphere of a community hit by a cholera epidemic in the early nineteenth century.

Cyrano de Bergerac played by Gérard Depardieu.

Claude Berri's (1934–) big-budget film of Zola's *Germinal* is another nineteenth-century offering. Here, the corpulent Gérard Depardieu takes the unlikely role of a starving miner during the mining strikes of 1870s northern France. In contrast, Berri's *La Reine Margot* is a sumptuous and bloodthirsty evocation of sixteenth-century France during the wars of religion. However, Berri's films of the Marcel Pagnol novels about rural strife, *Jean de Florette* and *Manon des Sources*, are better known outside France, as is his 1999 mega-production, *Astérix et Obélix contre César* (Astérix and Obélix versus Caesar) starring comedian Bernard Clavier and Gérard Depardieu. The film was intended as France's answer to *Titanic*, in other words to make an international top earner. Instead, it went on record as the country's most expensive film to date.

Colourful nineteenth-century Romantics are the subject of **Diane Kurys**' (1948–) 1999 film *Les Enfants du siècle* which chronicles the stormy relationship of the poet, Alfred de Musset and feminist novelist George Sand played by Juliette Binoche.

Cinéma du look

These stylish films, which sometimes abandon emotional depth in favour of action and image, are a far cry from the low-key, intimate films of *Nouvelle vague*.

Luc Besson's (1959–) first international success was with *Subway*, a slick thriller that takes place in the Paris *métro*. While *Nikita* was a breathtakingly exciting sequence of sexy combat, Besson's 1997 sci-fi blockbuster, *Le Cinquième Elément* (The Fifth Element), confirmed his reputation as an international film-maker. In 1999 he applied his particular brand of style and spectacle to France's enduring icon, *Jeanne d'Arc* in a star-studded production featuring John Malkovich, Faye Dunaway and Dustin Hoffman alongside Besson's ex-wife, the Ukrainian actress and supermodel Milla Jovovich as Jeanne.

The reticent and mysterious director **Leos Carax** (1960–) started out in a small way with *Boy Meets Girl* in 1984, but in 1991 made a phenomenal loss with his extravagant and spectacular romance about two tramps, *Les Amants du Pont Neuf* which at the time was France's most expensive film ever. However, by 1999 Carax had scraped together enough money to fund his next idiosyncratic film, *Pola X* starring Catherine Deneuve.

The stylized and visually arresting *La Haine* by **Mathieu Kassovitz** (1967–) goes deeper, tackling the very severe social problem of youth unemployment in France's depressed *banlieues*.

The French box office

Despite this wealth of home-grown talent, many French cinema-goers opt for American films which account for half of all films screened, while French films only constitute around a third of what is on offer at local cinemas. Serious or 'artistic' French films do not tend to be big crowd pullers. Instead, the French films that top the polls are usually comedies of varying degrees of sophistication. Until *Titanic* set a record for French box-office takings in 1998, the most popular film of the last fifty years had been *La Grande Vadrouille*, a 1966 comedy unknown outside France. Although the film's star, Louis de Funès, and comic actor Fernandel sometimes appeared in comic films that made it across the Atlantic, the French comedies best-known abroad are those of Jacques Tati. In a series of films ending with *Trafic* in 1971, Tati's screen persona, Monsieur Hulot, bumbles his way through the obstacles of modern life, a theme which continues to strike a chord in a country attempting to reconcile its attachment to the past with its hopes for the future.

Cannes film festival

The world-famous festival was due to open in 1939 but the war intervened. Instead, it became France's first great, post-war, cultural event in September 1946. Now the festival is both film mecca and media circus, hosting films, film-makers, stars and random starlets from all over the world ... and almost as many photographers. Over the years, *la Palme d'Or*, the festival's top prize, has been awarded to a very wide range of films, not all of which become box-office hits.

Television

Television, and particularly watching the 8 o'clock evening news together at the dinner table, is something of an institution for a lot of French families. In many dining-rooms, as in many cafés, the TV is positioned half-way up the wall for ease of meal-time viewing. On the other hand, there are also households where the television is most definitely not part of everyday life. This polarization seems to be sharper than in America or Britain where the average time over-fifteen-year-olds spend watching television is 7 hours and 4 hours respectively, compared with 3 hours twelve minutes in France. While multiple TV-ownership is very common in both America and Britain, only just over a third of French households have more than one television.

The quality of French television is patchy and, although it does not plumb the depths of some of America's worst channels, it is generally less good than what is on offer in Britain. This is surprising in a country which prides itself on the high standard of its other cultural entertainments such as music, art, cinema and theatre.

Perhaps this is the legacy of years of restrictive state control which only relaxed in the 1980s. Until then, French television producers and editors had to get a government thumbs up before making their programmes. Today, three of the six television networks are private, and even the state-run channels are half-financed by *la pub* (*publicité*, advertising). Now, digital television by satellite is taking off in France even faster than in Britain, opening up the possibility of multiple channels but not necessarily better programmes.

Although there are a fair number of American films and soap operas on French television these are not allowed to dominate home-grown programmes. Just as radio is obliged to play a quota of French music, so 40 per cent of what is broadcast on television must be French and a further 20 per cent has to be European.

Another feature of French TV is the approximate nature of programme times. Most programmes start late, on all channels except Arte which is scrupulously punctual – the German influence perhaps?

TV networks (in order of audience size)

TF1 (Télévision Française 1)
Owned by the Bouygues consortium. Low-brow variety shows, foreign soaps, plus news and culture; 8 p.m. news programme presented by elegantly handsome newscaster, Patrick Poivre d'Arvor (known as PPDA) whose alleged extra-marital relationship with fellow newscaster Claire Chazal satisfied the French love for celebrity gossip. The epitome of a TV *intello*, PPDA also presents the book programme *Ex-Libris*.

France 2
State-owned. Light entertainment, films and other special-interest programmes including *Bouillon de culture*, the lively culture programme presented by household name, Bernard Pivot (see p.25). F2's evening news bulletin is TF1's main rival for the 8 p.m. audience.

France 3
State-owned. More intellectual image than TF1 and France 2 and more regional; mainly films, documentaries and current affairs e.g. *La Marche du siècle* (The March of the Century).

M6
Owned by the Compagnie Luxembourgeoise de Télédiffusion (CLT) and Lyonnaise des Eaux. Variety programmes, films, mainstream music and documentaries.

La Cinquième/Arte
State-owned. La Cinquième broadcasts day-time educational programmes, while Arte (a Franco-German joint venture) shares the channel to offer high-brow, evening arts and culture programmes.

Canal Plus

Pay-TV cable network mainly owned by the media group Havas and Générale des Eaux; sport, films and documentaries, plus the very popular satirical puppet programme, *Les Guignols de l'Info* (see p. 177) broadcast nightly; one in five households subscribes to Canal Plus.

Radio

Part of a French person's early morning routine is tuning in to their favourite radio station. This long-standing radio habit shows no sign of weakening, particularly as there is no breakfast TV in France.

Since 1982 there has been a vast choice of private stations alongside the 53 stations of the state-owned network Radio France. Most of these are regional stations, while five are national: **France Inter**, **France Culture**, **France Musique**, **Radio Bleue** which plays endless golden oldies and **France Info** which provides a 24-hour news and weather service – the first of its kind in Europe.

The most popular private national radio stations are **RTL**, **Europe 1** and **Radio-Monte-Carlo** which are all on AM and FM bands. Other private stations, mainly found on FM, include **NRJ** a pop music channel, **Radio Beur** for North-African Arab listeners, **Rire et Chanson** for comedy, Skyrock for rock music, and over 30 regional stations.

The Press

The French are a nation of magazine readers rather than daily newspaper browsers. Between 1980 and 1990, the number of people reading daily newspapers dropped by a quarter, partly because of competition from television and magazines and partly because French newspapers are pricey (around 7 francs an issue) due to high production and distribution costs. On the other hand, weekly news magazines are doing well, alongside a vast choice of special interest publications such as the car weekly *Auto Plus*, the home and craft bi-monthly, *Art et Décoration* and the health monthly *Top Santé*. The biggest-circulation titles are television magazines (of which there are nine) and the women's weekly *Femme Actuelle* ('Today's Woman'). Outside France, the best-known French women's title is *Elle* which has changed beyond recognition since it was launched after the Second World War. With more than 2,500 such publications, France has more magazines per head than any other European country.

Children's magazines

French children read magazines too, although it is difficult to know if they really read from cover to cover of the tastefully and imaginatively produced educational titles on offer. Cheap comics and TV tie-in magazines, which still make up most of the Anglo-Saxon children's press, are much less evident in France where conscientious parents subscribe their offspring to charmingly illustrated, informative journals. Such are *Youpi* for littlies, *Astrapi* for ten year olds and *Okapi* for secondary-level children – with not so much as a plastic free gift or lurid lollipop in sight!

Bandes dessinées (cartoons)

In France, adults as well as children love cartoons, whether animated or published as albums, as newspaper strip cartoons or as satirical magazines. Even respected intellectuals Simone de Beauvoir and Jean-Paul Sartre rushed to the cinema to see Disney's *Blanche-Neige et les sept nains* (Snow White and the seven dwarves) in 1937. But closer to the French person's heart have been the exploits of Astérix and Obélix (see pp. 7–8) created by **Albert Uderzo** (1927–) and **René Goscinny** (1926–1977), and the adventures of Tintin and Milou (Snowy) depicted by Belgian artist **Hergé** whose real name was George Rémi (1907–1983). Tintin fans earnestly defended their comic-strip hero when critics recently cast aspersions about the young adventurer's politics. Hergé has been accused of passive collaboration with the Nazis, not only because Tintin was fired by anti-Communist zeal on early missions to the Soviet Union and the Belgian Congo, but because the artist worked for the Nazi-controlled, anti-semitic paper *Le Soir*. However, the plucky young cartoon character has reinvented himself over the years, ensuring his continued popularity and, consequently, big bucks for Nick Rodwell, the man who married Hergé's widow and who now controls the lucrative rights to Tintin.

French writer Jean-Paul Schulz claims to have discovered Tintin's real identity – the French war correspondent, and improbably-named, Robert Sexé who shared not only Tintin's love for foreign adventure and motorcycles but his looks as well ... right down to the distinctive quiff.

Weekly newspapers and news magazines

Unlike the Sunday-paper-reading Brits, the French catch up on the week's news and culture with *hebdomadaires* (weeklies) of a very different nature.

On the one hand there are serious magazines, similar to, but glossier than America's *Time* and Germany's *Der Spiegel*. The two leaders in this field are the right-wing weekly *l'Express* (formerly owned by Oliver Goldsmith and now part of Havas group) and the left-wing *le Nouvel Observateur* (*le Nouvel Obs* to afficionados), which over the years has departed from its earnest post-May-'68 image, carrying more advertising and appealing to the well-heeled intelligentsia.

Another left-wing news magazine is *Marianne* which, in the three years since its inception, appears to have won a faithful following for its hard-hitting investigative style.

Le Point, right-wing and owned by business magnate François Pinault (see p. 216) is more opinionated that its main rival *l'Express*, and has a smaller readership.

At the other end of the spectrum from these serious publications are the weekly scandal newspapers, *France-Dimanche* and *Ici Paris*. These are the French equivalent of the British gutter press *The News of the World* and *The People*. Similarly voyeuristic is the glossy magazine *Voici* which, like its cheaper competitors, shamelessly peddles sensationalist and frequently untrue stories about the rich and famous. Nonetheless, such publications offer an entertaining read for any student of the language!

Less scandalous, but often equally voyeuristic, is *Paris-Match* which for years was the only French publication to reach the shelves of American or British provincial newsagents. This photo-packed magazine, fêting topless-bathing royalty or mind-boggling celebrity divorce settlements, is France's top-selling news magazine.

The satirical weekly *Le Canard enchaîné* stands in a class of its own. It does not accept advertising and for nearly a century it has been dedicated to unearthing political scandals and keeping public figures on their toes.

Regional daily papers

France has 36 regional daily papers which are faring much better than the nationals. In fact they account for over two-thirds of total daily paper sales. This is not very surprising in a country where regional identity is so important. While some regional papers do not look far beyond the local cattle market, others are very well-respected for their good quality coverage of national as well as local issues and are frequently cited alongside the nationals on TV and radio.

The biggest regional is *Ouest-France* with a staggering circulation of 786,000. It covers the whole of the north-west and has forty different local editions. Next in size is *Sud-Ouest* based in Bordeaux, followed by *La Voix du Nord* in Lille, *Le Progrès* in Lyon and *Le Dauphiné libéré* in Grenoble.

National daily papers

In France there is no correlation between the shape of a paper and the seriousness of its contents, unlike the British press where broadsheet and tabloid roughly correspond to upmarket and downmarket journalism. The eminently respectable *Le Monde* is tabloid, while its august rival, *Le Figaro*, is broadsheet.

Only the Catholic daily *La Croix* is mainly sold on subscription. Readers of other titles prefer to buy their paper issue by issue from a kiosque or a *tabac*, there being no paper boys and girls in France where this Anglo-Saxon tradition is viewed with the same horror as sending children down the mines.

L'Equipe: sports daily giving the low-down on what is evidently closest to the French person's heart (*L'Equipe*'s circulation is higher than any other daily paper!).

Le Monde: serious and internationally-minded, top-notch left-wing paper; off-putting small print and few photographs; weekly culture supplements: *Le Monde des livres*, *Le Monde du cinéma et du théâtre* (known as *Aden*); separate monthly publications: Le *Monde diplomatique* and *Le Monde de l'éducation*; partly-owned by its journalists

Le Figaro: lively right-wing paper, more accessible than *Le Monde*; chatty Saturday supplements: *Le Figaro Magazine* and *Madame Figaro*; weekly supplements: *Le Figaro littéraire*, *Le Figaro économie.*

Libération: *Libé* to its readers; accessible, serious but punchy, left-wing paper founded after May '68 by Jean-Paul Sartre; a fifth owned by its staff

Les Echos: financial daily owned by publishers of the *Financial Times*, the Pearson Group

France-Soir: right-wing and populist evening paper

La Croix: Catholic daily owned by an Augustinian community

L'Humanité: Communist paper toeing the party line; minuscule sales compared with twenty years ago

Agence France-Presse

Alongside Associated Press in America and Reuters in Britain, Agence France-Presse (AFP) is one of the three largest news services in the world. With bureaux and correspondents in 129 countries it transmits news in French, English, Spanish, German, Arabic, Portuguese and Chinese.

Top French news photo services are Sygma, Gamma and Sipa.

New media

France online

For twenty years, the French have been able to check train times, buy tickets, find out what's on at the cinema and buy many other goods and services online – not through the internet but by means of France Télécom's Minitel service. Using terminals (Minitels) freely distributed to subscribers, telephone customers can access a huge range of electronic, public and commercial services. Minitels contain a chip to enable electronic payments; and because France Télécom guarantees the safety of the network, these payments are secure.

The success of the Minitel (owned by one fifth of the population) partly explains why the internet has been so slow to take off in France where at the end of 1998, only 1 in 20 people used the Internet, compared with 1 in 7 Britains and 1 in 4 Americans. In fact, only one in five French homes have a *micro-ordinateur* (personal computer), again far fewer than in Britain or America. However, the situation is changing rapidly as the French are overcoming their initial resistance to the internet. Given Prime Minister Jospin's pledge to push France onto *les autoroutes de l'information* (the information superhighway), the present Minitel's days are numbered.

France Télécom hopes to ride the tide of change with Internet Service Integrated (ISI) a joint project with IBM, intended to enable access of both the Minitel and the internet by means of a new screen-phone terminal. Meanwhile, France Télécom offers internet access through Wanadoo with internet directory voila.fr. The company's biggest rival, since deregulation of the French telecommunications market in 1999, is the media group Vivendi which has a major stake in AOL-Compuserve.

Computer games

Even though the French have been slow to buy home computers, when it comes to creating and marketing computer games, they are front runners alongside the United States and Japan. The four top French PC games companies are Havas International, Infogrames, Ubi Soft and Titus Interactive. Amongst newer up-and-coming games companies is Cryo Interactive, the creator of Casanova and other historical adventures set at the court of Versailles and in ancient Egypt.

Science

France's flair for science and new technology is epitomised by Futuroscope, the European Park of the Moving Image, which houses not only the world's most exciting cinema theme park, but also one of the *grandes écoles*, Ensma (l'Ecole Nationale Supérieure de Méchanique et d'Aérotechnique) training some of the country's top engineers. A tenth of France's physical science and engineering research is carried out in this exciting environment near Poitiers. Nearby is an experimental *lycée*, pioneering teaching with new technology. Also involved in technological training and research is the adjacent Centre National d'Enseignement à Distance (CNED) France's distance-learning body, similar to Britain's Open University.

France, and Paris in particular, became a hub of scientific discovery in the eighteenth and nineteenth centuries, with more scientific institutions than anywhere else in the world. Prominent amongst pioneering French scientists were the founders of modern chemistry, **Antoine de Lavoisier** (1743–1794) and **Louis Gay-Lussac** (1778–1850), the physicist **André Marie Ampère** (1775–1836) who discovered electromagnetism and gave his name to the amp, **Sadi Carnot** (1796-1832) the creator of thermodynamics, and zoologists **Jean-Baptiste Lamarck** (1744–1829) and **Etienne Geoffrey Saint-Hilaire** (1772–1844) whose research into animal organisms was taken further by Charles Darwin, culminating in the theory of evolution. A generation later, the chemist and biologist **Louis Pasteur** (1822–1895) studied fermentation and discovered the means of preserving first beer and subsequently milk; he later studied infectious diseases and developed vaccines against anthrax and rabies.

In the twentieth century, 22 French men and women have received the Nobel prize for their scientific achievements. The most famous of these is the physicist **Marie Curie** (1867–1934) who, with her husband **Pierre** (1859–1906), discovered radioactivity. She was the first of only ten women to be awarded the Nobel prize for science.

French firsts

France's reputation for innovation spans four centuries of achievements and discoveries which have transformed daily life.

Innovation:		**Invented or discovered by:**
1642	calculator *(la machine à calculer)*	Philosopher and mathematician Blaise Pascal
1668	champagne	Dom Perignon, the monk in charge of the vines of Benedictine monastery near Epernay
1681	pressure cooker *(la cocotte minute)*	Denis Papin developed this to feed the poor as it cooked otherwise-inedible, cheap, hard meat
1783	hot-air balloon *(la montgolfière)*	the Montgolfièr brothers invented this to help the French army survey enemy terrain; trial passengers were a cockerel, a sheep and a duck!
1792	guillotine	Ignace Guillotin's name was attached to the invention because he proposed it as a 'humane' way to finish off aristocrats; used for capital punishment from 1792 to 1981
1795	paper pencil	Conté's pencil was made of clay, lead and mercury and replaced the English graphite pencil
1797	parachute	André Jacques Garnerin made the first parachute jump from a hot-air balloon
1799	gas lighting	Philippe Lebon
1801	Jacquard weaving	Joseph Marie Jacquard; automatic weaving using perforated cards programmed with the pattern
1805	stethoscope	René Laennec's first stethoscope was a 20-centimetre wooden cylinder
1826	photography	Joseph Nicéphore Niépce was the first to fix a photographic image – but the pose took eight hours! In 1839 Jacques Daguerre reduced this to half an hour
1829	braille	Louis Braille, blind from the age of three, invented this alphabet which was adopted throughout the world in 1932
1860	pasteurization	Louis Pasteur
1869	colour photography	Louis Ducos de Hauron, precursor of Lumière brothers (see 1904)
1869	margarine	Hippolyte Mège-Mouriès invented an animal fat margarine for the army and navy as an economical and durable alternative to butter

Innovation:		Invented or discovered by:
1891	periscope	Jean Rey and Jules Carpentier
1892	concrete (*le béton armé*)	François Hennebique
1894	finger prints (*l'empreinte digitale*)	Alphonse Bertillon, head of the photographic service of the Paris police, was also the first to produce austere 'mug shots' of criminals; he devised an uncomfortable chair that forced the subject to sit bolt upright!
1895	cinema	Auguste and Louis Lumière gave the first public screening of films taken with their movie camera (see p. 147)
1895	tyre (*le pneu*)	Michelin brothers of Clermont-Ferrand
1898–1910		The elements polonium and radium discovered by physicist and chemist Marie Curie
1898	gearbox (*la boîte de vitesse*)	Louis Renault
1904	commercial colour photos	another first for the Lumière brothers
1909	first cross-Channel flight	Louis Blériot flew from Calais to Dover
1910	neon lighting (*l'éclairage au néon*)	physicist and industrialist Georges Claude
1921	TB vaccine	Albert Calmette and Camille Guérin
1924	wave mechanics (*la mécanique ondulatoire*)	physicist Louis de Broglie
1934	artificial radioactivity (*la radioactivité artificielle*)	physicists Frédéric and Irène Joliot-Curie
1938	nylon	the company Du Pont of Nemours (used for stockings by the Americans who introduced these coveted items to France in 1944)
1972	chaos theory (*la théorie des catastrophes*)	mathematician René Thom
1981	TGV	first line linked Paris and Lyon (see p. 202)
1983	AIDS virus (*le virus du sida*)	discovered by Luc Montagnier
1998	hand graft (*l'allogreffe de la main*)	first in the world performed by Jean-Michel Dubernard of l'hôpital Edouard-Herriot, Lyon

The montgolfière and its first passengers.

VOCABULARY

Film

le/la cinéaste *film maker*
le/la réalisateur/-trice *director*
le metteur en scène *producer*
le long-métrage *full-length film*
le court-métrage *short film*
tourner un film *to shoot a film*
le tournage *shooting*
le gros plan *close-up*
le plateau *set*
la mise en scène *production*
la bande sonore *soundtrack*
le scénario *script*
le montage *editing*
le cinéphile *cinema lover*
la salle de cinéma *auditorium*
le film policier *crime film*
analyser *to analyse*
décortiquer *to dissect/analyse*

Media

la télévision numérique *digital television*
la part d'audience *audience share ratings*
allumer la télé *to turn on the TV*
les téléspectateurs (m.f.) *viewing audience, viewers*
la chaine *channel*
la redevance télé *TV licence fee*
la télécommande *remote control*
l'antenne parabolique *dish aerial*
le quotidien *daily paper*
l'hebdomadaire (m.) *weekly paper or magazine*
le mensuel *monthly*
la presse éducative *educational press*
l'internaute (m.f.) *web surfer*
naviguer *to surf*

Taking it further

Places

Le Musée du Cinéma Henri Langlois, Palais de Chaillot, 1 place du Trocadéro, 75116 Paris; tel. 01 45 53 21 86

L'Institut Lumière, 25 rue du Premier-Film, Lyon; tel. 04 78 78 18 95 – cinema museum and info centre

Centre National de la Cinématographie, 12 rue de Lubeck, 75116 Paris; tel. 44 34 34 40

L'Institut National de l'Audiovisuel (INA) 4 avenue de l'Europe, 94366 Bry-sur-Marne; tel. 0149 83 20 00 – manages French TV archives

La maison de la publicité, 7 rue Bourdon, 75004 Paris, tel. 01 40 29 17 17 – study and info center with a collection of 300,000 advertising films and archive of press and poster campaigns

Musée de la bande dessinée, 121 rue de Bordeaux, 1600 Angoulême; tel. 05 45 38 65 65 – animation museum

Futuroscope, Poitiers; tel. 05 49 49 30 00

Cité des Sciences et de l'Industrie, 30 avenue Corentin-Cariou, 75019 Paris, tel. 01 40 03 75 00

Magazines
Les Cahiers du Cinéma, 9 passage de la Boule-Blanche, 75012 Paris, tel. 01 53 44 75 75 – in-depth analysis of the month's films

Le Nouveau Cinéma, 10–12 place de la Bourse, 75002 Paris; tel. 01 44 88 34 34

Books
Williams, Alan, **Republic of Images, A history of French film-making** (London: Harvard University Press, 1992)

Vincendeau, Ginette (ed.), **Encyclopaedia of European Cinema** (London: Cassell, 1995)

Films
Artificial Eye, 14 King Street, London WC2E 8HN, tel. 0207 2405353 – videos of subtitled French films

BFI Video, Stephen Mews, London IP0 AX, tel. 0207 957 8957 – black and white classics

Websites
France 3 – **www.france3.fr** (daily news from state-run TV networks, in Fr and Eng)

Le Monde – **lemonde.globeonline.com** (serious comment on politics and culture from France's top newspaper, in Fr)

Libération – **www.liberation.fr** (lively daily newspaper, in Fr)

9 | POLITICAL STRUCTURES AND INSTITUTIONS

Par devant l'Europe, la France, sachez-le, n'aura jamais qu'un seul nom, inexpiable, qui est son vrai nom éternel: la Révolution.

Know this, in the eyes of Europe, France will always have only one inexpiable name, her true name for all time: Revolution.

Jules Michelet (1798–1874)
Le Peuple – introduction

The touchstone of the French Republic is the 1789 revolution. It swept away for ever a monarchical system based on the divine right of kings and set in its place the beginnings of parliamentary democracy based on equality and freedom of speech. However, although prevailing political values changed after the Revolution, France's tradition of strong, central government did not. The country's hierarchical and centralized administration system introduced by the Romans, developed by Henri IV, strengthened by Louis XIV and perfected by Napoléon, was perfectly in tune with a fundamental principle of the Republic – unity and indivisibility.

La Déclaration des droits de l'Homme et du Citoyen

Les hommes naissent et demeurent libres et égaux en droits.
Men are born, and remain, free and equal in law.

Article 2

In September 1789, within a couple of months of the storming of the Bastille, the *Assemblée Nationale* voted for the sixteen articles of *La Déclaration des droits de l'Homme et du Citoyen* (The Declaration of the Rights of Man and the Citizen). As well as laying down the principles of individual freedom and equality, the

Declaration established the principle of citizenship which remains at the core of French society. Citizenship confers rights and responsibilities on the individual who is both entitled and obliged to play an active part in maintaining a just society, to not only support but challenge the established order. It is not surprising therefore that *la contestation* in street demonstrations, around the negotiating table or even around the dinner table, is a normal part of French life!

In 1793 the Declaration of Rights was incorporated in the constitution of France's First Republic. Unfortunately, scant attention was paid to *La Déclaration des Droits de la Femme et de la Citoyenne* penned by Olympe de Gouges who claimed that as women were citizens who could be sentenced to death for their opinions, they should equally have the right to free speech in the National Assembly. Her logic came a century and a half too early for her male fellow citizens who silenced her with the guillotine.

The Republic and its symbols

First Republic	1792–1804
Second Republic	1848–1852
Third Republic	1870–1940
Fourth Republic	1944–1958
Fifth Republic	1958–present

'Liberté, Egalité, Fraternité'

These words are etched into the French person's consciousness just as they are engraved in stone on the *mairie* of every sleepy village or on the *hôtel de ville* of the busiest town. Together with the tricolore flag that hangs above the entrance, and the bust of Marianne that is to be found inside, these three principles of the 1789 revolution have represented the French Republic from 1792 to the present day.

Le drapeau tricolore

The ancestor of the familiar red, white and blue flag was the 1789 revolutionaries' *cocarde tricolore* (three-coloured rosette), representing the union of king and people. Blue and red were the colours of the Paris national guard and white was the colour of the sash attached to the flagpole of the royal army.

Marianne

Marianne is the ubiquitous personification of the Republic. Wearing her revolutionaries' *bonnet phrygien* (the hat worn by the liberated slaves of ancient Greece), she had long graced French postage stamps and coins before she appeared on government documents as the country's first logo in 1999. Despite her origins in the 1789 revolution, the earliest representation of Marianne is in Delacroix's *La Liberté guidant le peuple*, painted forty-one years later to celebrate the revolution of 1830.

It is difficult to imagine the British Britannia bearing the features of, say, Kate Moss or Cindy Crawford, but successive representations of Marianne have borrowed the classic good looks of famous French beauties, such as Brigitte Bardot, Catherine Deneuve, and currently the model Laetitia Casta. Although communes are required by law to display a bust of Marianne, they are free to choose a different representation of her. In 1999, the *mairie* of the village of Frémainville adopted the country's first black Marianne as a symbol of racial integration.

La Marseillaise

Although the *Marseillaise* did not become the official national anthem until 1879, it was composed in 1792 by Captain Rouget de l'Isle as *Chant de Guerre de l'Armée du Rhin* (Battle song of the Rhine Army). Its rousing tune was soon heard all over Paris, sung by carousing revolutionary soldiers from Marseille who renamed it. Promising glory for the loyal and just desserts for tyrants and traitors, *la Marseillaise* appeals to the nationalism of both the Right and the Left who continue to sing it with equal passion, whether at a state occasion, a trade union convention or at an international football match.

Allons enfants de la patrie	Come, children of our country
Le jour de gloire est arrivé	The day of glory has arrived
Contre nous de la tyrannie	Against us is raised
L'étendard sanglant est levé	The bloody standard of tyranny
L'étendard sanglant est levé	The bloody standard of tyranny
Entendez-vous dans les campagnes	Do you hear the fierce soldiers
Mugir ces féroces soldats?	Bellowing through the countryside?
Ils viennent jusque dans nos bras	They are here in our very midst
Egorger vos fils et vos compagnes	To slit the throats of your sons
Aux armes citoyens!	and your women folk
Formez vos bataillons!	To arms, citizens!
Marchons, marchons,	Form your battalions!
Qu'un sang impur	March on! March on!
Abreuve nos sillons!	Let our furrows soak up
	The tainted blood!

The French constitution and the powers of the president

La France est une république indivisible, laïque, démocratique et sociale. Elle assure l'égalité devant la loi de tous les citoyens sans distinction d'origine, de race ou de religion ...

France is a republic that is indivisible, secular, democratic and social. She ensures equality before the law for all citizens irrespective of background, race or religion ...

Article 2 of the Constitution (1958)

The constitution, which is the legal basis of the French state, incorporates the Declaration of the Rights of Man and establishes the fundamental principles of liberty, equality and fraternity.

The present constitution, that of the Fifth Republic, was proposed by Charles de Gaulle in 1958 in an attempt to bring stability after two decades of political uncertainty. In the eyes of some people, the new constitution turned France into a kind of '*monarchie républicaine*' because it hugely strengthened the president's position at the expense of parliament.

Constitutional reform

Over the last thirty years, successive governments have tried to change the constitution and in particular to reduce the president's seven-year mandate which has resulted in three tricky periods of *cohabitation* (when the president and the government do not share the same political position). However, most attempts have been thwarted by the ultra-conservative Senate which is mostly made up of rural municipal councillors.

Another constitutional reform long sought by socialists is an end to *le cumul des mandats*, the widespread practice – illegal in other European countries – of holding several elected offices at the same time. For example, 84 per cent of deputies in the National Assembly and members of the Senate hold at least one other elected post such as mayorships and posts as regional or municipal councillors.

One important change achieved by Prime Minister Jospin's government concerns *parité*, equal representation for men and women in political posts. The philosopher Sylviane Agacinski, Jospin's wife, drew up a bill which finally gained the approval of both houses (the president had to lean somewhat forcefully upon the reluctant Senate), and Article 3 of the constitution was reworded to allow measures promoting equal access, for men and women, to political life and elected posts.

However, an attempt to change the constitution to allow official recognition of minority languages was unsuccessful, underlining the fact that the constitution recognizes equal citizens rather than communities of race, religion or region (see p. 31).

Presidents of the Fifth Republic	
Charles de Gaulle	1958–1969
Georges Pompidou	1969–1974
Valéry Giscard d'Estaing	1974–1981
François Mitterrand	1981–1995
Jacques Chirac	1995–present

Government

Toute nation a le gouvernement qu'elle mérite.
Every nation has the government it deserves.

Joseph de Maistre (1753–1821)

Central and local government

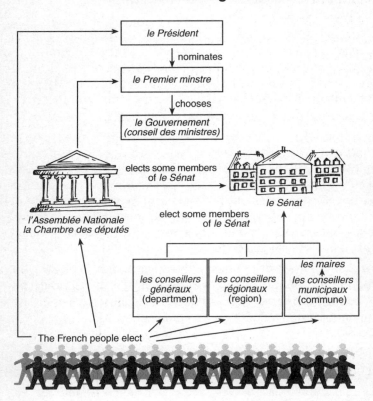

Le premier ministre (prime minister) is chosen by the president to be the head of government. The prime minister then chooses ministers and secretaries of state to form his *conseil des ministres* (cabinet), subject to the approval of the president. These members of government are not necessarily drawn from the *Assemblée*

Nationale. They may have a background in the law, banking or business or come from the higher echelons of the civil service. Often they are ambitious technocrats who have been trained for the top by one of the prestigious *grandes écoles* (see p. 195). The government chosen by *premier ministre* Lionel Jospin in 1997 was a broad left coalition (see *La gauche* pp. 176–178).

Parliament

Parliament consists of a lower and an upper house: *l'Assemblée Nationale* (the National Assembly) which meets in the Palais Bourbon, and *le Sénat* (the Senate) which meets in the Palais du Luxembourg. Both houses sit from October to June.

L'Assemblée Nationale

France's 577 deputies are elected for five years by direct popular vote in *les élections législatives* (general election). While political affiliation is not strong in France, deputies have huge local support. The 1997 general election resulted in a dramatic change in the pattern of power in the Assembly, which moved from a small right-wing majority to an absolute majority for the Socialists who won 245 seats compared with the Gaullist RPR's 140. Sixty-three women entered parliament, more than ever before and twice as many as in the previous Assembly.

New deputies are presented with a *tricolore* sash, the sign of parliamentary office, and take their seats in *l'Hémicycle* (the semi-circular chamber) to the left or right of the centre according to their political tendency. Wednesday usually sees a full house as this is when deputies can put direct questions to the government.

The President of the Assembly is elected by its members for the duration of that parliament.

Le Sénat

Je resterai député jusqu'à ma mort, après quoi j'irai au Sénat.
I shall stay a deputy until I die, then I shall go to the Senate.

Frédéric Dupont

There is no danger of young fire-brands stirring up proceedings in the *Sénat* as its 321 members must be over 35 years old. The predominantly conservative *sénateurs* are elected for nine years by deputies, general councillors and municipal council delegates.

The *Sénat* has little policy-making power. Its role is to vote on laws and the State budget. It may introduce a *proposition de loi* (bill) and it can modify the text of a *projet de loi* (government bill) before it receives a second reading in the *Assemblée Nationale*.

Elections

All elections take place on a Sunday. In the *élections présidentielles,* if an absolute majority is not achieved at the first vote, a *deuxième tour* (a run-off) is conducted a fortnight later for the two candidates with the most votes. The *élections législatives* go to a *deuxième tour* too in those constituencies where no candidate has obtained 50 per cent of the vote in the first round. The *deuxième tour* includes candidates who won at least 12 per cent of votes in the *premier tour*.

France has 577 *circonscriptions électorales* (electoral constituencies) each with about 100,000 inhabitants. Under the Fifth Republic, only the elections of 1986 were conducted with proportional representation.

Political parties

When le Parti socialiste came to power in the 1997 general election, it formed la Gauche plurielle (the broad left) with other left-wing parties: le Parti radical-socialiste (PRS), le Mouvement des radicaux de gauche (MRG), les Verts (the Greens) and le Parti communiste (PC). No such consensus exists at present between the parties of the Right which, despite former alliances, is deeply divided.

La Gauche (The Left)

Le Parti socialiste (PS)

France's old, somewhat doctrinaire Socialist party changed into a left-of-centre party in the 1970s under the leadership of François Mitterrand who became president in 1981 and whose imperious, inscrutable presence earnt him the nicknames of *Dieu* (God) and *Le Sphynx*.

The Socialists won the 1997 general election under the leadership of Lionel Jospin whose honest and serious image appealed to voters disenchanted by revelations of political corruption during the Mitterrand years. The satirical television programme *Les Guignols de l'Info*, which uses puppet caricatures of political figures, took delight in representing Jospin as an eager-to-please little man in a red and yellow car – Noddy or his French incarnation, *Oui Oui!* However this characterization was dropped when Jospin showed himself to be a strong prime minister capable of pushing through controversial measures such as the 35-hour week and the *Pacs* (see p. 238).

Le Parti communiste (PCF)

Founded in 1920, le parti communiste was the party of *la classe ouvrière* (the working class). It had a particularly large following in France's industrial north, was supported by many French intellectuals and artists and remained a significant political force until the 1970s. Since then, it has lost members to the Socialist party, partly due to the demise of communism in Eastern Europe and partly due to the decline of heavy industry from which its traditional electorate was drawn.

The rotund Robert Hue, *secrétaire général* of the PC, is one of three Communists in Lionel Jospin's government of *la Gauche plurielle*. Today's Communists are Eurosceptics who favour job-creation, welfare reforms, cuts in VAT and income tax, higher wealth tax and proportional representation.

Les Verts (the Greens)

Les Verts, the largest of the eight green parties, secured a government post for their leader Dominique Voynet in the 1997 elections. *Les Verts* want proportional representation and many environmental changes including the phasing out of nuclear power – an outcome which is highly unlikely, given France's long-standing commitment to nuclear energy which provides 75 per cent of her electricity. The Green's charismatic leader in the 1999 European elections was Daniel Cohn-Bendit, known to the world as Danny le rouge (Danny the red) when he led French student revolutionaries in May 1968.

Lutte ouvrière (Workers' struggle)

While this Trotskyist party has no seats in parliament it managed to win 20 seats on regional councils in the 1998 regional elections. Although Arlette Laguiller, the organization's long-standing leader, is a familiar face in the media, little is known about this secretive, 7000-strong organization. It has no headquarters, just a post box number, and members often use pseudonyms. For the 1999 European elections, LO joined forces with an even smaller Trotskyist outfit, *la Ligue communiste révolutionnaire* (LCR) led by Alain Krivine, in an attempt to further undermine support for the ailing Communist party.

La Droite (The Right)

Le Rassemblement pour la République (RPR) (the Rally for the Republic)

This is the descendant of the first Gaullist party, formed in support of de Gaulle. Reorganized as the RPR in 1976 by Jacques Chirac, it is a free-market, pro-Europe party. Since its rout in the 1997 general election, the party has lost support to a splinter group, Charles Pasqua's RPF (see below). Despite this, Chirac has been a fairly popular president, committed to repairing *la fracture sociale* (social breakdown) and a firm opponent of the Front National. His persona in *Les Guignols de l'Info* is a smooth Mr Fixit, a *commis voyageur* (commercial traveller).

L'Union pour la démocratie française (UDF)

The aristocratic Valéry Giscard d'Estaing founded the UDF, a federation of right-wing parties, when he was president in 1978. In past centre-right governments, the UDF partnered the RPR.

Severely weakened by its losses in the 1997 general election, the party's centrist image was dented when some of its members struck deals with the Front National in order to cling on to power in the regional assemblies. The federation was weakened further when its second largest party, la Démocratie libérale became independent in 1998.

Rassemblement pour la France (RPF)

Formed in 1999 by Charles Pasqua, former RPR stalwart and right-wing Minister for the Interior, this nationalist, anti-Europe party won Euro-sceptics away from the RPR in the European elections of June 1999.

Democratie Libérale (DL)

This party led by Alain Madelin split away from the UDF in 1998.

Le Front National (FN)

Although this extreme-right-wing party has no members in the *Assemblée Nationale*, 30 per cent of the population have voted for it at least once. Until recently it accounted for about 15 per cent of votes nationally, and it has many members on regional councils and controls several southern town councils. However, it divided into rival factions in 1998 and its popularity sank to 12 per cent of voters early in 1999.

Although he claims not to be racist, the long-time head of the party, Jean-Marie Le Pen, showed his true colours in 1997 when he claimed that the Nazi gas chambers were *un détail de l'histoire de la deuxième guerre mondiale* (a detail of the history of the Second World War). Le Pen's arch-rival, the diminutive and gimlet-eyed Bruno Mégret, heads the parallel far-right party Mouvement national. A sophisticated strategist, Mégret has attempted to cover with a veneer of respectability his proposals for *la préférence nationale*. These would exclude foreigners from benefits and reserve certain categories of jobs for French nationals – a frightening echo of the Vichy regime's anti-Jewish laws.

Political scandals

La politique c'est comme l'andouillette, ça doit sentir un peu la merde, mais pas trop.

Politics is like andouillette sausage, it should have a slight smell of shit, but not too much.

Edouard Herriot (1872–1957)

Like most countries France has its share of political scandals. But it is not usually sexual impropriety that will bring a politician down. The nation was not shocked when the existence of Mitterrand's mistress and eighteen-year-old illegitimate daughter Mazarine finally became public knowledge. The Lewinsky affair in America earnt Bill Clinton widespread sympathy in France where the right to privacy is enshrined in the *code civil* and where there has been tacit agreement amongst the press to keep clear of powerful politicians' personal lives. Similarly, the proposed 'outing' of a gay member of parliament, a nasty political practice not uncommon in Britain, was met with outrage in France.

What has caused political figures most grief in recent years is revelations of back-handers and gravy-train practices. *L'Affaire Dumas* involved payments made by the oil giant Elf Aquitaine to a certain Christine Deviers-Joncour allegedly employed to seduce the then Foreign Minister Roland Dumas and gain government favour for Elf business including arms deals. When the scandal first broke, the press made much of an incriminating gift from Mlle Deviers-Joncour to Roland Dumas – a £1,000 pair of hand-made shoes reportedly paid for by Elf.

A pay-roll scam, in which 300 RPR members were paid by the Paris Town Hall for, allegedly, non-existent jobs was the tip of an iceberg that drew the world's attention to the reality of many such hidden practices in French institutions. It also highlighted the president's immunity in such situations and led the influential paper *Le Monde* to decry *'cette présidence intouchable qui ne correspond plus aux nécessités démocratiques'* ('this untouchable presidency, which no longer corresponds to democratic necessities').

The 1999 revelations of inefficiency, corruption and nepotism in the European Commission caused a particularly big stir in France because the finger was being pointed at European commissioner Edith Cresson, a former Socialist French prime minister. Accused of flouting EU recruitment procedures and appointing a 70-year-old dentist friend to a research post for which he was unsuitable, Mme Cresson was unrepentant. She defiantly claimed that her actions would have been quite acceptable in France where the widespread practice of giving family and friends a step up the ladder is known as *le piston*.

The Administration

Les fonctionnaires sont les meilleurs maris; quand ils rentrent le soir à la maison, ils ne sont pas fatigués et ils ont déjà lu le journal.

Civil servants are the best husbands; when they come home in the evening they aren't tired and they've already read the paper.

Georges Clemenceau (1841–1929)

It is no coincidence that the word 'bureaucrat' comes to us from France where political decisions appear to be processed by a many-headed administrative monster that feeds on paper and red tape. France has about five million public employees, almost as many as in the whole of the United States. Civil servants may be moved around from one ministry to another or to a state industry, but they cannot lose their job. Only one category of *fonctionnaire* has the right to exactly the same job for life and that is *les magistrats de siège* (judges of the bench) who are *inamovibles*, in other words, cannot be shifted.

The centralized and hierarchical nature of the French administrative system harks back to Gallo-Roman times when all lines of power led to the Emperor in Rome. Napoléon copied this system with departmental *préfets* (prefects), unelected representatives of the State who were answerable only to Paris. The *préfets* were finally cut down to size by decentralization measures under François Mitterrand, which transferred much of their power to elected regional, general and municipal councils. However, many French people still feel that these local bodies should have more power and more independence.

Central administration

High-ranking civil servants and government ministers are most frequently drawn from an élite which has undergone a gruellingly rigorous academic training at one of the fiercely competitive *grandes écoles* which are a stepping stone not only to government but to top jobs in industry and commerce. Each government ministry has a tendency to recruit from a particular *grande école* although there is considerable flexibility. The two most prestigious *écoles* are the Ecole Polytechnique, which produces terrifyingly intelligent engineers who thereafter are known to be *un X*, and the Ecole Nationale d'Administration, the civil service *école* whose former students carry with them the respected nickname of *énarque* and who may address each other by the familiar *tu* even in the most formal context. Graduates of both institutions are guaranteed access to one of the world's most powerful and efficient 'old boy' networks. The former government minister Alain Peyrefitte described a *grande école* diploma as *une fusée longue portée qui, sauf accident, vous propulse jusqu'à la retraite* (a long range missile which, all being well, propels you through life until your retirement).

Les ministères

The three most important government ministries are the *ministères d'Etat*: le ministère de l'économie, finances et budget (Finance ministry), le ministère des affaires étrangères (Foreign Affairs ministry) and le ministère de l'intérieur (Interior ministry).

Each minister chooses thirteen or so senior civil servants to form his *cabinet* or private office. These include *ministres délégués* (junior ministers) who will attend the *conseil des ministres*, and the less senior *sécretaires d'état* (secretaries of state) who will not. The administration of specific areas of the ministry is overseen by *les grands commis de l'état*, the highest ranking civil servants, who are appointed by the government.

The most powerful civil servant in the country is the *inspecteur des finances* who runs *le Trésor* (the Treasury) within the Finance ministry, and who will almost certainly have been recruited from amongst the most brilliant students of the Ecole Nationale d'Administration.

Ministries and government offices are frequently referred to by their location or building:

l'Elysée – le Palais de l'Elysée, the president's office

l'Hôtel Matignon – the prime minister's office which, incidentally, boasts the largest private garden in Paris

le Quai d'Orsay – the Foreign ministry

Bercy – the Finance ministry

la Place Beauvau – the Interior ministry

Local administration

Local government is entrusted to three tiers of officials who are elected by universal suffrage every six years.

La commune

This is the smallest and oldest of France's administrative areas and the one with which French people most closely identify. Whether it is a hamlet or a city, each of France's 36,763 *communes*, has a mayor who is the hub of local life. He or she is responsible for seeing that the law is respected, for registering births, marriages and deaths and for issuing other official papers such as building licences. The *conseil municipal,* which elects the *maire,* shares many of his or her administrative duties including managing the budget for local amenities and the maintenance of local nursery and primary schools. Being mayor is a full-time post in large cities, but in smaller communes it is an onerous position often taken on by public-spirited citizens alongside their full-time work. Some mayors, however, have exploited their position for dodgy power-mongering. Such was Jacques Médecin, a former mayor of Nice whose corrupt networking caused him to flee to Uruguay. Far from being disgraced in Nice, on his death in 1998 Médecin was honoured with flags at half-mast and a minute's silence.

Le département

The next largest administrative unit is the *département* which was created in 1790 following the Revolution. The 100 *départements*, including five *départements d'outre-mer* (overseas departments), are each administered by a *conseil général* which elects a president who is now more powerful than the *préfet*. The *préfet*, who is an unelected government official answerable to the minister of the interior, is responsible for law and order and co-ordinating state services in the *département*. The *préfet*'s office, the *préfecture*, is in the main town of the department, the *chef-lieu*.

Départements of metropolitan France

01	Ain	24	Dordogne	49	Maine-et-Loire
02	Aisne	25	Doubs	50	Manche
03	Allier	26	Drôme	51	Marne
04	Alpes-de-Haute-	27	Eure	52	Haute-Marne
	Provence	28	Eure-et-Loir	53	Mayenne
05	Hautes-Alpes	29	Finistère	54	Meurthe-et-Moselle
06	Alpes-Maritimes	30	Gard	55	Meuse
07	Ardèche	31	Haute-Garonne	56	Morbihan
08	Ardennes	32	Gers	57	Moselle
09	Ariège	33	Gironde	58	Nièvre
10	Aube	34	Hérault	59	Nord
11	Aude	35	Ille-et-Vilaine	60	Oise
12	Aveyron	36	Indre	61	Orne
13	Bouches-du-Rhône	37	Indre-et-Loire	62	Pas-de-Calais
14	Calvados	38	Isère	63	Puy-de-Dôme
15	Cantal	39	Jura	64	Pyrénées-Atlantiques
16	Charente	40	Landes	65	Hautes-Pyrénées
17	Charente-Maritime	41	Loir-et-Cher	66	Pyrénées-Orientales
18	Cher	42	Loire	67	Bas-Rhin
19	Corrèze	43	Haute-Loire	68	Haut-Rhin
2A	Corse du Sud	44	Loire-Atlantique	69	Rhône
2B	Haute Corse	45	Loiret	70	Haute-Saône
21	Côte-d'Or	46	Lot	71	Saône-et-Loire
22	Côtes d'Armor	47	Lot-et-Garonne	72	Sarthe
23	Creuse	48	Lozère	73	Savoie

74	Haute-Savoie
75	Paris
76	Seine-Maritime
77	Seine-et-Marne
78	Yvelines
79	Deux Sèvres
80	Somme
81	Tarn
82	Tarn-et-Garonne
83	Var
84	Vaucluse
85	Vendée
86	Vienne
87	Haute-Vienne
88	Vosges
89	Yonne
90	Territoire de Belfort
91	Essonne
92	Hauts-de-Seine
93	Seine-Saint-Denis
94	Val-de-Marne
95	Val-d'Oise

French regions today

La région

The present French regions were created in 1964 in order to facilitate the administration of groups of *départements*. The 22 *régions* and four *régions d'outre-mer* (overseas regions) are run by a *conseil régional* (regional council) whose responsibilities include managing public land such as *les parcs naturels* (country parks) and building *lycées*. The government-appointed *préfet de région*, has a similar role to that of the *préfet de département*.

The legal system

The French legal system was set in place following the Revolution in order to unify the widely divergent laws around the country. These were subsequently refined and drawn up by Napoléon as *codes* or collections of laws which, with many modifications and additions form the body of today's laws.

Crime, trial and punishment

Certain aspects of the French legal process are different from the way things operate in Anglo-Saxon countries. To begin with, offences are not defined in the same way. The least serious offence is *une contravention* (e.g. traffic offences, unauthorized parking, breaking hunting regulations) sometimes punishable by an on-the-spot fine, as speeding holiday-makers know to their cost. Other civil offences concerning goods and property will be tried in the relatively informal context of a *tribunal d'instance* presided over by one judge. Un *délit* is a criminal offence against the person or property (e.g. theft, fraud and manslaughter), committed by *un délinquant* who will be tried in a *tribunal correctionnel*, before up to three judges but with no jury. The most serious offence is *un crime* which involves serious physical injury or weapons or incitement to riot; the *criminel* will be tried in a *cour d'assises* before three judges and nine jurors. In most cases a minor is tried by a *juge d'enfants* (children's judge).

Under French law, certain actions which are not punishable in other countries are an offence. For example, the legal action surrounding the death of Princess Diana in a Paris car crash, witnessed by press photographers, highlighted a law which requires an onlooker to an accident to stop and intervene themselves or call for help.

France's severe privacy laws are envied by Anglo-Saxon politicians and celebrities subject to press harassment in their own countries. Magazines and newspapers are liable to incur huge fines if they contravene Article 9 of the *code civil* which enshrines the individual's right to a private life. It was because of this law and the loyalty of newspaper editors that Mitterrand was able to conceal for so long the existence of his extra-marital family.

In France, the most severe sentence is *réclusion à perpétuité* (life imprisonment), familiarly known as *à perpette*, usually 30 years. The guillotine only disappeared from France in 1981 when the death penalty was abolished, twenty years later than in Britain.

The police

A French policeman in his *képi* (policeman's cap) is probably one of the world's most famous national stereotypes, but is he an *agent de police* or a *gendarme*?

The difference between the two lies in the division of the police into separate organizations: *la police nationale* which polices towns, and *la gendarmerie nationale* which operates in rural areas. The first is ultimately answerable to the *ministre de l'intérieur* known as *le premier flic de France* (France's top cop), and the second is a

Gendarme and **agent de police**

section of the army, organized in *brigades* and answerable to the *ministre de la défense*. In addition to *la police nationale*, a town may have a local police force, *la police municipale*.

There are many different sections of *la police nationale* which includes *la police de l'air et des frontières*, supervising customs, immigration and civil aviation, and the notoriously tough CRS *(Compagnie républicaine de sécurité)*, France's riot police. The 61 CRS units are specially trained to quell riots and disturbances but they also police *autoroutes* on motorbikes and intervene in emergencies such as mountain rescues. The most recent addition to the *police nationale* is a unit of nippy roller-blading *agents* recruited to keep up with the thousands of roller-blading citizens who throng Paris streets on Friday nights and Sunday afternoons. Faced with having to choose between banning what was becoming an increasingly popular but hazardous weekly event, and maintaining the strong French tradition of freely taking to the streets, the police established a traffic-free route and donned their blades, on the basis of if you can't beat 'em, join 'em!

The more grim side of the police is their record of brutality, to immigrants in particular. It was not until 1999 that the French state publicly admitted that dozens of Algerians on a peace march had been massacred by the Paris police thirty-eight years earlier. Human rights campaigners believe that at least 200 were killed and their bodies dumped in the Seine. In 1998 attention was drawn to police ill-treatment of detainees when a Council of Europe Commission found that the French police continued to flout international agreements outlawing racist attitudes. Such criticism evokes little soul-searching amongst the police whose unions launched a campaign of protest in 1999 when five of their members were given stiff sentences for savagely beating up and threatening with torture two Arab suspects in police custody. Given such attitudes, it is not surprising that a change in French law, allowing new detainees immediate access to a lawyer, was met with opposition from the police. Until 1999 the police had the right to make arrests without a warrant for questioning, conduct body searches and hold detainees for up to 24 hours without access to a lawyer.

VOCABULARY

le chef de l'Etat *head of state*
le septennat *seven-year presidential term of office*
détenir le pouvoir *to hold power*
le mandat *mandate to govern*
la législature *term of office*
le siège parlementaire *parliamentary seat*
la séance *sitting of parliament*
le projet de loi *bill*
présenter/adopter/rejeter/abroger *to introduce/pass/throw out/repeal (a bill)*
l'arrêté (m.) *official decision with the force of law*
la campagne électorale *election campaign*
le Journal Officiel *daily report of parliamentary debate*
le sondage d'opinion *opinion poll*
la côte *popularity rating*
pronostiquer les résultats *to forecast the results*
l'électorat *electorate*
se rendre aux urnes *to go to the polling station*
voter *to vote*
le scrutin *ballot*
s'abstenir *to abstain*
le bulletin de vote *ballot paper*
l'isoloir (m.) *voting booth*
le dépouillement *counting of the votes*
le système D (débrouillard) *'working the system'*
les collectivités (f.) locales *local council*
le conseil régional *regional council*
le Conseil Constitutionnel *Constitutional Council – France's highest court; it ensures that laws are constitutional, regulates elections and is empowered to impeach the president*
le Conseil d'Etat *Council of State – the final court of appeal in administrative cases; it also advises the government on new laws*
le palais de justice *law court*
le tribunal d'instance *magistrate's court*
le tribunal correctionnel *criminal court*
la cour d'assises *high court*
le juge *judge*
l'avocat *barrister*
le procureur public *prosecutor*
le parquet public *prosecutor's office*
plaider non coupable *to plead not guilty*
appeler un témoin *to call a witness*
témoigner *to give evidence*
prononcer le verdict *to give the verdict*
la réclusion à perpétuité *life imprisonment*
six mois de prison avec sursis *six month's suspended sentence*
faire appel *to appeal*
le juge d'instruction *examining magistrate who investigates a criminal case*
le casier judiciaire *police record*
le flic (slang) *cop*
la brigade criminelle *murder squad*
le limier (colloquial) *detective*
passer les menottes à quelqu'un *to handcuff someone*
le/la détenu(e) *prisoner*

l'Ordre de la Légion d'honneur *France's highest honour awarded in recognition of civil or military service (five classes:* grand-croix, grand officier, commandeur, officier, chevalier*)*

Taking it further

Events

Les journées de la justice (annual guided tours of law courts) tel. 01 41 96 31 31; **www.justice.gouv.fr** (in Fr)

Books

Laudet, Claire and Cox, Richard (ed.s), **La vie politique en France aujourd'hui** (Manchester: Manchester University Press, 1995)

Gunten, Bernard, **Les Institutions de la France** (Paris: Nathan, 1998)

Debray, Régis, **La République expliquée à ma fille** (Paris: Editions du Seuil, 1998) – clear explanation of the principles of the Republic and citizenship

Newspapers

For political comment: **Le Monde**, **Le Figaro, Libération** and websites as for Chapter 8

Websites

Prime Minister: **www.premier-ministre.gouv.fr** (in Fr)
      www.premier-ministre.gouv.fr/GB (in Eng)
President: **www.elysee.fr** (in Fr)
Le ministre de l'intérieur: **www.interieur.gouv.fr**
Law and legal system: **www.justice.gouv.fr** (in Fr)

CD-Rom

L'Assemblée Nationale, Histoire et Institution, Montparnasse Multi-média, Centre National de Documentation Pédagogique de Bourgogne

10 THE BASICS FOR LIVING

Education

> *'Alors? Pourquoi tu veux l'être, institutrice?'*
> *'Pour faire chier les mômes,' répondit Zazie*
>
> 'So why do you want to be a primary school teacher?
> 'To give the kids a hard time,' replied Zazie
>
> Raymond Queneau (1903–1976)
> *Zazie dans le métro*

For many foreigners their only contact with the French education system is the frenzy of *la rentrée* (beginning of the school year in September). Half-way through August when holiday-makers may still be trying to buy swim-suits or beach balls, the hypermarkets have shunted all their summer stock into storage to make room for piles and piles of strangely-lined school paper, exercise books, fancy pencil cases and colourful backpacks. Everywhere you look, advertising hoardings, magazines, shop windows and television commercials proclaim the imminent end of *les grandes vacances* (the long summer holidays). This tells the foreigner not only that *la rentrée* is big business, as French parents have to pay for school materials, but that education looms large in French daily life.

Never off the political agenda, the French education system has experienced a succession of reforms since the 1950s, all of which have resulted in debate, strikes and demonstrations involving teachers, students and school pupils alike (see p. 246). Everyone has opinions about education and knows someone who works for the education ministry which, with about a million people on the payroll, is France's largest employer.

Although reforms have meant that the education system is less rigid than it used to be and that little Pierre in Marseille is no longer studying *l'histoire* at exactly the same time of day as Marie-Laure in Paris, the French system remains highly centralized and hierarchical, in common with other aspects of French life rooted in the Revolution. The first constitution of the first Republic declared that secular schooling should be available for all. However, it was not until the first empire that education received the Napoleonic treatment – a tightly structured, centralized administration. Then in 1882, laws introduced by Jules Ferry (commemorated in thousands of *Ecoles Jules Ferry* throughout the land) made free, non-religious primary education a universal right and obligation. A further foundation stone of modern education was laid in 1905 when state education was formally separated from the Church. Since then, state educational establishments have been fiercely anti-religious (see p. 251).

Another distinguishing feature of education in France is its competitive ethos. Although in principle the system offers equality of opportunity regardless of money or social status, it is in fact an intellectual meritocracy designed to reward those who can stand the strain. After being subjected to years of school tests, French children may have to face the *concours*. These are competitive examinations which only a restricted number of entrants will pass, however high their standard. *Concours* is the normal means of entry to the civil service, the police and the various *grandes écoles* (see below). Just to keep everyone on their toes, final exams for trainee secondary teachers and *grande école* students are by *concours* too.

Schools

Today 80 per cent of schools are state-run, most of the remaining 20 per cent being private Catholic schools. On the principle of maintaining freedom of choice, the private schools receive a state subsidy. This means that opting for a private education in France need not break the bank and is not the exclusive preserve of the middle classes.

Although schooling is obligatory from age six to 16, nearly all three year olds and about half of two year olds, attend an *école maternelle* (nursery school) which is often attached to a primary school. Long before the child leaves the nursery classes he or she will have been introduced to *le graphisme* (handwriting) and by six or seven will have mastered the charmingly loopy French script which reminds admiring Anglo-Saxons of times gone by – great-grandfather's school books perhaps. However, the uniformity of handwriting style and its importance in the curriculum suggests another difference between French and Anglo-Saxon classroom practices – the place accorded to individual expression.

Looking at the neat rows of desks in a French school, compared with classrooms designed for group work in British and American state primary schools, one could believe that child-centred, discovery-based learning had passed France by. In fact France has produced many progressive educationalists, including Cousinet, Freinet and Piaget whose theories challenged traditional 'talk and chalk' teaching methods in the 1960s.

Jean Piaget
(1896–1980)

A pioneering child psychologist who explained how children progress towards abstract thought by the ages 11–14. He influenced the trend to learning through discovery, in classrooms throughout the world.

However, because of its tradition of intellectual rigour and its centralized administration, French education is not conducive to gradual change and experimentation at local level. Tentative initiatives in play-centred primary school learning led to fears of falling standards in the 1970s and were swiftly succeeded by a return to the three Rs. Although French schools have absorbed new ideas, they remain temples of information rather than creativity. Corridors are not usually enlivened by pupils' artwork, and primary school playgrounds are often dull stretches of tarmac without wild-life corners or climbing frames. Academic success is the school's main business and this it monitors with plentiful *contrôles* (tests) and lashings of homework, even in primary school.

The long school day begins at 8 or 8.30 am, with a two-hour lunch break, and ends at 4.30 pm. There are few after-school activities, partly because of the constraints of time and resources, but also because a French school does not see itself as a community in the way that a British or American school does. All of the staff, including the *directeur* (head teacher), are appointed by the education ministry in Paris. However, because of a deeply-ingrained belief that such restrictive centralization is the price to be paid for equal treatment of staff, teachers have opposed proposals to give head teachers more control over appointments and administration.

Le baccalauréat

State schooling is non-selective until a child is fifteen, at which age he or she will be considered suitable for one of several local *lycées*, some of which offer vocational courses. However, most *lycées* prepare pupils for the *baccalauréat* exam, usually taken at 18. Familiarly known as *le bac*, this world-famous qualification was created by Napoléon in 1808. Today pupils choose a specific *bac* option so that while continuing to study a broad range of subjects they will specialize in, for example, maths and science, philosophy or commerce.

University and other tertiary colleges

There are about eighty universities, many of which are overcrowded as students simply need the *bac* in order to study where they choose. However, many students are weeded out after the first year exams. In the humanities, sciences and law there are two, three and four-year courses, leading to the DEUG, *licence* (degree) and *maîtrise* (masters degree). Many other students study at one of the hundred IUT (*Instituts universitaires de technologie*) which are technical universities preparing students for the DUT qualification (*diplôme universitaire de technologie*) and careers in industry or technology. A slightly less academic technical qualification, the BTS (*Brevet de technicien supérieur)* can be obtained at a specialist section of a *lycée d'enseignement professionnel* offering vocational training.

A very few post-*bac* students, *la crème de la crème*, are admitted to *cours préparatoires*, known as *prépa*, which are two-year intensive courses, usually run in exclusive Paris *lycées* such as Henri IV or Louis-le-Grand, and which lead to the *concours* for entry to the power-houses of the French establishment, the *grandes écoles*.

Les grandes écoles

Of the hundred or so *grandes écoles*, the most renowned is the Ecole Polytechnique which was founded by Napoléon in 1804 as an élite corps of military engineers. Many other *grandes écoles* are engineering schools, known collectively as the *Corps des mines*. Hence, although *ingénieur* may simply mean someone who draws up plans for a new stretch of *autoroute*, it more often means a brilliant mathematician who has survived a three-year grind at a *grande école* and who is en route for a dazzling career at the top of the tree in politics, commerce or industry. The preferred route to government and the high échelons of the civil service is via the prestigious Ecole Nationale d'Administration which has groomed many presidents and prime ministers including Valéry Giscard d'Estaing and Jacques Chirac (see p. 181).

Health

You only have to call in at a French pharmacy to understand that the French take their health seriously. An atmosphere of professional calm invites you to talk in whispers as though you were in a doctor's waiting room, which is not so far from the truth. The pharmacist will advise on all ailments, suggest treatment, including homeopathic remedies and recommend seeing a doctor if necessary. The pharmacy combines the French qualities of good taste and practicality – discreet displays of creams and potions alongside alarmingly graphic posters explaining how to deal with an adder bite.

The French gulp down more medicines than any other country. They consume an average of 33 boxes of medicines per person per year, compared with 15 in Germany, 10 in Britain and 6 in the United States. The French figure has doubled in the last twenty years which they explain by the higher proportion of old people in the population – pill-popping over-80s swallow down 97 boxes of tablets per person per year.

Does all this mean that the French are ill more often, or better cared for than other nations? There certainly appears to be a national attitude that equates better health with 'taking something' whether it be *une infusion* (herbal tea), a particular brand of mineral water or prescription medicines. This, together with the lower price of medicines in France compared with other developed countries, and the plentiful supply of doctors may explain the French medicine habit. On average, a French person visits the doctor eight times a year which is more frequently than the British (6 visits) although not as often as the Germans (12 visits). In addition, the French person enjoys more time with the doctor – an average of 14 minutes compared with 9 minutes in Germany and 8 in the UK.

La crise de foie (liver touble)

The French person's legendary complaint, *la crise de foie* includes varying degrees of indisposition, from mild indigestion to cirrhosis of the liver. The high incidence of the latter has undoubtedly been due to the country's record-breaking alcohol habit. Excessive drinking is responsible for 60,000 deaths a year, three-quarters of which are male. The French are still amongst Europe's biggest tipplers, even though changing lifestyles have caused the consumption of alcohol, and wine in particular, to drop. Today French people drink an annual average of 65 litres of wine per person compared with nearly double that amount in the 1950s. Increasing prosperity has meant that fewer people are knocking back harmful quantities of coarse *vin ordinaire*, preferring better quality wine instead, while many others, particularly women and young people, astound foreigners by touching nothing stronger than mineral water. However, this was still not good enough for Bernard Kouchner, the former Health Minister, who to the fury of France's wine industry, hoteliers and restaurateurs classified alcohol as a dangerous drug, alongside cannabis and heroin. In practice this means a tough government campaign to cut alcohol abuse and alcohol-related illness which account for 25 per cent of hospital admissions. Alcohol also plays a part in nearly half of France's horrifyingly high number of road accidents.

Le tabagisme (cigarette-smoking)

This is the other evil on the Health Minister's hit list because of worrying statistics that show half of French 19 to 24 year olds, a quarter of pregnant women and a third of doctors to be regular smokers. However, in the population as a whole cigarette smoking is decreasing. The French now smoke considerably less than the Americans and Japanese, a little less than the Germans and only slightly more than the British and Italians. In 1991, the Evin law prohibited tobacco advertising and made smoking in confined public spaces illegal. Cafés and restaurants are exempt if they provide a smoking area, but even smoke-filled bars are now likely to smell of Marlborough rather than *Gitanes* as many smokers have switched to milder American brands. But notwithstanding these changes, and with lung cancer the main cause of death amongst French men, the government deems there is no room for complacency.

One curious fact to emerge from French statistics is a correlation between smoking and politics. A member of the political Left will light up more often than a right-winger, but extremists of any political persuasion are the heaviest smokers.

La maladie cardiovasculaire (Heart disease)

Although heart disease is the main cause of death for French women, far fewer die from it than in most other developed countries – there are 61 cases per 100,000 inhabitants compared with 200 cases in Britain, 176 in America and 173 in Australia. In France, deaths from this cause have been cut in half over the past decade, no doubt as a result of good preventive care and medication. The French now consume 15 times more medication for cardio-vascular disease than the British.

Le cancer

In cancer care too, France has an impressive record. According to the World Health Organisation, France has one of the highest cancer survival rates in Europe, while Britain has one of the lowest. Although high spending on drugs does not always mean better treatment, it indicates a country's priorities. Spending £2.93 per head of population on anti-cancer drugs, France is ahead of

Germany (£2.31) and Britain (£1.01), although far behind the United States (£4.93).

The health service

Successive governments have attempted to rein in France's runaway health expenditure and streamline the system to provide better cover for all. The public health system administered by the CPAM (Caisse Primaire d'Assurances Maladie) is paid for by compulsory employer and employee contributions which entitle a French person to go to whichever general practitioner, specialist or hospital they wish, pay the doctor's set fee (120 francs in 1999) and then have about 70 per cent of this and the cost of medicines reimbursed. Eight out of ten people top up this cover by joining a complementary private insurance scheme, known as a *mutuelle*, through their employer.

Attitudes to doctors

Perhaps because they have the freedom to pick and choose their doctors, the French appear to be less in awe of the profession. It is not routinely glamorized by French TV which does not dish up its own hospital melodramas, although over the years French viewers have been no strangers to a dubbed *Casualty* (*Urgence*).

The image of the health service has not been helped by revelations of medical blunders and by the high number of patients admitted to hospital because of the side effects of medication. But the most shocking blow to the French health service came from the scandal over *le sang contaminé* (HIV-contaminated blood) which began in 1984 when 4,000 people, including half of France's haemophiliacs, received infected blood transfusions, resulting in a thousand deaths. In 1999, the former Prime Minister Laurent Fabius and his Health and Social Affairs Ministers found themselves in the dock accused of deliberately delaying the introduction of an American test to detect the presence of HIV in blood, so that a French test could be perfected by the Institut Pasteur. While Laurent Fabius and his Social Affairs Minister were acquitted, the former Health Minister was convicted.

> ### *Les sapeurs-pompiers*
> ### (Firemen)
> These are France's local heroes. In a crisis, the French ring 18 and – fire or no fire – *les pompiers* are ready to help. Their ambulance and first-aid service is likely to get to the scene of an accident faster than the SAMU (*Service d'Aide Médicale d'Urgence*), and they still find time to rescue kittens from trees and dispose of wasps' nests.

Housing

To the delight of foreign romantics, much inner-city accommodation is still elegant and spacious appartments with twirling wrought iron balconies, or else crumbling nineteenth-century blocks converted to provide flats and *studios* (bed-sitters) that are quaint, albeit pricey and cramped. But one institution of French urban life, the *concierge*, is dying out. This combination of caretaker and nosey parker was once posted on the ground floor of every block of flats to keep tabs on comings and goings and take in the inhabitants' mail. Now, personal letter boxes, intercom systems and number-coded locks on street doors do the job instead.

Beyond the city centres lie the suburbs. These have continued to grow since the post-war baby boom when the French government introduced low-rent public housing, the HLM (*habitations à loyer modéré*), to cope with a drastic housing shortage. Many HLM erected outside big cities in the 1950s and '60s were grim high-rises in a concrete desert. Since then, French planners have attempted to avoid the social problems which inevitably arose in these areas deprived of community life, schools or shops. The new town of Evry south of Paris is one of nine ambitious developments which appear to have successfully combined attractive HLM and private housing, good facilities and a mixed blue- and white-collar population.

Today, one in five French households occupies an HLM and these are not always flats. During the 1980s property boom there was a sudden surge of house-building with the result that, today, well over

half of all French people live in *maisons individuelles* (individual houses), which is quite high compared with some European countries – only 38 per cent in Germany and 32 per cent in Italy, but 80 per cent in Britain.

There has been a trend away from renting too. Before the Second World War, only about a third of French homes were owner-occupied, whereas by 1996 the proportion had risen to a half – no longer so different from Britain (two-thirds) where, as everyone knows, the Englishman's home is his castle.

The fact that the French now spend more on their homes than in the past indicates a clear change of priorities. Forty years ago, only a fifth of household income was spent on housing, compared with a third on food, whereas today the figures are the other way round.

Despite being the European country with the highest proportion of second homes, France has around half a million homeless, *les SDF (Sans domicile fixe)*. Homelessness became a severe problem during the recession of the 1980s and attracted the help of l'Abbé Pierre, a priest well-known for his work with the poor, and the popular comedian Coluche who joined forces to raise funds for soup kitchens known as *les restos du coeur* (restaurants with a heart). In 1998 the *Assemblée Nationale* passed an anti-poverty bill intended to help the 60 thousand people living below the poverty line, through provisions for more low-cost housing and the requisitioning of empty apartments to house the homeless. The urgency for the measures to be implemented was highlighted the following winter when ten homeless people sleeping rough died of hypothermia.

Social security

La Sécu (Sécurité sociale) is France's welfare system. It covers health care, pensions, unemployment benefit, housing benefit and a range of family allowances. Although France is Europe's most generous country when it comes to family allowances, she is the only one to pay nothing for the first child, a legacy of past attempts to encourage large families. But, despite such inducements, large families are now rare (see p. 234).

Martine Aubry, the Labour Minister and daughter of Jacques Delors, has been trying to get to grips with France's enormous social security deficit as well as to improve provision for the most needy. The introduction of *la CMU (Couverture Maladie Universelle*, universal health cover) will mean that any person living in France on a low income will receive free medical, dental and optical care without having to go through the usual system of paying the bills and obtaining partial reimbursement of the cost.

Transport

Although the French public transport system, *les transports en commun*, is extensive and efficient, the French still snarl up their cities with cars. The Socialist government's Green party Environment Minister, Dominique Voynet and the Communist Transport Minister, Jean-Claude Gayssot, are both concerned to woo more people away from their cars and on to public transport, as Strasbourg town council has done. The city's bold investment in a new tram system and a large bicycle network combined with draconian parking penalties has achieved a 30 per cent increase in public transport use. In many other towns, a car-free day which has turned into an annual autumn event entitled *En ville sans ma voiture* (In town without my car) allows seasoned motorists to flirt with bus and tube, walk to work or exchange their car keys for a day's free cycle hire. But it remains to be seen if commuters will forsake their precious cars more than once a year.

French railways

France's state-owned railway company, the SNCF *(Société nationale des chemins de fer français)*, was dramatically resuscitated and modernized after near-death in the Second World War. It has since built up a world-wide reputation for innovation and efficiency. While the TGV *(train à grande vitesse*, high-speed train) is the SNCF's glamorous star, the company's comfortable electric and diesel trains are hardly bumbling country cousins. They run punctually and speedily on a dense network of track which radiates out from Paris.

Le TGV

The TGV, the world's fastest train, first ran in 1981 on new track from Paris to Lyon and halved the journey time to two hours. Since then, a total of 800 miles of special track have been built and the distinctive bullet-nosed trains now dash from Paris, north to Lille and on through the Channel tunnel to Britain (the Eurostar), or on to Brussels and the Netherlands (the Thalys), south as far as Valence and soon to Marseille, and west to Tours and Le Mans. Built by the French engineering company Alsthom the trains travel at around 300 kph, with a top speed of around 515 kph, slashing previous journey times. TGV technology has been so successful that it has been snapped up for new lines around the world – in Australia, Taiwan, Spain and in the US for the Houston-Dallas-San Antonio line and other inter-city projects, thus making France the world's top railway exporter. However, the TGV is not without its opponents in France because it is costly, requiring new track which often scars the landscape. Although a long-planned route east to Strasbourg, and another connecting Mulhouse with the Rhône valley, will probably be completed, it is likely that in the future the government will opt for the cheaper but slower option of tilting trains used in Italy and Sweden, which run on conventional track.

La RATP (Régie Autonome des Transports Parisiens)

This is the Paris public transport authority which was established in 1948. It owns and runs the *métro*, the RER (*Réseau Express Régional*) whose trains connect Paris with the suburbs, the buses and the Saint-Denis-Bobigny tramway. Parisian public transport compares well with systems in other cities, not only on efficiency but on price. While the average cost of a bus or train ticket is 4.5 fr. in Paris, it is the equivalent of 9 fr. in New York, 14 fr. in London and 6 fr. in Berlin.

Le métro

Short for *chemin de fer métropolitain*, the Paris *métro* is known throughout the world for its distinctive Art-Nouveau station entrances, many of which have remained unchanged since they were built a hundred years ago at the time of *l'Exposition universelle* (the universal exhibition) in 1900. Now there is a *métro* in Lyon, Marseille, Lille and Toulouse. The latest Parisian *métro* line, the first to be constructed since 1935, is the futuristic *ligne 14* which connects west and east Paris and runs with fully-automated, driverless trains, *les Météors*. These complete their seven-kilometre journey from La Madeleine to the Bibliothèque Nationale de France in 12 minutes, stopping at only eight lavishly-decorated stations. For example, the *Météor* station at the Gare de Lyon features a large and stylish greenhouse full of tropical plants while Les Pyramides station gives pride of place to modern art exhibitions. On a more sombre but practical note, *Météor* stations are fitted with glass walls between the platform and the rails in order to reduce the *métro*'s annual total of 130 suicides and attempted suicides. With further *Météor* line extensions planned, the RATP claims that its costly, ultra-modern showpiece is twenty years ahead of its time.

The RATP's zest for innovation extends to the conventional *métro* too. In 1997, in order to cheer up its passengers and prevent mediocre buskers passing round the hat in train carriages, it set up a new department *Métro chords* to audition and license buskers, and so raise the standard of music in its stations. It even acts as an intermediary between its musical hopefuls and appreciative passengers wanting to hire performers for weddings and parties.

Also with passengers in mind, the RATP has funded years of research into ways of masking the *métro*'s pungent smell. Successive attempts with lavender, eucalyptus and strawberry-based products had distinctly unsubtle results. It remains to be seen if the RATP is successful with its latest deodorant, a chemical powder romantically named *Madeleine*. But for nostalgics nothing will compensate for the disappearance of the *métro*'s familiar whiffy aroma.

Roads

France has a dense and good road network connecting every region with Paris, a legacy first of Roman engineering and much later of Napoleonic centralization. Consequently, France was relatively slow to develop *autoroutes* (motorways). However, the country now has 9,000 kilometres of *autoroutes*, compared with only 3,000 in Britain and 11,000 in Germany. Since 1969 the *autoroutes* have been privately-run toll roads dotted with *péages* (toll gates).

> **Some roads have glamorous names!**
>
> La Francilienne – A104/N104
> L'Autoroute du soleil – A6/7
> L'Océane – A11
> L'Occitane – A20
> La Provençale – A8

Cars

The French love their cars. With 79 per cent of households owning a car and 28 per cent owning two, France is third in terms of car ownership in the European Union, behind Italy and Germany. It seems fitting in a country of such strong regional identities that the last two digits of a French car registration number should designate the owner's *département*. When the owner moves out of an area their new place of abode is immediately evident from the new registration number they have been obliged to obtain from the *préfecture*.

The noisy rumble of economical and hard-wearing diesel engines is common in France, and in 1995 diesel cars reached a peak of popularity, accounting for almost half of new cars. However, this figure has since dropped to less than a third because of concerns about pollution, and fears that the government might bump up the price of the previously cheap *gazole*. Even so, France still has the highest proportion of diesel cars in Europe.

French cars have been renowned for their combination of style, sturdiness and idiosyncracy. The last quality has been best exemplified by the world-renowned Citroën 2CV (*deux-chevaux* i.e. two horse-power engine) which was designed in 1948 to carry *'deux cultivateurs en sabots, cinquante kilos de pommes de terre ou un tonnelet'* (two farm workers in clogs, fifty kilos of potatoes or a wine cask). The 2CV, known as *quatre roues sous un parapluie* (four wheels under an umbrella), was loved by farmers, students and low-budget families alike until it finally went out of production in 1991. Another Citroën innovation, hydro-pneumatic suspension, still distinguishes many present-day models just as in the past it helped hoist into action Général de Gaulle's favourite car, the impressive and whale-like Citroën DS. Today's French cars are

designed not only with comfort and style, but with low-fuel consumption and women drivers in mind – as testified by Renault's long-running TV advertising campaign featuring 'Nicole' and her Clio. In 1997 the Clio was France's second best-selling car, only slightly behind the Renault Mégane. Another international hit was the pioneering Renault Espace which set a new trend for *monospaces* (people carriers).

The French still prefer their own, but foreign cars have gradually been making inroads. However, it was still a shock to French pride when in 1999 French car manufacturers lost their monopoly of official vehicle production, half of which was offered to the American company Ford. Henceforth not only *les fourgons de police* (police vans) and *les camions de pompier* (fire engines) but, *quelle horreur*, even the official car of the prime minister, may no longer be French.

Air travel

Unlike other forms of public transport, French air travel has developed dramatically in the last ten years. it has increased by 60 per cent, whereas use of the train, including the splendid TGV, has only risen by 17 per cent. France now leads Europe with her dense network of frequent domestic flights which are used for both business travel and family visits home. It is an ideal means of conveying unaccompanied Parisian grandchildren to their far-flung *Mammie et Papi* (Granny and Grandpa) for the long French summer holidays.

French aviation has been a source of national pride ever since Louis Blériot became the first person to fly across the English Channel in 1909. Although the French aircraft industry was well-nigh finished by the end of the Second World War, it was resuscitated by Georges Héreil and his Caravelle aircraft in the 1950s and '60s. The prestige project of the 1970s was Concorde, and that of the 1980s was the Airbus. The latter, a joint venture with Germany, Spain and Britain has been a far greater commercial success than the Anglo-French Concorde whose production was bedevilled by delays and cross-Channel disagreements.

VOCABULARY

Education
le système éducatif *education system*
la scolarisation *schooling*
l'enseignement (m.) *teaching*
enseigner *to teach*
apprendre *to learn*
l'école primaire (f.) *primary school*
l'instituteur/-trice *primary-school teacher*
le collège *secondary school*
le/la professeur *secondary-school teacher*
le directeur/la directrice *head teacher*
passer le brevet (BEC) *to take the general certificate of studies at the end of* collège, *usually at age 15*
passer en seconde *to go into 2e (first year of* lycée)
le/la proviseur *head of a lycée*
le dossier scolaire *school record*
le bulletin *report*
le contrôle continu *continuous assessment*
l'examen blanc (m.) *mock exam*
le bachotage *cramming for exams*
etre reçu à *to pass (an exam)*
rater to fail *(an exam)*
se faire coller *to be failed*
avoir son bac *to pass one's baccalauréat*
le bachelier/la bachelière *someone who has passed the* bac
passer un concours *to take a competitive exam*
l'Ecole Normale Supérieure *prestigious teacher training college – the most famous one is known as* la rue d'Ulm
le normalien *student of an* école normale supérieure
la licence *bachelor's degree*
la maîtrise *master's degree*
l'agrégation (f.) *postgraduate competitive examination*
le doctorat *doctorate*
la formation continue *adult education*

Health
être en bonne santé *to be in good health*
se sentir malade *to feel ill*
les premiers soins (m.) *first aid*
le médecin généraliste *general practitioner*
le médecin référant *GP for referrals to specialist*
le/la spécialiste *specialist*
le cabinet de consultation *surgery*
le centre hospitalier *general hospital*
se faire soigner *to get medical attention*
suivre un traitement *to have treatment*
l'ordonnance (f.) *prescription*
être hospitalisé(e) *to go into hospital*
se faire opérer *to have an operation*
l'assurance-maladie (f.) *medical insurance*
Médecins sans frontières *International humanitarian organisation established by French doctors. (1999 Nobel prize winner)*

Social security
les charges sociales (f.) *payments deducted from salary for social security, unemployment insurance and pension*
les prestations (f.) *benefits*
les allocations (f.) familiales *family allowance*
les allocations (f.) chômage *unemployment benefit*
les bureaux (m.) de l'Assedic *unemployment benefit office*

Housing
le logement *housing*
le propriétaire *owner*
l'agence immobilière (f.) *estate agency*
le loyer *rent*
le locataire *tenant*
le bail *lease*
le banlieusard *suburb dweller*
la cité *blocks of flats*
le grand ensemble " "
la zone à urbaniser en priorité (ZUP) *priority development area*

le parc immobilier *number of properties nationwide*
le parc social *stock of low-rent housing*
Transport
le parc automobile *number of cars nationwide*
le réseau routier *road network*
les heures de pointe (f.) *rush-hour*
la circulation *traffic*
le week-end noir *dangerously busy weekend*
l'embouteillage/le bouchon (m.) *traffic jam*

le Bison fûté *government-sponsored traffic advice service*
rouler *to drive*
le numéro d'immatriculation *registration number*
la plaque minéralogique *number plate*
la berline *saloon*
le break *estate car*
le réseau ferroviaire *railway network*
circuler *to run*
les cheminots (m.) *railway workers*

Taking it further

Books

Michaud, Guy and Kimmer, Alain, **Le nouveau guide France** (Paris: Hachette, 1996)

Info

Ministère de l'Education nationale, de la Recherche et de la Technologie, 110 rue de Grenelle, 75337 Paris; tel. 01 55 55 10 10; **www.education.gouv.fr**
Ministère de la Santé, www.santé.gouv.fr
Ministère de l'Equipement, des Transports et du Logement, 246 Boulevard Saint-Germains, 75006 Paris; tel. 01 40 81 21 22; **www.equipement.gouv.fr**
Ministère de l'Aménagement du Territoire et de l'Environnement, 20 avenue de Ségur, 75302 Paris, tel. 0142 19 2021, **www.environnement.gouv.fr**
le Musée de l'automobile de la Sarthe, Circuit des 24 heures du Mans, 72000 Le Mans, tel. 01 43 72 72 24

11 | FRANCE AT WORK AND PLAY

Le travail est souvent le père du plaisir.
Work is often the father of pleasure.

Voltaire (1694–1778)
Discours sur l'homme IV

Nowadays, the traditional French peasant, once the mainstay of the country's agriculture, is more likely to feature in a TV food commercial than to be found working the soil. Industrial workers in blue overalls are still to be seen flooding through the gates of Renault factories in Longwy and Le Mans or of the Aérospatiale works in Toulouse, but their numbers have fallen by a quarter since 1980. Today two-thirds of the working population are employed in service industries as technicians, administrators, managers, teachers, sales representatives and assistants. The last fifty years have seen an explosion of white collar jobs and of *cadres* (executives or managers), a term borrowed from the army whose rigid hierarchical structures are echoed in the formal culture of many French companies.

As for leisure, the French have a lot of time for it, thanks to their generous holiday entitlements and moderate working hours, not to speak of the unwelcome gap created in many people's lives by high unemployment. But long before the birth of the leisure industry, in the days when peasant small-holders and Lorraine miners worked from dawn to dusk, the daily activities of cooking, eating and drinking together were a source of French pride, pleasure and relaxation. They remain so in today's very different consumer society with its hypermarkets, sports clubs and computer games.

Economic change and *le dirigisme* (state intervention)

Although the transition from agriculture to manufacturing industry and subsequently to technology and services is common to the economies of other developed countries, the transformation has been particularly swift and dramatic in France. Until the Second World War, France was dependent on labour-intensive agriculture (over a quarter of the working population were peasant farmers) and on her old iron and coal industries run by a hotchpotch of small firms. A multitude of crafts people and small shopkeepers completed the picture of an impoverished, inward-looking nation struggling to survive. France emerged from the war with these limited resources badly battered. Rapid industrialization was the only remedy for the country's crippling poverty.

To this end, in 1946 Jean Monnet and a group of fellow visionaries hatched up France's first economic plan which directed state investment to heavy industry. This was followed by further *plans quinquennaux* (five-year plans) which fixed growth targets in every economic sector. The Plan of 1981 focused on decentralization.

Nationalizations

The French state's long involvement in many aspects of the economy goes back to the seventeenth century when Louis XIV nationalized the tobacco industry. However, it was not until the 1930s that the railways and the new aircraft industry were nationalized. Then, after the Second World War and in conjunction with the first economic plan, the largest commercial banks, insurance companies, the coal, gas and electricity industries, and the Renault car company were all nationalized. When the Socialists came to power during François Mitterrand's presidency in the 1980s, a further sweep of nationalizations turned 10 per cent of the French work force into industrial public sector employees, giving France the largest public sector in Europe. Then in 1987, the right-wing government of Jacques Chirac set about reversing these nationalizations. This trend has been taken up with even more enthusiasm by the current Socialist Prime Minister Lionel Jospin who has swung away from the interventionist dogma dear to the former president Mitterrand, in order to raise much-needed cash for social reforms and job creation schemes. Now, the industrial public sector (not including the Post Office) has been halved by the sale or partial sale of numerous companies including insurance and armaments companies, Aérospatiale, France Télécom, Air France, Crédit Lyonnais and the gas and electricity industries.

Industry

Today, France's coal and iron industries are virtually dead, and steel and textiles are far less important than the newer *industries de pointe* (high-tech industries) – aerospace, chemicals, pharmaceuticals, glass and plastics.

France still has many small companies, but her largest ones are world players. Her two car groups, Renault and Peugeot-Citroën, account for over a fifth of all car sales in western Europe; and since its partial acquisition of the Japanese car manufacturer Nissan, Renault has become the fourth biggest vehicle manufacturing group in the world. Other international household names are Alcatel/Alsthom (engineering and telecommunications), Michelin (tyres), Rhône-Poulenc (chemicals), St Gobain (glass). Aérospatiale (missiles, helicopters and the Airbus), Elf-Aquitaine and Total (oil), L'Oréal (cosmetics), Danone (food).

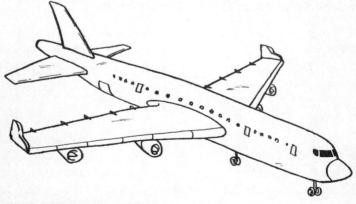

France's pride – the Airbus.

Agriculture

The traveller through France, and particularly across the plain of Beauce south and west of Paris, cannot fail to be impressed by the vast expanses of French wheat, one of her main agricultural exports. France has the largest agricultural sector of the European Union and, in terms of world trade in agricultural produce, she is second only to the United States. Widespread mechanization and industrialization of farming has meant a huge drop in the numbers of agricultural workers but increased productivity. Many small-scale farmers have improved their businesses by sharing machinery and jointly marketing their produce through co-operatives.

For the French, farming has much greater importance than its small part in the national economy which is only 2.4 per cent of GDP. Farming represents the fine food and wines in which France takes such pride and in which the rest of the world also takes such pleasure; it represents the disappearing way of life of *la France profonde* (traditional rural France). Perhaps for this reason French farmers have been particularly cosseted and have received generous subsidies (49 fr. billion in 1997 including 40 fr. billion from the EU) although these are by no means equally distributed. The poor Auvergnat receives considerably less help for his small cattle farm than does the Beauceron large-scale wheat producer. Farming unions have vigorously and often violently defended their members' interests, obstructing roads and even railway lines with surplus artichokes, cauliflowers and manure (see p. 257).

Services

It was the consumer society of the 1950s and '60s which saw the beginning of rapid growth in retailing, tourism, catering, financial services, teaching and the health service. But since the 1970s, automation and an increasingly self-service culture, together with France's high social security contributions (see *Les charges sociales* below), have steadied job growth.

In services, as in industry and agriculture, France has been forced to think big, while struggling to hold on to the traditions which have been part of her national identity. This is particularly true in

French farming, forestry and fishing

- 🐂 Cattle
- 🐑 Sheep farming
- 🌾 Cereals
- 🍎 Fruit
- 🍇 Grapes
- 🌲 Forestry
- 🥕 Vegetables
- 🐟 Fishing

retailing where *les petits commerces* (small local shops) and small-town markets survive alongside vast hypermarkets. Marseille's Carrefour hypermarket is one of the largest in the world.

The abundance of weekly and twice-weekly markets shows the importance placed by the French on fresh local vegetables and fruit, and traditionally-prepared local cheeses. However, there are only half as many small shopkeepers today as fifty years ago and the last twenty years have seen one in two of those pillars of the community, bakers and café owners, shut up shop. Unable to compete with the range of goods and low prices of supermarkets, small shops survive by selling specialist goods or by becoming franchises. Meanwhile, a third of all household purchases pass through the supermarket checkout.

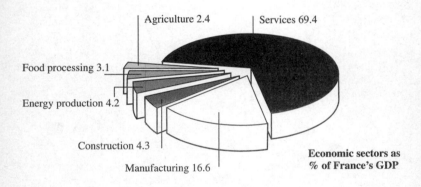

Agriculture 2.4 · Services 69.4 · Food processing 3.1 · Energy production 4.2 · Construction 4.3 · Manufacturing 16.6

Economic sectors as % of France's GDP

The workers

French railway workers' or lorry drivers' strikes which hit the headlines now and then might give the impression of a militantly unionized country. In fact France has the lowest level of union membership in Europe. Only around seven per cent of French employees are union members compared with 15.6 per cent in the US, nearly 33 per cent in Germany and 39 per cent in Britain. However, one in five French public sector employees are members of a union. The rapid drop in union membership in France began in the 1970s with the decline of heavy industry and its workforce, the traditional working class. However, weak unionization does not mean no strikes. French workers of all categories, including doctors, dentists, the police and lawyers, may strike whether or not they are union members and they are more inclined than workers in many other countries to state their claims by means of street demonstration.

The main unions

The CGT (La Confédération Générale du Travail)
The oldest of the French unions, its membership has fallen from half of the workforce in 1946 to just 2.5 per cent of it today. Long associated with the Communist party.

The CFDT (La Confédération Française Démocratique du Travail)
Originally a Catholic Socialist organization (CFTC), this union turned militant during the events of May '68. In recent years it has adopted a more conciliatory approach, seeking influence through co-operation with employers.

FO (Force Ouvrière)
This union was formed by break-away members of the CGT in 1948. Once a more moderate union, its present leadership adopts a hard-line, anti-capitalist position.

La CFTC (Confédération Française des Travailleurs Chrétiens)
This small, Catholic trade unionists' organization survived a split when the majority of its members left to form the CFDT in 1964.

The bosses

Le Mouvement des entreprises de France (Medef) is the federation of French employers. Once a staid and conservative body, it has recently changed its internal structure, its image and its name. Today it has dropped its former opposition to the Anglo-Saxon free-market model and it has vigorously campaigned against the introduction of the 35-hour week which it accuses of destroying, not creating, jobs.

The Medef represents nearly all French employers. Some are old family firms which have mostly changed with the times. Michelin, for example, was renowned for the patriarchal culture that pervaded its eighty factories world-wide, but widespread changes were expected when Edouard Michelin, great-grandson of one of the company's founders, took over in 1999. Like many of today's industrial and commercial bosses he has American-style management experience as well as *grande école* training (see p. 195). In fact, such dual training is prized in the top échelons of international business on either side of the Atlantic. However, the only British citizen at the head of a big French publicly-quoted company is the Welshman Lindsay Owen-Jones who worked his way up through the ranks at l'Oréal and who in 1998 received the *Légion d'honneur*.

Two of France's richest bosses are arch rivals Bernard Arnault and François Pinault. Arnault is head of Luis Vuitton Moët Hennessy, the world's biggest luxury goods business which includes brands such as Christian Dior and Moët Chandon. His wealthy background and Ecole Polytechnique training is typical of traditional French business leaders. Pinault on the other hand is the archetype of a self-made man. The son of a Breton wood-cutter, he left school at 16 and made his fortune as an astute entrepreneur before acquiring the smart department store group Au Printemps. He hit at the heart of the British cultural establishment in 1998 with his purchase of the leading London auction house Christies.

Les charges sociales (social security contributions)

Hiring staff in France is a far more expensive business than it is in Britain or the US. France's welfare state is funded by *charges sociales*, payments made for each employee by deductions from their gross wages as well as by hefty employer contributions. Although the latter are due to be reduced by the Jospin government, many other taxes and bureaucratic rules affecting employers have not helped remedy France's unemployment problem.

Even though income tax is relatively low and paid by only half of workers, French employees pay nearly half of their earnings in high social security payments and other state taxes. These deductions are amongst the highest in Europe coming behind only the Scandinavian countries and Belgium. Because of this, many young French high-flyers are being tempted to take up posts in Britain and America where employees pay less of their earnings to the state. It is not just the young who are defecting. France is losing some of its brilliant scientists such as Luc Montagnier, the co-discoverer of the HIV virus and Jean-Loup Chrétien, the first French astronaut; both are past the French retirement age of 60 and have accepted lucrative offers in the US .

Working hours and holidays

France was notorious for its short working hours even before the Socialist government succeeded in persuading many private firms to accept a 35-hour week as part of its job creation programme. Until 1998, the official working week was 39 hours, the shortest in Europe, although in practice the average in France was 41 hours, compared with 44 hours in Britain. Of course, many self-employed French people work far longer hours – a typical *boulanger artisanal* (independent, traditional baker) for example, works 65 hours a week. Amongst employees, ambitious or conscientious *cadres* regularly work far longer than the legal maximum. However, in 1998, worried that such executives could undermine the purpose of the 35-hour week, the government authorized *inspecteurs du travail*, a kind of job police, to monitor individuals' use of computers and snoop around company car parks after normal office hours.

Although France's public sector is not renowned for burning the midnight oil, the rest of Europe was shocked when a government report revealed that a 35-hour week would mean many French civil servants having to work more, not less. The most workshy were employed in the justice and culture ministries where a 29-hour week was not uncommon. In some ministries, staff were able to boost their annual six-week holiday entitlement with a variety of special days off including *jours-valises* (suitcase days) tacked on to the beginning and end of a holiday for packing and unpacking!

Paid holidays

These date from 1936 when Léon Blum's *Front Populaire* government introduced two weeks paid holiday and a 40-hour working week. Today the French statutory paid holiday is five weeks, although, with seniority entitlements or as a result of individual company agreements, 28 per cent of workers enjoy more than this.

Pay

For the French, discussing money was once a terrible taboo. This has changed as France, like all other western nations, has become a consumer society. In the 1980s, the French media made much of fortunes amassed and lost by wheeler-dealers like the Olympique Marseille football team chief, Bernard Tapie, and it continues to drool over the lavish life-styles of celebrities. However, the French remain prudish about sharing the secrets of their pay packet.

For many years, France had the widest *éventail des salaires* (salary range) in the West. This diminished in the mid 1990s, whereas at that time the gap between the richest and the poorest grew in the US and Britain. However, embarrassingly for the Socialist government, during their first year in office, the fortunes of the country's top earners shot up, while more and more workers were earning the minimum wage. The assets of France's wealthiest woman, l'Oréal heiress Liliane Bettancourt, is frequently used as a barometer of fat-cat fortunes. In 1997/8 her wealth rose from £4.2 billion to £6.5 billion – £7 million for each working day.

Air-line pilots and dentists are amongst the highest-paid employees. While in industry the highest salaries are earnt in petrochemicals, the lowest are in the clothing industry and retailing. However, this is not true for every category of employee in these industries. In general, factory workers in the aeronautics industry earn more than those in petrochemicals and twice as much as those in clothing.

The number of people earning *le Smic* (*le salaire minimum interprofessionnel de croissance*), France's minimum wage, has trebled since it was introduced in 1970. In 1998, 2.2 million people

(11 per cent of the population) known as *smicards* received the minimum wage of 6,700 fr. a month for a 39-hour week. This is just over half of the average wage, making *le Smic* the world's most generous minimum wage. However, as it is established at an hourly rate, it cannot prevent the income of many part-time workers falling below the poverty line of 3,500 fr. a month.

Women at work

Nearly half of the French workforce is female, making France the country with the highest proportion of women workers in the European Union. However, less than a third of *cadres*, and only a tenth of company directors are women. Women are more affected by unemployment (one in seven women is jobless compared to one in ten men) and in the private sector they earn an average of 20 per cent less than men, although the gap is narrower in the public sector.

Unemployment

Unemployment in France has risen gradually from an official figure of one million in the 1970s to over three million in 1999, 11.2 per cent of the population – one of the highest unemployment rates in Europe. Even this gloomy picture is not accurate as these figures only take account of those registered for full-time work. The real number of French unemployed may be closer to five million.

International unemployment (% of labour force – mid 1999)	
Spain	15.8
Italy	12.0
France	11.2
Germany	9.1
UK	6.1
US	4.3
Euro 15 average	9.4

Successive governments have attempted to tackle unemployment which affects a quarter of the country's young people. The Jospin government's initiatives include a scheme to create thousands of short-term jobs for young people, as well as the introduction of the 35-hour week intended to encourage employers to take on more workers. However, it remains to be seen if this will be successful. France's rigid labour laws are one of the reasons why French bosses are very cautious about taking on more staff despite the economic upturn. These regulations covering safety, holidays, maternity leave and job security mean that those French workers who are lucky enough to have a job are amongst the best-protected in Europe. The high social security contributions payable by employers have been another impediment to new jobs.

L'ANPE

L'Agence Nationale pour l'Emploi, the French national employment agency has hundreds of job centres throughout the country. It offers support for people seeking training, careers advice and employment. Unemployed people must register with their local ANPE in order to receive their *allocation de chômage* (unemployment benefit).

Holidays

Summer holidays in France have a special place in the nation's psyche and August has long been a sacrosanct period when day-to-day worries give way to single-minded hedonism. For this reason, government attempts to relieve the pressure on roads and resorts by staggering school holidays and encouraging people to take their holidays at other times, have only succeeded in spreading the crush to July as well as August. More people are taking winter breaks but these are usually second holidays making no difference to the congestion of these two vital months when four-fifths of French people, not to mention thousands of foreign tourists, are hurtling along the *autoroutes*.

Although lake, country and mountain holidays, often with healthy pursuits such as *la voile* (sailing), *la randonnée* (walking), *l'escalade* (climbing), *le VTT* (mountain biking) or *le rafting*, have become increasingly popular, the pull of the sea, bathing and *bronzage* (sun-bathing) is still irresistible. According to French sociologists, a French person's chosen beach indicates their social status. Research shows a preponderance of senior managers on the Côte d'Azur, the middle classes in the Languedoc-Roussillon resorts west of Marseille, the working classes on the Channel coast, and a mixture of *catégories socioprofessionnelles* on the Breton and Atlantic coasts.

Seaside holidays have a long history in France and have been celebrated in countless films, novels and songs. However, when they began at the end of the eighteenth century their purpose was strictly medicinal. Just before the Revolution, Boulogne became France's first *station balnéaire*. Then, with the development of the railways, resorts quickly sprang up all along the Channel, Atlantic and Mediterranean coasts. However, until paid annual leave was introduced in 1936, holidays remained the privilege of a wealthy élite. The Côte d'Azur in the nineteenth and early twentieth centuries was the playground of rich foreigners seeking winter sun. It was particularly loved by English aristocrats who funded the construction of Nice's Promenade des Anglais, an elegant seafront thoroughfare which is now an eight-lane, five-kilometre-long highway.

The Club Med

Another aspect of French holiday culture taken up by foreigners is the Club Med. Gilbert Trigano, the son of a French industrialist, founded le Club Méditerranée in 1950 to provide cheap family holidays. At first quite primitive, the clubs offered informal and egalitarian community life in idyllic surroundings. A new breed of *animateur* (organizer) was born, the Club's friendly and relaxed *gentils organisateurs* (GOs) whose lack of deference shocked some well-to-do French holiday-makers in the 1950s. On the other hand most participants, known as *gentils membres* (GMs), felt liberated by the absence of the usual social barriers. Over the years, the club became more luxurious and middle class and the organization's name was trimmed because of American GMs' alleged inability to pronounce it in full. After six years in the red and now with former EuroDisney chief, Philippe Bourguignon, in control, the Club is, sadly, planning to drop further Gallicisms, but surely not to translate *gentil membre* as 'nice member', which, on certain Club naturist beaches, might give quite the wrong impression.

Colonies de vacances

It is not as common nowadays as it was thirty years ago to see young, harasssed *moniteurs* and *monitrices* in charge of long crocodiles of *petits Français* marching to or from the beach. *Colonies de vacances* (state-subsidized summer camps) began at the end of the nineteenth century to give town children a breath of sea or country air, and they continued to be popular with working parents as childcare for their offspring during the long school holidays.

Destinations

French people like French holidays. Only just over one in ten French holiday-makers venture outside *l'Hexagone*, whereas the Germans and Dutch spend half of their holidays abroad, and the British a third. However, the seemingly ubiquitous Americans and Japanese are, according to statistics, even more stay-at-home than the French, taking only 4 per cent of their holidays abroad.

A fortnight in a *gîte rural* (rented country holiday home) may be the foreigner's idea of a typical French holiday, but it is one disproved by the French who spend only 3 per cent of their summer holidays this way. Camping and rented flats in resorts are popular, but the favourite French holiday mode is to stay rent-free with friends or family, which accounted for nearly half of French holidays in July or August in 1997. A further 10 per cent of holidays are spent in a *résidence secondaire* (second home) – the French are the largest second-home owners in Europe. Given these holiday habits, it is hardly surprising that fewer than one in ten French holiday-makers choose to go on a package holiday.

Spare time

Traditionally the French have enjoyed their spare time at home *en famille*, doing a bit of *bricolage* (DIY), digging over their vegetable garden, cooking five-course meals or watching the television. But in recent years they have gone out more and now spend an estimated quarter of their income on cultural or other leisure activities. In addition, the French are overcoming their traditional wariness of clubs and associations. Now, one in five French people belongs to a sports club, amateur dramatics group or other cultural society.

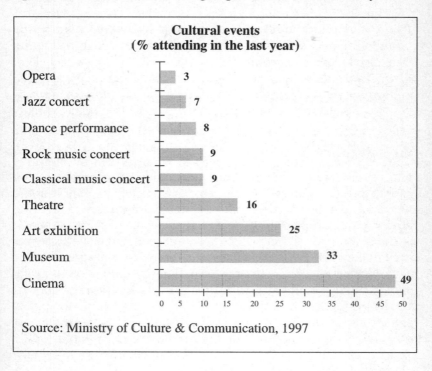

**Cultural events
(% attending in the last year)**

Opera	3
Jazz concert	7
Dance performance	8
Rock music concert	9
Classical music concert	9
Theatre	16
Art exhibition	25
Museum	33
Cinema	49

Source: Ministry of Culture & Communication, 1997

Sport

Until relatively recently, the French preferred the role of spectator to participant. However, this changed in the 1980s and '90s as the preoccupation with health and fitness that started in the United States swept across Europe. With government funding, smart new sports centres sprang up in many French towns, the most impressive of which is Le Palais Omnisports de Paris-Bercy which hosts many international competitions. Now, French sports clubs have 14 million paid-up members, 1.8 million of which belong to football clubs. However, apart from football and rugby which arouse strong passions and local loyalties, the French prefer non-team sports.

Cycling

Le Tour de France is France's top annual sporting event, a gruelling 2,500-mile cycle race through some of France's toughest terrain. The route is modified each year, sometimes making a loop into neighbouring countries, but always finishing around 14th July in the elegant Champs-Elysées.

Cycling and the Tour in particular are an essential part of French life. Every weekend young cycling enthusiasts, many from modest backgrounds, participate in competitions and test their stamina against hundreds of others all hoping to reach the next grade and eventually, maybe, follow in the cycle tracks of their heroes up steep Pyrenean passes, across remote plateaux and through the villages and towns of the Tour de France. The pressures on participants have always been enormous from the first Tour in 1903 when cyclists had to do their own repairs and carry their own provisions, to the present-day race with its media hype, not to speak of the *dopage* (drug-taking) investigations that seriously disrupted most of the 1998 Tour. The affair, which revealed widespread use of performance-enhancing drugs, caused much Gallic navel-gazing and led many eminent cycling enthusiasts (including Jacques Delors) to defend the sport's ideals as well as to call for much greater monitoring and support of cyclists. As a consequence, the French cycling federation must now conduct an in-depth health check every three months on all top cyclists in order to reveal any physical changes linked to drug-taking.

Tour de France know-how	
le peloton	main pack of cyclists
le maillot jaune	yellow jersey worn by the leading rider
le maillot vert	green jersey worn by leader on points
le maillot à pois	red polka-dot jersey worn by *'le roi des montagnes'* ('the king of the mountains')
les domestiques	long-suffering assistants who cycle alongside their team members with food and water
un grimpeur	a climber (good uphill cyclist)
la Grande Boucle	the Tour

Football

Only the French could make a philosophy out of football. Preparations for the 1998 world cup gave rise to excited polemic over the *footbalisation de la société* and *le supporterisme* and to discussion of the stadium as un *espace socio-psychique* (a socio-psychic space). However, in the euphoria at France's unexpected and dazzling victory, even the sociologists shut up and got on with popping champagne corks and dancing down the Champs-Elysées.

Football used to take second place to cycling in the country's affections, but after the '98 world cup, membership of the *Fédération française de football* (French football federation) rose by 200,000 and attendance at matches picked up. However, even French first-division matches draw only half the number of punters at German, Italian or English matches. Perhaps most French supporters are in front of the TV cheering *'aux chiottes l'arbitre'* ('send the ref to the bogs'), with un *pack* of Krönenberg 1664.

France's famous football clubs

Auxerre	Association Jeunesse Auxerroise
Bordeaux	Les Girondins de Bordeaux
Guingcamp	En avant Guingcamp
Lens	Racing Club de Lens
Marseille	Olympique de Marseille (OM)
Monaco	Association Sportive de Monaco
Nantes	Football Club Nantes Atlantique
Paris	Paris Saint-Germain (PSG)

Turnstile takings are not helped by the defection of local stars to wealthier foreign clubs which can afford to poach France's best players – sixteen members of the former World Cup team play abroad, these include French heroes Zinedine Zidane, playing for Italian team Juventus and Didier Deschamps at English club Chelsea. French clubs are considerably poorer than those foreign counterparts which have made a success of merchandising or which have become limited companies. In 1999, Paris Saint-Germain, owned by television station Canal Plus, was the only French team to feature in the list of the world's top 20 wealthiest clubs which included six Italian, five English and three Spanish clubs. However, this situation may change with a recent law enabling French football clubs to become limited companies, although stock market listings are prohibited.

Le Championnat de France de Football

This is the competition for France's 20 first-division clubs. The winner plays in the European Cup Winners' Cup and the second- and third-place clubs compete in the UEFA Cup.

La Coupe de France

The Coupe de France gives every small-town team the chance to compete against the greats as well as the possibility of far-flung travel if they reach the seventh round. This is when teams from France's *départements d'outre-mer* (overseas departments) join the competition and either fly to Paris, where they are fêted by expatriots, or else receive on their home ground those metropolitan French teams lucky enough to qualify for what amounts to an all-expenses-paid, exotic holiday. Of course, considering the staggering distances involved, the travelling teams may not be up to giving of their best – in 1998 the Armentières *équipe* flew 10,400 miles to play JS Traput Lifou in New Caledonia in the Pacific Ocean, whilst hopefuls from Pirae in French Polynesia spent a day in a plane before confronting the Corsican team Ajaccio at the Parc des Princes in Paris.

Rugby Union

The oval-shaped ball rules in the south-west, the French rugby heartland. However, as a national sport, rugby has far fewer participants than football, tennis or *pétanque*. Rugby's top teams are Brive, Bègles-Bordeaux, Castres, Montferrand, Pau, Toulouse, Stade Français and Racing de Paris who always have players in the national side lined up against England, Ireland, Scotland and Wales in the Tournoi des Cinq Nations (the Five Nations).

Pétanque

This variant of *boules* is another southern passion, played wherever there is sufficient shade and a flat sandy or gravelly surface. In keeping with the foreigner's image of France, many *pétanque* fans are indeed old men in berets, but the game also has a younger following and many local, and even international, championships. *Pétanque*, which is France's fourth most popular sport, was allegedly introduced to France by sailors from the island of Rhodes in the seventh century. The name is derived from *provençal – pé tanco*, meaning feet fixed to the ground. There are many variations throughout the country including *Boule de fort* played in the West, *Boule Parisienne* and *Boule Lyonnaise*. The little wooden ball or jack is called *un cochonnet* in some areas and *un but* in others. Traditional *boule*-playing lore has it that a piece of *gruyère* will calm the nerves and that a squeeze of lemon with sugar will sharpen the reflexes!

Boule lyonnaise

The player takes a run when throwing the *boule*.

Pétanque

The player stands inside a circle with his feet together.

The aim of the game – to get your *boule* as near as possible to the *cochonnet* (small ball), and also to knock your opponents' *boules* out of the way!

Sailing

Sailing, along with tennis, golf and horse-riding, is traditionally a sport popular with the French middle and upper classes. Many French, and Bretons in particular, have won transatlantic yacht races. In 1957 Florence Arthaud, the first woman to win an ocean race, set a new world record when she crossed the Atlantic in nine days twenty-one hours. However, France's favourite sailor was the inventive and courageous Eric Tabarly who was lost at sea in 1998 when racing Pen Duick, the boat in which he had learned to sail 60 years earlier.

Motor racing

L'Automobile Club de France, which was founded in 1895, was the first association of its kind in the world. Every year, France still hosts the best international drivers at a string of glamorous competitions: 24 heures du Mans, le Grand Prix de Pau, le Rallye de Monte-Carlo, le Tour de Corse and at the trials for the world championship in Castellet.

Gambling

Although gambling has been illegal in France since the time of Napoléon, the French, like other nations, enjoy a flutter on the horses, in the casino or even on *les planches à gratter* (scratchcards). The prohibition was circumvented by according a monopoly on gambling to the State which dispenses gambling licences to private bodies such as France's 159 casinos. In 1997 the French State earnt 3.1 billion francs from its casinos. However, most of this sum was fleeced not from languid aristos at the gaming tables but from ordinary French people trying their luck at *les machines à sous* (fruit machines).

Other forms of gambling are run by the state-owned company La Française des Jeux and by the Pari Mutuel Urbain (PMU), an association of off-course horse-race betting offices which are supervised by the Ministry of Agriculture. La Française des Jeux is responsible for a multitude of *jeux instantanés* including Loto, Millionnnaire and Astro which are purchased at newsagents and *tabacs* many of which are also agents of the PMU and sell tickets for the horse-betting game, le Tiercé. To place a Tiercé bet, punters must indicate the three winning horses of a race.

Horse-racing has been a popular French spectator sport since the Middle Ages. Today, elegant society rubs shoulders with ordinary Parisians at the capital's race courses at Auteuil, Longchamp and Vincennes. One of the biggest races is the Grand prix de Paris, run at Longchamp on the last Sunday in June.

La chasse (hunting and shooting)

Much of France's wildlife is fair game for hunters – deer, wild boar, grey wolves tentatively returning to the Alps after 40 years' absence, migrating birds, blackbirds, thrushes. France has Europe's longest hunting season and the most hunters – 1.6 million and a further 3.5 million who use their shotguns occasionally, in all twice as many as in Britain.

The hunting tradition is so strong in France because of the country's rural past and because of an unsentimental attitude towards wild animals which have been viewed first and foremost as meat for the table. Hunting is also a powerful symbol of peasant rights as, until the Revolution, it was the privilege of the aristocracy. Nonetheless, today 60 per cent of the population claim to be against blood sports. However, even though they are a minority, members of the French hunting lobby have enormous power (many rural mayors and councillors are hunters) and have repeatedly forced parliament to defy European Commission directives to shorten the hunting season.

Feelings run high at the beginning of the season when hunters are confronted on marsh and moor by ecologists pleading for the lives of precious migrating birds, including the endangered *ortolan*, 150,000 of which find their way onto gourmets' plates each year. Shortly before he died, President Mitterrand invited his nearest and dearest to a farewell lunch at which, in the manner customary for savouring the full flavour of *ortolans*, he covered his head in a large napkin and crunched his way through two of the minuscule, but exceedingly rich, song birds.

VOCABULARY

l'exploitation (f.) agricole *farm*
l'agriculteur (m.) *farmer*
la grande culture *large-scale farming*
cultiver *to grow/to cultivate*
la PAC (politique agricole commune) *Common Agricultural Policy*
les subventions (f.) *subsidy*
la FNSEA (la Fédération nationale des syndicats d'exploitants agricoles) *farming union*
les OGM (les organismes génétiquement modifiés) *genetically- modified organisms*
la culture biologique *organic farming*
moderniser *to modernize*
le bâtiment *building trade*
la sidérurgie *steel industry*
les métallos (m.) *steel workers*
l'industrie automobile (f.) *car industry*

l'industrie alimentaire *food industry*
l'industrie pétrolière *oil industry*
le tourisme industriel *industrial tourism*
les PME (petites et moyennes entreprises) *small and medium-size businesses*
le PDG (président-directeur général) *managing director*
la direction *management*
le cadre moyen *middle manager*
le cadre supérieur *top manager*
le personnel/les effectifs (m.) *staff/workforce*
le contremaître *foreman*
l'ouvier/-ière *worker*
l'ouvrier spécialisé *skilled worker*
le col blanc *white-collar worker*
le col bleu *blue-collar worker*
le commerçant *shop keeper/tradesperson*
l'artisan (m.) *craftsperson*
le/la fonctionnaire *civil servant*

l'insertion (f.) professionnelle *getting into the job market*
la formation professionnelle *job training*
effectuer un stage *to do a course*
le/la stagiaire *course participant*
le contrat de travail *contract*
travailler à temps partiel *to work part-time*
travailler à plein temps *to work full-time*
embaucher *to take on staff*
débaucher *to get rid of staff*
le syndicat *trade union*
adhérer à *to join*
la côtisation syndicale *union dues*
la grève *strike*
la revendication *demand*
le/la délégué syndical(e) *union representative*
le comité d'entreprise *works council (mandatory in companies with over 50 staff)*
le délégué du personnel *staff representative on works council*
gagner *to earn*
le bulletin de salaire *pay slip*
le treizième mois *an extra month's pay received annually by civil servants and many private sector workers*

le smicard *person receiving national minimum wage*
ête au chômage *to be out of work*
toucher les Assedic *to get unemployment benefit*
les vacances (f.) vertes *country holidays*
les vacances (f.) bleues *seaside holidays*
le vacancier *holiday-maker*
l'aoûtien/-ienne *August holiday-maker*
le/la juilletiste *July holiday-maker*
les grands départs *departures for summer holidays*
bronzé *tanned*
blanc comme un cachet d'aspirine *white as a sheet (lit. as an aspirin)*
le/la spectateur (-trice) *spectator*
participer *to take part*
jouer dans un club *to play in a club*
pratiquer un sport *to play a sport*
le permis de chasse *hunting licence*
la carte de pêche *fishing licence*
la pelote *Basque ball game*

Taking it further

Books

Ardagh, John, **Rural France** (London: Century, 1983) – agriculture and rural life in the French regions

Ardagh, John, **France in the new century** (London: Viking, 1999)

Mermet, Gérard, **Francoscopie: Comment vivent les Francais** (Paris: Larousse, published annually) – chapters on French work and leisure trends

L'Annuaire du Sport (Paris: Transfort Conseil) – annual listing of sports organisations and events, also sports clubs and sportsmen and women

Info

INSEE (Institut nationale de la statistique et des études économiques), Insee Information Service, Tour GammaA, 195 rue de Bercy, 75582, Paris; tel. 01 53 17 88 77; **www.insee.fr**

Ministère de l'Agriculture et de la Pêche, 78 rue de Varenne, 75349 Paris; tel. 01 49 55 49 55; **www.agriculture.gouv.fr**

Ministère de l'Emploi et de la Solidarité, 127 rue de Grenelle, 75700 Paris; **www.travail.gouv.fr**

Ministère de l'Economie, des Finances et de l'Industrie, 139 rue de Bercy, 75572 Paris; tel. 01 40 04 04 04; **www.finances.gouv.fr; www.industrie.gouv.fr**

PME (Petites et moyennes entreprises), Commerce et Artisanat, 80 rue de Lille, 75700 Paris; **www.pme.commerce.artisanat.gouv.fr**

Ministère de la Jeunesse et des Sports, 78 rue Olivien de Serres, 75739 Paris; tel. 01 40 45 90 00

Fédération française de cyclisme, Bâtiment Jean Monnet, 5 rue de Rome, 93561 Rosny-sous-bois; tel. 01 49 35 69 00; fax 01 48 94 09 97

Tour de France: **www.letour.fr**

l'Equipe (daily sports paper), 4 rue Rouget-de-Lisle, 92793 Issy-les Moulineaux; tel. 01 40 93 20 20

Places

French Tennis Open (last week May, first week of June), Stade Roland Garros, 2 ave Gordon-Bennett, 75016 Paris; tel. 01 47 43 48 00

Circuit des 24 heures du Mans (third weekend of June), tel. 02 43 72 72 24; www. 24h-le-mans.com

Hippodrome de Longchamp (horse racing), Bois de Boulogne, 75016, Paris; tel. 01 44 30 75 00

Parc des Princes (football), 24 rue du Commandant-Guilbaud, 75016 Paris; tel. 01 42 88 02 76

Stade de France (football) (Paris; www.stadefrance.fr)

12 PEOPLE

Who are the French today? In 1998, television viewers throughout the world saw France united in celebration at the triumph of their multi-racial football team in the world cup. It was a victory not only for *le bleu, blanc, rouge*, but for a France of *blacks, blancs, beurs* (blacks, whites, arabs) who waved the *drapeau tricolore* with equal pride. The ethnic backgrounds of France's population are only one marker of the profound changes that have taken place in French society over the last fifty years. In that time France has moved from being a largely agricultural nation to become a modern industrial society, but one where 12 per cent of the active population is unemployed. The difference between rich and poor has grown wider and rifts in society (*la fracture sociale*) have grown deeper. The old certainties provided by the Church, marriage and the traditional family are fading fast.

The French population

Population in 1997 (in millions)	
France	58.6
United States	267.6
United Kingdom	59
Germany	82.1
Source: World Bank	

In the first half of the twentieth century, France's population was dwindling, mainly due to the terrible loss of life in the two world wars. To encourage people to have more children, the government introduced generous family allowances which remain the highest in Europe, although they are only paid to families with more than one child. This incentive, the post-Second World War *bébé-boom* and a big influx of mainly North-African immigrants in the 1960s, caused the population to leap from 41 million in 1946 to 54 million in 1982. However, in common with the rest of Europe, France's population is expected to dip again during the next fifty years.

The days when many French families had four or more children are long gone – the average French family now has two children, and a fifth of all families have just one child. Amongst other social factors, one reason for this change was the legalization of contraceptives in 1967 and, later, the widespread use of *la pilule* (the pill), despite the Pope's repeated condemnation of contraception, which pragmatic Catholics have chosen to ignore.

Where the French live

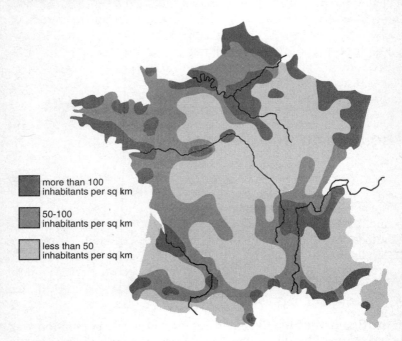

more than 100 inhabitants per sq km

50-100 inhabitants per sq km

less than 50 inhabitants per sq km

With a notional 108 people per square kilometre, France's population density is less than half that of Britain (244) or Germany (230), but nearly four times that of the United States (28). Of course the reality in France is not of inhabitants evenly sprinkled over areas as diverse as the wooded hills of the *Massif central* or France's commercial hub, the *Ile de France*. Three-quarters of French people today are *citadins* (urbanites) or *banlieusards* (suburb dwellers). The Paris area is the biggest conurbation in Europe with 11 million inhabitants.

Although France is still experiencing *l'exode rural* (rural exodus) which began in the nineteenth century, recent years have seen something of an *exode urbain* (urban exodus). Between 1975 and 1994, 164,000 Parisians, equivalent to the entire population of rural Cantal, decamped to the less hectic suburbs. Others have moved up to 100 kilometres out of town and rely on the TGV to get to work. Despite the urban nature of daily life, France has strong rural roots (see p. 212) which probably explains why Paris empties at weekends and why one in eight French families have a second home, the highest proportion in the world.

The family

The family is still a cornerstone of French society, but it has changed beyond recognition since the time when Napoléon's *code civil* declared that since a woman bore a man children *'elle est donc sa propriété comme l'arbre à fruit est celle du jardinier'* ('she is his property, just as the fruit tree is that of the gardener')! However, autocratic fathers and husbands continued to lay down the law until well after the Second World War.

In France it is significant that *parents* means all relations, not just mother and father. When members of big extended families of several generations lived close to each other, duties to aunts and uncles and cousins were as important as ties to the nuclear family and certainly took precedence over links with outsiders. However, as the young have abandoned rural communities to seek work in the towns and as the urban world of work has changed, with fewer sons carrying on old family businesses, so peasant, bourgeois and working class family dynasties have declined. These changes, together with the freer social and sexual values which took hold in the 1960s and '70s, have contributed to a radically different picture of family life. The formerly rigid family ties have been replaced by much looser links, including friends, ex-partners, new partners and step-children who would not necessarily all sit down happily together at a traditional French family Sunday lunch.

Nonetheless, children still tend to live near their parents, two-thirds of whom are less than 12 miles away. In addition, French children are tending to leave home later than a few years ago. While this is no doubt largely due to high youth unemployment, it also indicates that living with your family is more socially acceptable for French young people than for their Anglo-Saxon peers.

Nom de famille

The most common surname is **Martin** (400 in every 100,000 inhabitants), followed by **Bernard** (200), **Durand** (168) and **Richard** (163).

Certain surnames are common in particular regions:

Fabre in the south-east, **Schmitt** in the east, **Marie** in the Cotentin peninsula south of Cherbourg.

The couple

Next to Sweden, France is the European country where couples are least likely to get married. Since the 1970s, the number of marriages has dropped by about a third and the number of unmarried couples living together has risen sharply to constitute about 15 per cent of all couples, compared with only 3 per cent in 1968. Nowadays, nine out of ten couples live together for a preliminary period even if they subsequently decide to marry. This dramatic change of attitude and behaviour is reflected in current language. The somewhat pejorative term *concubinage* (common-law marriage) has been dropped in favour of *la cohabitation* or *l'union libre* (living together). Equally, children born out of wedlock are no longer branded *illégitimes* (illegitimate). After all, they now constitute more than a third of French babies, compared with only 10 per cent in 1980. Only the traditionally permissive Swedes, Norwegians and Danes have an even higher proportion of children born outside marriage.

Further proof of France's general tolerance of *l'union libre* is the widespread support for Prime Minister Jospin's bill to introduce *le Pacs (pacte civil de solidarité* – civil solidarity pact) which would entitle any two people whether heterosexual or same-sex, who have lived together for two years or more to benefit from the same fiscal and social rights enjoyed by married couples. Fiercely debated in the *Assemblée Nationale*, the bill was applauded by libertarians but condemned by many Church leaders and right-wing politicians who claimed it would sanction gay marriage and lead to the decline of the family. At the time of the controversy it gave rise to a new verb, *pacser*, used for fun as a pick-up gambit: *Voulez-vous pacser avec moi ce soir?* (Would you like to enter into a civil solidarity pact with me tonight?)!

The *Pacs* bill was welcomed by the French gay community which is estimated at up to two million inhabitants, of whom up to a quarter live as a couple. However, it is only relatively recently that such openness has been accepted. Although homosexuality was never criminalized, as it was in Britain, discreet behaviour was the price to be paid for public tolerance.

Divorce

The fact that there are four times as many divorces in France now as in 1960 is further confirmation of the breakdown of the traditional family. With one in three marriages ending in divorce, France has the highest divorce rate amongst Mediterranean countries, although in England, Belgium, the Scandinavian countries and the US, the rate is even higher. France's formerly severe divorce laws were relaxed in 1975 to allow divorce by mutual consent after six months (more than half of divorces today), divorce at the request of one partner after six years' separation, or divorce because of a partner's unreasonable behaviour.

Les Chemins de la liberté – pour les Françaises! (Roads to freedom – for French women)

In France as elsewhere, a shift in attitudes, greater sexual freedom and the legal recognition of women's rights, have changed the balance of power between men and women. Perhaps the changes have been all the more dramatic in France because former norms of social and private behaviour were so prescribed and restrictive. Even though the most misogynist clauses of the *code civil* had been revoked by 1938, the official view of women in the first half of the twentieth century was simply as procreators of the nation.

Although a minority of women had campaigned for equal rights as long ago as the French Revolution (see *Déclaration des Droits de la Femme et de la Citoyenne* p. 169), women did not win the vote until 1944 which was already much later than in Britain and the US. While the vote was granted partly in recognition of women's wartime work and the involvement of many in the Resistance, it was also prompted by the fact that de Gaulle's provisional government needed women's predominantly-conservative vote to stop a communist land-slide in the 1945 municipal elections. Hardly a feminist, de Gaulle later countered a proposal for a ministry of Women's Affairs with *'Un ministère? Pourquoi pas un ministère du tricot?'* (A ministry? Why not a ministry of knitting?').

Given that this summed up the attitude of many French men, it is not surprising that the publication in 1949 of Simone de Beauvoir's *Le Deuxième Sexe* outraged the French male establishment and horrified the Church who put the book on their Index of forbidden texts. Boldly asserting *'on ne naît pas femme, on le devient'* ('you are not born a woman you become one') de Beauvoir analysed French patriarchal society and challenged the idea of marriage and motherhood as woman's natural destiny. Male writers of Right and Left condemned the book – François Mauriac declared that it made him want to vomit, and Albert Camus responded with hurt male pride: *'Ce livre déshonore le mâle français.'* (This book dishonours the French male'). It was not until the 1960s and early 1970s that de

Beauvoir's ideas took hold, influencing a new groundswell of feminist thinking and the formation of the French women's liberation movement, the MLF (*Mouvement de Libération des Femmes*). Even so, *Le Deuxième Sexe* has had much higher sales in the US than in France.

The MLF was a loose association of diverse feminist groups, the best-known of which was *Psych et Po*, short for *Psychanalyse et Politique*. As its name suggests, this group approached feminism from a psychoanalytical perspective and in particular from the extremely complex theories about language and gender developed by the analyst Jacques Lacan. This very intellectual approach was quite at odds with the pragmatism of the Anglo-Saxon women's groups, but perfectly in tune with trends in French philosophy, sociology and linguistics departments where Lacan's dry and difficult ideas gave rise to impassioned debate.

Three feminist stars of the 1970s who took Lacan's theories further, and who still have considerable intellectual clout, are the psychoanalysts Luce Irigaray and Julia Kristeva, and the novelist and poet Hélène Cixious.

1944	Women won the vote (1918 in UK, 1920 in US)
1965	Married women allowed to make independent financial decisions without their husband's permission – e.g. open a bank account or obtain a passport!
1967	Contraception legalized
1970	Creation of the MLF
1972	Equal pay legislation. First female Polytechnique student
1974	Cost of contraception reimbursed by social security; contraception available for minors without parents' consent
1975	Sex discrimination illegal
	Abortion (IVG) legalized
	Divorce available by mutual consent
1980	Women granted equal rights at work
1981	First woman admitted to Académie Française
1982	France's first *bébé-éprouvette* (test-tube baby), Amandine. France holds the test-tube baby world record with 20,000 such births before 1996 (US 16,000, Britain 15,000)
1983	Cost of abortion reimbursed by social security
1987	Advertising contraceptives permitted
1991	First woman prime minister – Edith Cresson (1981 in UK)
1992	Law against *le harcèlement sexuel* (sexual harassment)
1999	Women granted equal representation in political life

L'homme nouveau (the new man)

Although twenty years ago few French men would have been caught with a tea-towel in their hands, today nearly half of them, allegedly, help with the washing-up. While they far outshine reluctant Italian males, only one in twenty of whom lifts a finger near the sink, French men still fall behind their British counterparts, nearly three-quarters of whom claim to do the dishes. Of course the critical question is whether such help in the house is substantial or just a token gesture ...

However, the younger generation appears to be less fixed in its ways and attitudes. In a recent survey of French men aged between 25 and 34, 80 per cent considered having a job to be just as important for a woman as for a man. Most respondents put having a good relationship with their partner as their top priority in life, followed by having children and spending time with them. When the French have a word for something it is usually grounded in reality, so *le nouveau papa* (the new dad) and *coparentalité* (shared parenting) must be more than wishful thinking. France was one of the pioneers in introducing *congé de paternité* (paternity leave) entitling men to time off work following the birth of their child.

Despite these changes of attitude, old habits die hard. If a woman is introduced to a man by her Christian name and surname, nine times out of ten, the man will enquire *'C'est Madame ou Mademoiselle?'* No wonder the title 'Ms' never caught on in France!

A backlash to feminism, *Le mouvement de la Condition masculine*, was formed in 1975 and is still going strong. Many of its 30,000 members are divorced men protesting against the size of maintenance payments expected of them. The movement has had some legal successes though, notably in changing the *code civil* to give a formerly-cohabiting father and mother equal rights over children in separation cases.

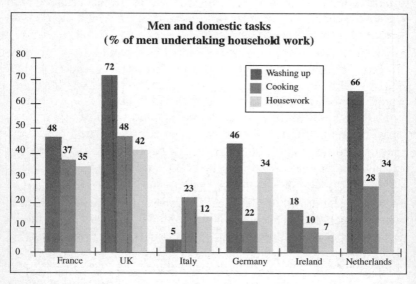

Source: Eurobaromètre

L'amour à la française (love French-style)

En amour, être français, c'est la moitié du chemin.
In love, being French is half-way there.

> Paul Morand (1888–1976)
> *L'Europe galante*

For generations of foreigners, the French woman has personified style and sexiness, and the French man has epitomized charm and passion. But have the big changes in French society left these stereotypes intact? Where did they come from? And do the French really leave the rest of the world standing when it comes to romance?

France's reputation as an amorous nation goes back much further than the steamy Brigitte Bardot films of the 1950s and '60s or the appearance of the dapper Maurice Chevalier on British and American screens in the 1940s and 50s. It is to medieval French *troubadours* that we owe the notion of 'romance'. These early poets developed *le roman courtois*, stories about courtly love in which a knight woos his lady with religious fervour and in accordance with the strict rituals of *chevalerie* (knighthood) from which the English notion of 'chivalry' derives.

However, France very early became associated with a more libidinous kind of love. Early condoms were named 'French letters'. However, the French equivalent is *la capote anglaise* (English hood) allegedly because in 1749 Louis XV ordered a consignment of 300 condoms from England because a papal ban prevented him from obtaining supplies at home. The French and English names have stuck, probably because of long-standing mutual suspicion – when Anglo-French relations were strained, anything beyond the Channel was seen as treacherous, immoral or licentious. Even so, the *capote anglaise* may be a French invention as there is evidence from explicit cave paintings in the Dordogne that condoms were used as early as AD 100. However, it is not clear whether the Frenchman's second-century ancestor was concerned with contraception or protecting his manhood against the elements.

In nineteenth-century Britain where any public display of sexuality was prohibited, Paris gained a reputation amongst foreigners for sexual permissiveness. While this was born out by what the foreign visitor might have seen at the Folies Bergères and le Moulin Rouge in the naughty 1890s or by the abundance of *maisons closes* (brothels), it was certainly not the case for Parisian and provincial families for whom the appearance of propriety and good manners were of paramount importance. Consequently, girls were chaperoned in their outings with young men, and extra-marital affairs were conducted with the utmost discretion. The greater sexual freedom of Parisian Left Bank bohemia was always something of an exception until the 1960s when growing sexual permissiveness swept away France's rigid codes of behaviour. Even so, attitudes were slower to change in small towns than in the metropolis. In addition, France's efficient and well-funded AIDS health education campaign in the 1980s and '90s put the brakes on promiscuity.

The French mistress

At one time, the French mistress was a tacitly accepted part of man-centred middle class life. The long-suffering wife turned a blind eye while the man kept his regular *cinq à sept* rendezvous (after-work-and-before-home tryst) in a hotel or his mistress's love nest. Not only are fewer erstwhile mistresses prepared to remain loyal if their man is unwilling to leave his wife, but fewer wives will put up with persistent infidelity now that divorce is easier and now that they are less financially dependent on their husbands. In addition, in these days of broken families, few men are able to fork out for a 'kept woman' on top of contributing to the finances of their estranged family and maintaining a new household. French sociologists claim that the once common 'archipelago' mode of relationship – a central marriage and mutliple extra-marital relationships – is giving way to the Anglo-Saxon norm of serial monogamy, despite the fact that according to recent statistics, one in five French men and women cheat on their partners.

The French lover

French men have long basked in their reputation as adept and irresistible lovers who are *toujours prêts* (always ready). This long-cherished image was somewhat dented by the huge demand in France for the anti-impotence drug Viagra, and also by recent research into French sexual habits which revealed that around 20 per cent of men over-eighteen experience impotence at some time or other. This is not a higher proportion than for any other nationality, but nonetheless, a blow to the Frenchman's legendary sexual supremacy.

Often dismissive of other nationalities in the romance stakes, French men were probably not too pleased when in a 1997 Paris-Match poll, Kevin Costner was voted the world's sexiest man, followed by Paul Newman, Mel Gibson and Tom Cruise. Alain Delon was twelfth and Gérard Depardieu only nineteenth.

La séduction

Out and about in France it is impossible to ignore a profound difference between the French and the British or Americans. Most French men and women are very conscious of appearance and would not be seen dead, even on holiday, wearing shapeless shorts or plastic water-proofs. They have been born into a culture of *séduction*. The word does not have the exclusively sexual innuendo of its English equivalent. In French *séduire* means 'to please, to charm, to delight ...' and not just the opposite sex. Yves Saint Laurent sums it up as *'La séduction: s'aimer un peu pour plaire beaucoup'* ('Seduction: to love oneself a little in order to please a great deal'). It is therefore not surprising that the French are the biggest spenders in Europe on cosmetics and toiletries. Eight out of ten women use *eau de toilette* or perfume, compared with only one in ten forty years ago; and a growing number of men, six out of ten, use after-shave, *eau de toilette* or perfume. Even when they are just pottering about, doing the weekend chores or digging the garden, most French men and women will smell delicious and be wearing clothes that they have chosen for the occasion, rather than ancient jeans and some disgusting old jersey.

In France there is an atmosphere of readiness for being seen, for being appreciated. It is no myth that the French stare. But what a Brit or American may take for rudeness is simply unguarded curiosity, or in the case of looks exchanged between men and women, undisguised appreciation. The British look while pretending not to, afraid of embarrassing the other person or of being embarrassed themselves. It does not occur to the French person that their lingering look might cause embarrassment; they are used to being stared at. For the French, sexuality is more conscious and less concealed. After all, there is no pithy equivalent in English for *le dragueur* (someone on the look-out for a pick-up).

Given this difference in attitude it is not surprising that the French are generally more accepting of nudity than the British and Americans. The French seem to like their bodies, and into old-age continue to strip off and soak up the sun on holiday beaches. It was French and Italian women who were the first to go topless in the 1970s. The near-naked displays at the *Crazy Horse* or *Moulin Rouge* have always been defended on the grounds that they were produced with the utmost good taste. The large number of bare female bodies in adverts and on French television – more than on British or American TV – is no doubt also justified in terms of *le bon goût!* French women have been less ready than American and British feminists to crusade against gratuitous female nudity. What many reconstructed Anglo-Saxons see as leery exploitation is for many French people simply artistic appreciation of the beautiful female form. However, feminists and politicians of the Right and Left drew the line at Galeries Lafayette's spring '99 human window display. The Paris store outraged the public and many of its own staff by using live models to display skimpy underwear to passers by. The designer of the lingerie and organizer of the show, Chantal Thomass, claimed that she had avoided vulgarity by not including suspenders!

Youth

C'est la fièvre de la jeunesse qui maintient le reste du monde à la température normale. Quand la jeunesse se refroidit, le reste du monde claque des dents.

It is the fever of youth that keeps the rest of the world at normal temperature. When youth goes cold, the rest of the world finds its teeth chattering.

Georges Bernanos (1888–1948)

It is more than thirty years since the turmoil and heady optimism of *les événements de mai '68* when French students manned make-shift street barricades made of paving stones and overturned cars to fight the CRS (the riot police). While striking workers claimed more pay and better conditions, the students were concerned not only with changing an archaic, under-resourced education system, but with realizing utopian ideals. The graffiti of the time proclaimed an end to the materialist society of *métro, boulot, dodo* (metro, work, kip). *'Soyez réaliste, demandez l'impossible!'* ('Be realistic, demand the impossible!') urged the slogan writers, or more poetically *'Sous les pavés, la plage!'* ('Under the paving stones, the beach!').

Today's students are less idealistic. With high youth unemployment, they are more concerned to get a job and fit in to society than to change it. Nowadays, the issues are strictly practical but just as passionately debated. In 1998, hundreds of thousands of *lycéens* (over-16 school students) demonstrated throughout the country in protest at low staffing levels and crumbling, cramped premises.

Unemployment has been a major factor in the alarming increase in juvenile crime which has doubled since 1992. A quarter of all crimes in France are now committed by under-18s. The problem is particularly acute in *les banlieues*, the run-down suburbs full of desolate concrete high-rises which surround Paris and other big cities like Lyon, Toulouse and Nancy. There is an atmosphere of growing racial tension in many suburbs which have a large immigrant population and where more than one in two young people are unemployed. Repeated waves of urban rioting, including annual mayhem at *La Saint-Sylvestre* (New Years Eve) and the increasing violence of gang warfare have prompted the Socialist government, formerly unwilling to take a hard line, to introduce no-nonsense measures. Fifty high-security detention centres and a hundred re-education units for convicted juveniles are planned, together with an extra 7,000 policemen for problem areas.

It is a sad sign of the times that the short-bladed *Opinel*, the handy and multi-purpose knife favoured by the French peasant to prune his vines and kept by every French worker in the pocket of his *bleus* (overalls), has become the chosen weapon of intimidation and defence for France's disaffected youth.

Of course outside urban ghettoes French youth culture is not dominated by violence. Like the youth of other developed countries French young people are concerned not only with their studies and with getting a job but with enjoying themselves. Fashions in music and dress are influenced by America and Britain but also by *beur* culture. Young second- and third-generation North-African immigrants have contributed to *le look* of loose trousers, layered tops and back-to-front baseball caps. They are often the most accomplished *verlan* speakers (see p. 39) and *rappeurs*, (see p. 108), and they are amongst the most stylish skate-boarders and bladers.

Old people

Just as 'old' has been replaced by various euphemisms in English, so the French prefer to speak of *les personnes âgées* (the elderly), *le troisième âge* (the third age), *les aînés* (elders) and *les seniors* rather than *les vieux* (old people). Whatever the terminology, the over-60s in France, just like those in other western countries, are a steadily growing group now constituting 20 per cent of the population and expected to include more than a quarter of the nation by the year 2020.

With a life expectancy of 82 years, the longest in Europe, French women appear to be particularly sprightly. They live three years longer than the British and Americans (in terms of statistical averages at any rate) and in the world they are only outlived by Japanese women. Until 1997, the oldest person in the world was a French woman, Jeanne Calment who died at the age of 122. French men however, are not so lucky. Their life expectancy of 74 years is eight years less than than that of their female compatriots, a bigger gap between the sexes than in any other European country. Analysts have attributed this to France's seriously high levels of alcoholism, smoking and reckless driving, predominantly male foibles. Although these levels are now falling, the impact on male longevity is yet to become apparent.

Trade union discussions in 1910, about fixing the retirement age at 65, illustrate the enormous difference between today's life-expectancy and that of nearly a century ago. The Communist union, the CGT, claimed the proposal meant retirement for the dead, given that life-expectancy in France was only 43 years for men and 47 years for women! The extra thirty or so years of life now enjoyed by today's French *seniors* is equivalent to the whole life expectancy of a French peasant at the end of the eighteenth century.

La retraite

Pour tout Français, la retraite est le but suprême de l'existence. C'est avec joie qu'il envisage sa vie de vieillard. Mastiquer avec une machoire édentée semble être le comble de ses délices.

For every Frenchman, retirement is the ultimate goal of his existence. He anticipates old-age with joy. For him, chewing with toothless jaws seems to be the height of ecstasy.

George Mikes (1912–1987)
Little Cabbages

In France, retirement has for decades been a sacrosanct *acquis* or hard-won right. The offical retirement age is 60, but very generous agreements for France's 4.5 million public service employees have meant that by 58 only half the active population is still working. The average retirement age in France is 57 – a world record! Particular categories of public employees are entitled to retire even earlier – railwaymen wave goodbye to the station at 55, and ballet dancers hang up their pumps at 40. However, this cushy picture is likely to change when the Socialist government implements plans to extend working life to at least 66 in order to afford full pensions for an increasingly long-lived population.

Despite their early pension entitlement many retired people are unhappy about the low level of the state pension. In 1998, a 20,000-strong, grey-haired crowd marched through Paris in protest – which just goes to show that in France you are never too old for *la manif!*

Immigration

Being at the cross-roads of Europe, France has a long history of immigration. In the seventeenth century France became a *terre d'asile* (country of refuge) when she welcomed Irish and Scottish Jacobite exiles, and she has continued to receive refugees. In the twentieth century these included Poles, White Russians, Spaniards, Chileans, Argentines and Yugoslavs. However, most twentieth century immigration was instigated by France in times of economic need. After the First World War, a huge wave of Italians, Spanish and Polish responded to France's need for workers to rebuild the country. Following the Second World War and until 1974, a further wave of immigrants (this time from Portugal and French former colonies in North Africa, black Africa and south-east Asia) were recruited to realize government plans for rapid industrialization. Coming from poor, less-developed countries than France, these immigrants had few, if any, qualifications and filled low- and unskilled jobs in the building trade, heavy industry and road construction. As these areas were hard-hit by recession in the 1970s and '80s, and as technological change has meant even fewer unskilled jobs in industry, it is not surprising that immigrants have suffered the most from unemployment. Today, a quarter of immigrants are out of work, compared with 11 per cent of France's total active population.

France has at least 4.2 million immigrants, including 1.3 million who have acquired French nationality. In addition, there are many *immigrés clandestins* (illegal immigrants) estimated at between 300,000 and one million. A third of all immigrants are *les Maghrébins* (North Africans including Algerians, Moroccans and Tunisians) often known as *les beurs*.

Immigration legislation

Until 1974 foreigners had the right to stay in France if they found work. But since then, immigration has been restricted to certain asylum seekers, a small number of workers coming to fill specific jobs, and to members of an existing immigrant's close family.

The introduction of harsh immigration laws and a policy of repatriation for illegal immigrants in 1993 led to violent demonstrations and the occupation of a Paris church, l'Eglise Saint-Bernard, as a place of refuge for *les sans-papiers* (illegal immigrants). Before this date, a person born in France had *le droit du sol*, that is they automatically held French nationality. But under the new law, a young person born in France but whose parents were born abroad, which is the case for many North Africans, could not become French before the age of 16, when he or she was required to formally *manifester leur volonté* (register their willingness) to be French. Subsequent modifications to the law lowered the age limit to 13, and nationality is now automatically given at 18 provided the young person has lived in France for five years since the age of 11.

Main immigrant communities in France (in thousands)

Portuguese	646
Algerian	620
Moroccan	585
Italian	254
Spanish	216
Tunisian	207
Turkish	201
Yugoslav	52
Polish	46
Senegalese	45
Cambodian	44
Malian	35
Laotian	32
Vietnamese	31
Camerounais	19
Ivoirien (Ivory coast)	17

INSEE census, 1990

Racism

Despite the fact that most twentieth-century immigrants were invited to the country to build up the French economy, they have often found themselves in the role of *bouc émissaire* (scapegoat) in times of economic hardship, accused of stealing French jobs. Today, Arabs in particular are the butt of racist criticism and aggression, partly because they are such a large group and because of the perceived differences between them and the native French – they are Muslims, tend to have larger families (although native French and immigrant birth rates are converging) and many live in deprived areas with high crime rates. Young Arabs are far more likely than white youths to be stopped for identity checks by squads of CRS who are not renowned for a kid-gloves approach (see p. 188).

The French have traditionally favoured *assimilation* of foreigners rather than *intégration*, the former being a 'when in Rome ...'

attitude and the latter an acceptance of immigrants' distinctive cultures. This polarity illustrates the innate contradiction in the origins of the Republic. The principles of *liberté*, *égalité* and *fraternité* were only established throughout the land through enforced centralization and the very unfraternal repression of local identity formerly evident in local laws and regional languages and dialects (see p. 30). Today, many people still believe that embracing the cultures of ethnic minorities poses a threat to the French identity and republican values. Americans and British were bemused at the fuss in French schools when Muslim girls refused to remove a sign of their religion, *le foulard* (headscarves). But for the French this was not simply a question of racial tolerance. What was at issue was the principle of a secular state, a principle which had been hard-won, through revolution; secular education represented equality of treatment and opportunity based on rationalism, not privilege or superstition. Any hint of religion in school smacks of the *Ancien Régime*. Nonetheless it is difficult to imagine the teachers who went on strike in 1998 over the *foulard* issue, doing the same thing if Catholic girls refused to remove their crucifixes.

Of course racism is not only directed at foreigners. France is no stranger to anti-semitism, as the famous Dreyfus case testifies (see p. 16), and is still coming to terms with the part played by French collaborators in the Holocaust. Every so often, anti-semitism rears its head again, as in the early 1990s when extreme right-wing youths desecrated graves in Jewish cemeteries in the south of France.

For all its tensions, France is a multi-racial country of extraordinary vitality. This is no better exemplified than by its 1998 world cup football team which included four players born in Ghana, New Caledonia, Senegal and Guadaloupe, and a further six players who are second-generation immigrants and whose parents come from Armenia, Italy, Guadeloupe, the former Yugoslavia and Algeria. For a few heady summer days, France's victory united all her races and all her political parties. However, there have been longer-lasting consequences. This manifestation of unity, like other more serious, political events in French history, represented a certain *prise de conscience* (becoming aware), in this case of a national desire to end racial conflict. Perhaps it is no coincidence that throughout the following year, support for the racist Front National began to ebb (see p. 179).

Religion

Le vingt-et-unième siècle sera spirituel ou ne sera pas.
The twenty-first century will be spiritual or it will not happen.

André Malraux (1901–1976)

France was once known as *la fille aînée de l'église* (the oldest daughter of the Church), but today France's Sunday morning congregations are small. Although three-quarters of French people describe themselves as Catholic, fewer than one in ten go to mass regularly and half go to church only for baptisms, weddings, funerals and perhaps the Christmas Midnight Mass. Church christenings and marriages have fallen off as well – since 1970 baptisms have dropped by a third to 58 per cent of children, and only one in two couples tie the knot in Church, compared with 95 per cent thirty years ago. France's shrinking priesthood (one priest for every ten thousand inhabitants, compared with seven in 1965) is further evidence of the Catholic Church's diminished role in French life.

The religions of France	
Catholics	36,000,000
Muslims	4,000,000
Protestants	800,000
Jews	600,000
Buddhists	600,000
Various sects	400,000

Islam is France's second religion, reflecting the size of her immigrant population. Muslims are by no means a homogenous group, the majority coming from North Africa but many coming from other black-African ex-colonies and from Turkey. About three-quarters of a million Muslims have French nationality and only half of all Muslims in France practise their religion, following a variety of interpretations of the Koran. Despite fears aroused by the activities of the extremist Front islamique du salut in Algeria and terrorist bombs in Paris in the early 1990s, there are very few *intégristes* (Islamic fundamentalists) in France. While most Muslims are from modest backgrounds, some are highly educated members of an intellectual élite.

Set against the tradition-bound and ritualistic Catholic Church, French Protestantism, from the time of the Huguenots (see pp. 12–13), has come to represent the values of simplicity, innovation, enterprise and, most significantly, dissent. In the twentieth century, however, it was the Protestant Church in particular which took ecumenical initiatives, seeking dialogue between its own Lutherans and Reform Church members and with Catholics too. The general dip in church attendance includes Protestants, 60 per cent of whom never go to church.

France's Jewish minority is over one per cent of the population, a higher proportion than in any other country of the European Union. Most French Jews live in the Paris region – the fourth *arrondissement* and the rue des Rosiers are famous Jewish areas – although substantial numbers also live in Lyon and in Provence.

The Buddhist population is now equal in size to France's Jewish community. Most Buddhists are refugees from south-east Asia and China. However, an increasing number of native French are attending the country's 300 Buddhist prayer centres.

A 1996 survey revealed that France has 172 sects with about 800 branches. While French Jehovah's witnesses, the country's largest sect, are generally tolerated, France is quick to investigate any group suspected of posing a threat to society or to its own members. There have been long-running legal battles with Scientologists, who in Britain and America are usually left alone. But France is understandably edgy, having investigated and banned four sects which claim to be *autodestructrices*, that is their leaders could order mass suicides along the lines of what happened to the Sun Temple sect in Switzerland in 1994.

Although France's relationship with institutional religion has changed, she is far from being a nation of non-believers. Two-thirds of French people claim to believe in a deity, and a third of under-30s say that religion plays an important part in their lives.

VOCABULARY

la pièce d'identité *identification*
la carte nationale d'identité *national identity card*
le livret de famille *official family record book in which marriage, births and deaths are recorded*
l'extrait de naissance (m.) *birth certificate*
la fiche d'état civil *certificate of civil status*
le carnet de santé *health record*
les mœurs (f.) *social habits*
la natalité *birth rate*
la nuptialité *marriage rate*
la baisse *drop*
la hausse *increase*
la rupture d'union *marital breakdown*
vivre ensemble *to live together*

la naissance hors mariage *birth outside marriage*
la fécondité *fertility*
diminuer *to fall*
augmenter *to increase*
la famille nombreuse *large family*
la vie intime *personal life*
la cité *block of flats*
la violence urbaine *urban violence*
SOS racisme *anti-racist organisation*
la xénophobie *xenophobia*
le harcèlement policier *police harassment*
les croyances (f.) *beliefs*
la pratique religieuse *religious practice*
le/la pratiquant(e) *church-goer*
se rendre à l'église/à la mosquée/à la synagogue *to go to church/ the mosque/the synagogue*

Taking it further

Books

Mermet, Gérard, **Francoscopie: Comment vivent les Français** (Paris: Larousse - published annually)
Zeldin, Theodore, **The French** (London: Collins, 1983)
Temine, Emile, **France, terre d'immigration** (Paris: Gallimard, 1999) – well-illustrated and very readable historical picture of immigration
Dupaquier, Jacques, **Les noms de famille en France** (Paris: Archives et Culture, 1998)
Service des droits des femmes, **Les femmes** (Paris: INSEE, 1995)
Duchen, Claire, **Women's rights and women's lives in France** (London: Routledge, 1994)
Mernick, Jeffrey and Ragan, Bryant T (ed.s), **Homosexuality in modern France** (New York: OUP, Inc, 1996)

Websites

Parents and children's rights: **www.enfance.com**
Centre d'information et de documentation jeunesse: **www.cidj.asso.fr**

POSTSCRIPT – FRANCE IN THE WORLD TODAY

The chic, sophisticated image that France chooses to project to the world has changed little since Marianne first bore Brigitte Bardot's glamorous features in the 1960s. In 1999 the country chose supermodel Laetitia Casta to be the face of France on stamps, coins and in *mairies* throughout the land. And yet France today is very different from forty years ago. Far-reaching social and economic changes have forced her to reassess her fundamental values, her relations with other countries and her role in the global economy.

France in Europe

France has been at the centre of the European Union since its very beginnings in the 1950s. One of its founders was the brilliant French administrator Jean Monnet, known as *le père de l'Europe*. He and the politician Robert Schuman saw economic and political co-operation with other European countries, and with Germany in particular, to be vital for France's post-war economic recovery and her national security. Together, Monnet and Schuman drew up plans for the European Coal and Steel Community which began in 1951 with France and Germany pooling their coal and steel industries and thus renouncing national sovereignty over strategic assets. Italy, Belgium, the Netherlands and Luxembourg followed suit. Six years later, the Treaty of Rome created the CEE (*La Communauté économique européenne*, European Economic Community) and the beginnings of *le Marché commun* (Common Market). Then in 1992 the Treaty of Maastricht formed *l'Union européenne* which was further revised by the Treaty of Amsterdam in 1997.

For much of this period, and with something of de Gaulle's belief in his country's civilizing mission, France has called the tune in

Europe. After the war, Germany was subordinate to France out of atonement and economic necessity. Since then the two countries have been each other's principal trading partners. Today, however, the balance of power has tilted in Germany's favour. Now a confident and wealthy country, the unified Germany is less dependent on France. Consequently, France can no longer take for granted her former supremacy nor the so-called Franco–German axis at the core of the Union. Nonetheless, France still sees herself as the champion of European values, a plucky Astérix, squaring up to what she perceives as the dehumanizing aspects of American culture.

France and Britain

Anglo-French rivalry goes back at least to the fourteenth century and the Hundred Years War. Shakespeare's *Henry V*, documenting the French army's dismal showing at Agincourt in 1415 ('Ten thousand French that in the field lie slain ... Where is the number of our English dead? ... But five and twenty'!) was not performed in French until 1999 at the Avignon festival.

However, the French claim that they no longer ridicule the English in the way that the English tabloid press continues to mercilessly stereotype the French at the first sign of any trade dispute. It is only eccentric French nationalists who now and then try to provoke the seemingly phlegmatic British. In 1998, the French author and traveller Jean Raspail invaded a miniscule patch of British territory, the Minquier reef twelve miles south of Jersey, and raised not the French flag but that of the non-existent Kingdom of Patagonia. In 1999, a more serious-minded, but equally cheeky, move came from a senior French politician with the distinctly bellicose name of Longueépée (Long sword). He requested that London's Waterloo station be renamed since this constant reminder of Napoléon's defeat at the hands of the English was bad for European relations! Unaware of British ignorance in European history, he even threatened what he imagined to be a crushing humiliation, the renaming of la Gare du Nord as la Gare de Fontenoy, in memory of Louis XV's victory against the English. No doubt British bewilderment was interpreted as *sang-froid*.

When it comes to clashes over lamb, veal, fish or beef, however, the old mutual suspicion is rekindled, and Henry V's challenge echoes down the centuries – but now on both sides of the Channel: *'Encore une fois sur la brèche, précieux amis'* ('Once more unto the breach dear friends')!

France and the United States

France has a love-hate relationship with the United States. It was Americans who helped the British and the Canadians to defeat the Germans in Normandy in 1944. It was Americans who introduced French youth to the delights of nylon stockings and jazz, and later to pop music and *le rock* (jive). It was Americans who first created tough crime films and fiction, for which France has had a lasting passion. However, the French are ambivalent about other aspects of American culture which have become part of French life: they have been unable to resist hypermarkets but regret the resulting demise of many small shops; they enjoy the convenience of fast food chains and the novelty of McDonald's but remain proud of France's gastronomic heritage and family-run restaurants whose survival is threatened; similarly, they flock to see American films but believe their own film industry should be protected.

Although modern France embraces all of these contradictory elements, when French interests are under severe threat, attitudes swiftly polarise. Then, French food, language and films represent France's endangered way of life, and everything American comes to symbolize the United States' unwelcome political and economic power, as illustrated by a recent Franco-American food spat. When France refused to import growth-hormone-injected, American beef, the United States retaliated by slapping punitive tariffs on imports of cherished French products such as Roquefort cheese. Angry French farmers and Roquefort producers then resorted to direct tactics – they upturned the familiar plastic effigy of Ronald McDonald and buried it under a mound of rotting apples. Even though French farmers' direct action does not always earn them foreign sympathy, on this occasion papers throughout the world gleefully carried the image of American commercial might brought low.

The American liberal economic model, underpinned by belief in Thomas Jefferson's claim that less government is better government, has long been anathema to the *dirigiste* French for whom unfettered market forces mean inequality rather than liberty. By contrast, the centralized and protectionist French state has seen its role as guiding the economy and protecting its citizens. Nonetheless, France is a signatory of the GATT free-trade agreement (General Agreement on Tariffs and Trade) having insisted on exception clauses to protect French music and film. When in 1998 the United States pressed for the removal of these clauses, thousands of French film makers, actors and intellectuals united in protest. Now, France is entitled to continue offering subsidies to her own industry without, as was proposed, having to extend the same financial help to multi-national media groups in France making Hollywood films – a nonsensical situation which would have meant death to the French film industry.

Despite continued fiery public debate demonizing the free market, French attitudes are changing. In the last few years her public sector has dramatically diminished as the government has sold off many of its state-owned industries, banks and other public services. A recent *Le Monde* survey revealed that two-thirds of French people accept a market economy and over half consider globalization to be a good thing for France. In spite of their fears, the French see little point in attempting to withstand inevitable change, but they are torn about the consequences. Most of all, they do not want to sacrifice the qualities which have made their culture the envy of the world – humanity, diversity, creativity, independence. At a time when the French feel these to be under threat, they have flocked to see Luc Besson's blockbuster *Jeanne d'Arc*. The film's runaway success confirms the national heroine's enduring power as a symbol of French defiance against the enemy. But in the global economy, France is less sure-footed. To protect her culture and her interests, France will have to cross swords not only with foreign governments but with more elusive adversaries. In this age of e-commerce and digital communications, it is multi-national corporations, crossing boundaries at the speed of light, that threaten to take France by stealth.

French kings and heads of state from the fifth to the twenty-first century

457–751	multiple **Merovingian** kings of which the most famous was Clovis I, crowned in 481
751–986	**Carolingians** including Pépin le Bref (751) and Charlemagne (768)
987–1328	**Capetians** of whom the first was Hugues Capet (987)

Valois

1328	Philippe VI
1350	Jean II, le Bon
1364	Charles V, le Sage
1380	Charles VI
1422	Charles VII
1461	Louis XI
1483	Charles VIII

Valois – Orléans

1498	Louis XII

Valois – Angoulême

1515	François I
1547	Henri II
1559	François II
1560	Charles IX
1574	Henri III

Bourbons

1589	Henri IV
1610	Louis XIII
1643	Louis XIV
1715	Louis XV
1774	Louis XVI

First Republic

1792	Comité de Salut Public (Robespierre and Danton)
1795	Directorate
1800	Consulate (Napoléon Bonaparte as Consul)

First Empire

1804	Napoléon I

Restoration of the monarchy

1814	Louis XVIII
1815	Return of Napoléon I (100 days)
1815	Return of Louis XVIII
1824	Charles X
1830	Louis-Philippe

Second Republic

1848	Louis-Napoléon Bonaparte

Second Republic

1852	Napoléon III

Third Republic

1870–1940	A succession of presidents including Sadi Carnot (1887) and Raymond Poincaré (1913)

Vichy government

1940	Philippe Pétain

Fourth Republic

(Provisional government)

1944	Charles de Gaulle
1946	Gouin, Bidault and Léon Blum

Presidents:

1947	Vincent Auriol
1954	René Coty

Fifth Republic

1959	Charles de Gaulle
1969	Georges Pompidou
1974	Valéry Giscard d'Estaing
1981	François Mitterrand
1995	Jacques Chirac

INDEX